THREE FRENCH COMEDIES

THREE FRENCH COMEDIES

❊ ❊ ❊

TURCARET

LESAGE

THE TRIUMPH OF LOVE

MARIVAUX

EATING CROW

LABICHE

❊ ❊ ❊

Translated and with an Introduction by
James Magruder

C. B. Coleman, GENERAL EDITOR

Yale University Press   New Haven and London

Designed by James J. Johnson and set in
Fournier Roman types by Tseng Information
Systems, Inc.
Printed in the United States of America.

*Library of Congress Cataloging-in-Publication
Data*

Three French comedies / translated and with
    an introduction by James Magruder ;
    C.B. Coleman, general editor.
    p.   cm.
Contents: Turcaret / Lesage—The triumph of
love / Marivaux—Eating crow / Labiche.
    ISBN 0-300-06275-3 (cloth : alk. paper). —
    ISBN 0-300-06276-1 (pbk. : alk. paper)
    1. French drama (Comedy)—Translations into
English.   2. French drama—18th century—
Translations into English.   3. French
drama—19th century—Translations into
English.   I. Magruder, James, 1960-   .
II. Coleman, C. B.   III. Le Sage, Alain René,
1668–1747. Turcaret. English.   IV. Marivaux,
Pierre Carlet de Chamblain de, 1688–1763.
Triomphe de l'amour. English.   V. Labiche,
Eugène, 1815–1888. Chasse aux corbeaux.
English.   VI. Title: Turcaret.   VII. Title:
Triumph of love.   VIII. Title: Eating crow.
PQ1240.E7T495   1996
842'.052308—dc20   95-40001

A catalogue record for this book is available
from the British Library.
The paper in this book meets the guidelines
for permanence and durability of the
Committee on Production Guidelines for
Book Longevity of the Council on Library
Resources.

10   9   8   7   6   5   4   3   2   1

In memory of my father
Frederick Elliott Magruder

CONTENTS

Acknowledgments

ix

Introduction: From Court to Boulevard

1

I. Turcaret

25

II. The Triumph of Love

83

III. Eating Crow

127

ACKNOWLEDGMENTS

Bridging as it does the academic study of French literature and the craftier world of the living stage, this work is the result of many encouraging voices from a number of disciplines.

I began my graduate career in the French department of Yale University. It is there I came under the charming influence of Jacques Guicharnaud, who proved to be an invaluable first example of the dedicated scholar who is also a true man of the theater. I am also indebted to Georges May, the *dix-huitièmiste* who introduced me to the works of Lesage and Marivaux. Thence I defected to the Yale School of Drama, due in large measure to the sardonic genius of Leon Katz, an inspiration as scholar, pedagogue, and cultural synthesizer. I thank him for guiding my pre-doctoral work on eighteenth-century theater. I also thank Richard Gilman for assiduously scouring the deconstructionist residue from the French department out of my prose.

I owe my theatrical career to Robert Moss, who always believed in my writing and who got me started writing plays, which got me started translating plays. Thanks to New York Theater Workshop, the sadly departed Los Angeles Theater Center, Baltimore's Center Stage, and the New York Shakespeare Festival for holding readings of the dramatic texts in this book. I am indebted also to Michael Mayer and Lisa Peterson; their directorial expertise led to invaluable revisions and refinements in the Lesage and Marivaux texts. They've given me friendship, great rewrites, and scintillating productions. All honor to Irene Lewis for her brilliant premiere of *The Triumph of Love* but, more important, for providing me with meaningful work and an artistic home at Center Stage.

Thanks to my agent, Peter Hagan, C. B. Coleman, and Cynthia

Wells and Noreen O'Connor at Yale University Press for guiding the manuscript to publication.

More private but no less essential have been the enduring emotional contributions of Carolyn Blum, Deidre Dawson, Nancy Hoffman, Raymond Hoffman, Jill Rachel Morris, David Nolta, Julia Reidhead, Catherine Weidner, and Sam Wolfe. In the cases of Peter Ashjian and the late Virginia Vappi Ashjian, their support extended to the material as well. My love and gratitude to them all.

Finally, I wish to thank Gordon Rogoff—mentor, advisor, editor, raconteur, friend, and kindred spirit.

INTRODUCTION
FROM COURT TO BOULEVARD

In his seventh *Epître*, written in 1677 and dedicated to the tragedian Racine, Boileau lays the following wreath upon Molière's reputation:

> With Molière lovable comedy was laid low,
> Vainly sought to recover from such a rude blow,
> For to stand in his buskins she was now too late.
> Such was our comic theater's fate.

Coming as it does only four years after Molière's fatal onstage collapse in *The Physician in Spite of Himself*, this postmortem for French comedy seems premature, but its author was given to the grand gesture, as literary mandarins tend to be when theorizing on the right side of an absolute monarch. Boileau's *L'Art poétique*, a four-canto poem which stands as the ultimate summation of French neoclassical aesthetic doctrine, prizes the enduring, if somewhat workaday, literary value of clarity. Although its most famous dictum, one that French schoolchildren still record in their notebooks, is "what has been clearly conceived can be clearly stated," I find Boileau's epitaph for Molière perversely unclear. What exactly does he mean when he says, "With Molière lovable comedy was laid low/Vainly sought to recover from such a rude blow"? The preposition *with* is unsettling. Doesn't he mean *after?* Is he saying that the Italianate origins of Molière's comedy lowered the genre? Or was the subcategory of love comedy—not a prevailing interest for Molière—laid low? In his estimation, how low and rude is comedy to begin with? Is Boileau insinuating that the success of Molière's art, however impressive, was far from lovable? Could the "rude blow" refer both to Molière's demise and to an unseemly usurpation of the comic mode? As for the matter of the buskins, a benign reading would have Boileau lamenting that no one will ever be able to fill the shoes Molière stretched with his talent; in a spiteful reading, Boileau might be complaining that Molière's big feet got there first and left no room for anyone else. "Such was our comic theater's fate." Is this a threnody or a sideswipe? Boileau is brisk with this conclusion, yet with Molière dead, Corneille in extreme dotage, and Racine about to forsake secular tragedy to become historiographer for the Holy Realm, he may have sensed the shadows lengthening over the greensward. He is again premature, for both he and Louis XIV will live on for another forty years. In 1680, three years after the publication of Boileau's *Epîtres*, the king chartered the Comédie-Française, a monopolistic *maison de culture* designed to keep the sun from setting on a set of dramatic masterpieces and a declamatory style of acting. In the three hundred years since this typically French act of Kunstpolitik, the choice to stand in Molière's shoes and retrace his steps, or to break with cultural tradition and beat some brand new measure in them, has been a challenge for all of France's comic playwrights from Beaumarchais to Musset, from Jarry to Giraudoux. Never review intentions, or so I'm told; we may never know what Boileau meant in this puzzling quatrain. Truth to tell, as one of the mightiest hairsplitters in French literature, he probably never recovered from the age of classicism he helped engineer, enduring season after season of dessicated, formulaic comedy and musty tragedy written to his specifications at "the House of Molière," to finally expire of nostalgia in 1716, one year after his king. For the task at hand, however, I find myself interested in drawing out this other, delicately subversive Boileau, a critic who, although keenly aware that a moment has passed with Molière, nevertheless appears to be making room — between the lines or off to the side — for the comic gifts in France's future. Might he not be saying, "We have lost Molière — *hélas*. Playwrights, start your engines"?

The French make peace with the shade of Molière through uninterrupted reappraisals of his plays, duly paying him reverent and irreverent attention in the theater. Three centuries later, in this country, in a theater culture that had only begun to establish its own aesthetic since O'Neill, Americans are too willing to take Boileau — a footnote to a footnote as far as most people are concerned — at his word. Received wisdom is better than none, and a lack of imagination among theater artists in a nation heroically resistant to foreign tongues means there is room in our repertory for only one notoriously big-footed Frenchman. This anthology is intended, therefore, as both a contribution to the repertory and as an act of New World restitution for the authors I include. If a stylistically wider range of French comedy is made available to the American theater, it is my modest hope that someday we can expect resident theater decision makers, when filling that "continental comedy" slot in the season, to consider something fresher than one more go-round with *The School for Wives* or *The Miser*. The aim is not to supplant Molière (as if that were possible). Yet, just as bardolatry casts an enduring shadow over the brilliant achievements of Marlowe, Jonson, and Webster, room needs to be made for the worthy successors of Molière's genius. The three authors in this collection—Lesage, Marivaux, and Labiche—need no plaintiff for their talents. Each in his own lifetime was prolific, well-compensated, and popular with the critical establishment and with the public. Each abandoned a law practice for the comic muse—an odd coincidence that might guarantee, for Lady Bracknell at least, a respectability of character. Their works remain current in the European repertory. *Turcaret, Le Triomphe de l'amour,* and *La Chasse aux corbeaux* are each representative of their author's oeuvre and the theatrical culture that flourished around them. All they require is vigorous, fluid, and, most important, stageworthy translations.

Then as now, Molière was a tough act to follow. He shifted styles and combined genres as it suited him, always managing to summon enough tact in his prefaces to end-run the official tastemakers and retain Louis's personal patronage. By 1660, his genius for melding the anarchic, improvisational spirit of the commedia dell'arte with a growing, highbrow proclivity for Terentian comic form inspired a ministry intent upon willing a national culture into existence for a civilization meant to exceed that of ancient Athens. After the death of Cardinal Mazarin in 1661, the twenty-three-year-old Louis XIV decided to govern France on his own and write himself into the constitution as an architectural ideal, becoming in the process both the arbiter and the guardian of form. Every detail of the *ancien régime,* from monuments and comic types to lace cuff lengths and the salt tax, was constructed for his *gloire* and in his image. The rules of dramatic art, articulated and modified through a series of aesthetic imbroglios that only the French seem to have the energy for, were, by the time Boileau codified them in *L'Art poétique,* a series of conventions, unities, action, and act structures that set the precepts for a theater whose artifacts travelled up the sunbeams for the godhead's perusal and approval. The absolute, baroque passions and defects of a Phèdre or an Alceste are extreme, off the map, and fitted for an absolute monarch.

As early as 1631, the theorist and playwright Mairet, re-reading

Aristotle to suit his methods in his preface to *Silvanie*, doggedly insists upon three laws of comedy: a believable story, a single action, and a unity of time. Also at this time the newly chartered Académie Française unveils the twin peaks of *vraisemblance* and *bienséance*. The rhetorical concept of *vraisemblance* (verisimilitude) was decreed as the "active and emotional presentation of things as if they are truly happening on the stage." *Bienséance* (seemliness or decorum), according to the conservative theoretician Chapelain, required that "each character speak according to his condition, his age, and his sex." The nagging question of dramatic decorum will, as time goes on, carry with it the weight of moral propriety. Although a conscious literary artist, Molière was also an actor loath to lose a laugh to legislation; his views on the subject of suitability waffle early in his career: "The play has pleased its audience and that is the greatest of all rules," he wrote in *Critique of the School for Wives* in 1663. Later in that year he appears to shift his bias when he writes in *The Versailles Impromptu* that comedy must depict "a reality recognizable to all." A commitment to "realism" provided a handle with which comedy could proclaim its utility, to recall that "theater is the school for man," in which "comedy corrects men's vices by exposing them to ridicule" (preface to *Tartuffe*, 1669).

After Molière's death in 1674, his imitators, chief among them Regnard and Dancourt, continued to work, with more diligence than élan, the vein of character comedy. Their five-act plays are careful to occur within one revolution of the sun. They take place in what Corneille termed the theatrical fiction of a neutral room that belongs to no one character but is available to all for private conversation. There is no mingling of tragic and comic tone; lovers are of incidental interest and incidental humor; and servants motor the plots. In the name of verisimilitude, the action is not permitted to skip forward from scene to scene—time intervals may occur only between the acts. A strict pattern of entrances and exits—the famous "French scenes"—maintains scene liaisons, such that dragging transitional scenes impede the action. Characters are consistent; in order that they don't appear too simple a representative of a custom, a vice, or a social class, they are provided with a modicum of psychological complexity.

The comic impulse, hamstrung as it was by neoclassical doctrine, received a severe setback in 1697 when Louis XIV banished Luigi Riccoboni's commedia troupe from France. The Théâtre des Italiens, which had enjoyed a royal monopoly on prose comedy and farce, had been planning to mount *The Prude,* a thinly veiled portrait of Madame de Maintenon, the king's second wife. As the century turned, people of all classes flocked to the theaters of the seasonal St. Germain and St. Laurent fairs, where rope dancers, three-legged calves, and obscene one-act *parades* like *The Shit Merchant* provided more immoderate, unmediated pleasure than the from-the-neck-up bombast of the "great players" at the Comédie-Française, who were mercilessly satirized by the feisty Italiens. The Quarrel of the Ancients and the Moderns waged between Boileau and his partisans and the Perrault brothers, who believed that the authors of antiquity "tho' great, were men as well as we," intensified, so much so that the balance and purity of the French national drama became imperiled by satiric interlopers. Unpopular and ill-attended, official comedy was in such a state of desuetude that the moral philosopher Pierre Bayle felt compelled to write in his "Continuation of Miscellaneous Thoughts" in 1704 that "comedy must be thought of as a feast given for the people, and therefore what is important is that the food appears good to the guest, and not that it was prepared according to the rules of the art of cuisine."

Did you ever see such a big fat dupe? — *Turcaret*

Literary historians the world over genuflect before the big novel, so Alain-René Lesage is revered most for the picaresque sprawl of his twelve-volume *History of Gil Blas de Santillane,* although his other lasting achievements include the mendacious *Turcaret,* more than one hundred short plays for the outlawed fair theaters, and *The Devil on Two Sticks,* a delightful novel of manners. Boileau himself is said to have boxed the ears of a lackey who had the audacity to bring a copy of *The Devil on Two Sticks* into his home, and it is not hard to see why. In it, the crippled Asmodeus, one of Beelzebub's wittier minions, takes Don Cléofas on a guided nocturnal tour of Madrid—that is to say, Paris. Asmodeus charms the roofs off the tenements so that he and Don Cléofas can peer in at the leading citizens after they have removed their social armor. *The Devil on Two Sticks* is an extended character assassination— a wealth of telling gestures, vanities, and peccadilloes—that eschews the neoclassical values of moderation, restraint, and decorum to reveal the tight, hot hearts beating beneath the humanist sang-froid of France's enlightened century. Indeed, there had been no room in Boileau's inventory of *genres* for Lesage's little imp, but by this time, new, irregular literary forms like the epistolary novel, the philosophic *conte*, the weekly journal, and the comedy of manners had arisen in accordance with a new temper that had little use for doctrinal intransigence.

Starting with the generation of 1680, as Versailles grew pious under the influence of Madame de Maintenon, the physical movement of bored, disaffected nobles away from Versailles and back to their private *hôtels* in Paris signals a concomitant shift away from the emulation of a glorious, constructed ideal—the public courtier—toward a new focus on the private self in all its weak, willful, and pleasurable mediocrity. The years 1680 to 1720 mark a period of aristocratic decadence, fiscal anxiety, and extreme social flux. Foreign wars and the completion of Versailles were bankrupting the monarchy; historians estimate that seven of every eight francs collected in taxes between 1680 and 1715 were spent on Versailles. The revocation of the Edict of Nantes in 1685 and the displacement of the Huguenots meant an irrevocable loss of Protestant capital and commercial know-how. To raise money, Louis and his ministers increased the manufacture of noble titles, but without land or church property to guarantee them, they were a devalued currency from the outset. Addicted to gambling and desperate for money, the aristocracy began to borrow heavily from rising bourgeois merchants. The state issued worthless bonds, raised taxes, inflated the money supply, and doubled its deficit in the first ten years of the eighteenth century. When Louis died in 1715, public debt stood at 750 billion francs. A typical solution for squeezing more money from the Third Estate was to recruit more tax farmers from the middle class; as long as these royally enfranchised publicans fulfilled the terms of their leased office, they were free to enrich themselves by levying ever higher taxes from the poor and pocketing the difference or lending to aristocrats at outrageous rates of interest.

In this economic climate of intense speculation, a clerk could become a banker, and a usurer could transform himself into a financier who was indispensable to the treasury. These arrivistes aped the manners of the gentry, consumed conspicuously, and married their daughters into families that could no longer afford to despise them. When money begins to supercede birth and everyone is for sale, price tags begin to appear in European literature. Lesage, for example, states at the outset of *Gil Blas* that "all men have coins for souls in this age." Among highborn dramatic heroes and heroines, wealth had heretofore been assumed and was never referred to except in general terms; in the newer genres, money becomes the central preoccupation and a spanking new source of comic material.

The moment is propitious, then, in 1708 for Lesage's new *grand caractère*, Turcaret the tax farmer, to make his debut at the Maison de Molière. At this point in his career, the forty-year-old Lesage, who came to Paris from Brittany to study law, had already translated several Spanish playwrights, including Calderón. In 1707 *The Devil on Two Sticks* was published, as well as the successful premiere of his one-act comedy *Crispin, Rival to His Master* (also freely adapted from a Spanish source) at the Comédie-Française. Private readings of *Turcaret* were held for the censors; but, because the title character was etched so acidly, a cabal of financiers threatened to shelve the project indefinitely. After an apocryphal intervention by either the Duc de Bourgogne or Fénélon or the Grand Dauphin, *Turcaret* premiered on 14 February 1709, in the middle of the severest winter France had experienced in seventy years. After seven performances, it was hastily withdrawn from the repertory, again under mysterious circumstances. Soon thereafter, Lesage forsook the state theater for the fairs, and *Turcaret* was not produced again until 1730. With Lesage's son Montmesnil playing the title role, this revival was an unqualified success, and *Turcaret* entered the permanent repertory, and eventually, the national school curriculum.

Formally, *Turcaret* combines neoclassical comedy of character with comedy of manners. Its plot, although stuffed with shady deals, is simple: the Baroness, an unscrupulous coquette, has secured the attentions of Turcaret, a parvenu tax farmer who promises to marry her. Daily, she accepts his expensive gifts and passes them on to her lover, the Chevalier, who for his part is bilking her to remain solvent at the gaming tables. The Chevalier, in turn, is being cheated by his lackey Frontin, whom he has managed to advantageously place in Turcaret's service. Frontin hopes to gain the wherewithal to marry Lisette, an amoral maid whom he has hired out to the Baroness. Money flows outward from Turcaret without interruption until the inconveniently extant Madame Turcaret turns up at a dinner party given by the Baroness. In the midst of the ensuing uproar, Turcaret is informed that he has been bankrupted, and the Chevalier learns that the money he extorted from the Baroness and entrusted to Frontin has been seized by Turcaret's creditors. In a final reversal, Frontin reveals to Lisette that he has lied about the confiscated funds. They now have enough money to marry and set themselves up in the ruined Turcaret's place.

There had been satiric portraits of tax farmers before, notably in Molière's *Countess of Escarbagnas* (1671) and Noland de Fatouville's *The Bankrupter* (1688), but whereas in Molière's world the hoarding or squandering of money provokes ridiculous laughter, in Lesage it is an occasion for irony. Harpagon has buried a bag of gold in his courtyard; both its balance and its provenance remain unspecified. *Turcaret*, by contrast, is strewn with immodestly specific lines like "That rotten bastard we lent nine thousand francs to last year at 200 percent is behind in his payments." The monetary transaction shows people up for what they really are, and every character in the play, without exception, is an irredeemably craven chiseler. Although they may, when in dramatic extremis, invoke the classical allegiances of honor, love, and birth, eventually their masks fall to reveal that the only true allegiance in this world is to the self, here understood to be a pre-emptive, unilateral greed. Money is the only relationship among people. The objective for the characters, and the source of *Turcaret's* comedy, is to keep the masks on through the constant twists of fortune Lesage drops into the plot.

Unlike some of his contemporaries, Lesage does not entirely renounce action for manners; his characters aren't merely caught behaving in juxtaposable slices of life; all of the scenes in *Turcaret* work within the double action frame of Turcaret's fall and Frontin's rise. On the other hand, Lesage's adherence to the unities of time and place—a day spent in the antechamber to the Baroness's boudoir—is not chosen out of slavish deference to *vraisemblance*, but rather for its theatrical possibilities. High finance is predicated on crisis; an escalating series of surprise entrances within this space serves to take Turcaret apart. Lesage appears to be winking at classical convention when he has Frontin run down for the audience the six separate errands he must complete before Act Three can start, or when Lisette says "Twenty thousand francs! And all in one day!"

Formally, then, *Turcaret* would appear a proper enterprise for the court theater, yet Lesage uncomfortably crowds onto the great stage more of French society than it had hitherto been accustomed to. Circling around the tycoon is a swarm of grotesques worthy of Gogol; François Mauriac once referred to the cast of *Turcaret* as "gilded insects." By presenting high-born characters in tatterdemalion, low-born domestics with seditious mindsets, or horrifying freaks disguised as drop-in guests, Lesage pushes the limits of *bienséance* with every entrance. A far cry from the classical *jeune premier*, the decidedly ignoble Chevalier is incapable of love and acknowledges that he is no match for the "superior genius" of his servant Frontin; for fun, his crony, the outrageously dissipated Marquess, has taken to humiliating bulky countesses at costume balls. Marine, the Baroness's first chambermaid, initially appears to resemble her clear-sighted, good-natured relations in Molière, but she storms out at the end of Act I because she and her mistress are not realizing enough profit on their swindles. The scold is soon replaced by the tart: no standard-issue soubrette, Lisette declares herself sexually available to the highest bidder and even threatens to sell Frontin out in order to rise in station. Messieurs Rafle and Furet, the loan shark and the confidence man, respectively, are grizzled representatives of the louche, fiscal demimonde that has sprung up to accommodate a cross-pollinating French society. Madame Jacob, Turcaret's off-color sister who peddles secondhand trinkets door to door, and the blowsy Madame Turcaret behave like tinseled bawds sprung from the St. Germain fair.

Frontin is part of an interesting continuum in French dramatic literature, that of the calculating manservant. Molière's wily Scapin performs tricks that are, for him, works of art, proof of his virtuosity and his commedia dell'arte identity, as well as a source of pleasure for himself and the audience. With *Dom Juan*'s Sganarelle, we move closer to Frontin: obedient, somewhat respectful, Sganarelle is alternately amused and frightened by his master, yet, as the curtain falls, he is shrieking for his wages. Unlike Molière's servants, Frontin is completely guided by his cupidity, and, although he is pleased to deploy his "superior genius," unlike Scapin he won't entertain any more than is required for the task at hand, even going so far as to complain about his workload. In fact, he seems slightly miffed that Turcaret, the Baroness, and the Chevalier are all too easy to dupe—as if Lesage hadn't set up enough of a challenge for his talents. Like Figaro, whom he forecasts, Frontin is at war with his master, resents his attentions to his intended, yet manifests no personal rancor. Frontin alone is aware of the extended "deliciously deceitful food chain" that describes the play, and even if he can joke, his is a dry and cold-hearted humor. His triumph at the end of the play is one of intelligence, not charm.

The Baroness is the most difficult character to grasp in the play; her heartlessness is not as securely tied to an action as the others; since she never appears visibly in the Chevalier's thrall, we never know why, for example, she loves him. When she discovers his faithlessness, her rupture with him lacks comic force and resolution; instead of banishing him, she retreats weakly into the wings. Her most interesting moment is perhaps her most false: very late in Act IV, she experiences a suspiciously tardy wave of remorse for Turcaret: "Do you know I'm beginning to pity him? . . . I'm feeling the birth pangs of integrity." Is her regret to be taken at face value, or is Lesage working too hard to exonerate his inhumane heroine? Lisette, as ever, is quick with her counsel — "Let's not pity the pitiless!" and the matter is summarily dropped.

Whether this is appropriate to the Baroness's character or not, Lesage nevertheless has to beg the question: is Turcaret more to be pitied than condemned? Easily shamed, socially insecure, humiliated in love, ridiculed by his servants, loathed by his wife and sister, Turcaret the guileless cash cow is ultimately both repulsive and endearing. "Have you ever seen such a big fat dupe?" marvels the jade Lisette. No match for his surroundings, like Molière's poor Monsieur Jourdain in *Le Bourgeois gentilhomme*, he does all he can to improve himself, subscribing to the Opéra, writing poems to his lady love, ordering carriages for her, building her a château. His love is pathetically authentic, and when he breaks things, he pays for them.

He is generous, even magnanimous — with other people's money. Lest anyone pity Turcaret unblushingly, Lesage shrewdly includes a scene of Turcaret conducting business; shrewder still, he places it in the very center of the play. Rafle arrives to present his dossier of hard-luck cases to his boss. The sight of Turcaret liquidating the defenseless is as amusing as the thought of Ralph Kramden running Proctor & Gamble, but the scene is nonetheless a chilling portrait of corporate efficiency. Monsieur Jourdain, the would-be gentleman, arrives without us seeing how he got there. Lesage's fiscal realism reminds us that we can never forget at whose expense Turcaret has come to power. Cheating a locksmith out of his life savings in a split second, Turcaret has created the surroundings he eventually falls prey to. Like all great dramatic characters, Turcaret embraces irreconcilable extremes, and Lesage refuses to take sides. Turcaret combines the pugnacious bluster of the braggart warrior with the pathos of Lopahkin, his distant Russian cousin in Chekhov's *Cherry Orchard*.

What is finally important about *Turcaret*, not to say revolutionary for the course of dramatic literature, is its utter lack of a moral cynosure. Lesage places no value on virtue, scruple, ingenuity, or purity. The only public statement he ever made about the play was made indirectly, through the mouth of little Asmodeus, who, spying Lesage in a loge at the opening of *Turcaret*, offhandedly says to Don Cléofas: "He took it into his head to render vice hateful." What is missing from this neutral statement is a helpful correlative and a host of qualifiers. Which vice? Hateful to whom? Render vice hateful in order to . . . ? Lesage poses the question: when watching a play unencumbered by ethics, where *is* an audience supposed to look?

Turcaret provides the first test case in Western drama for what happens when money replaces the older, ordinal motives of the agon. Today, in our own careening, multifariously bankrupt society, even the serial-killing antiheroes of our theater and cinema have to have their sympathetic sides in order to get the green light from producing organizations. Who are we to *care* about in *Turcaret?* They're a pack of weasels, equally and refreshingly bad. When Frontin the pupil surpasses his master, does one root for his guile or for the revenge of the Third Estate? The love between Frontin and Lisette sets no example. *Turcaret* is not a political play, and Lesage is no moralist. The only comfort one can adduce from the game is that evil destroys itself and that one day Frontin will get his own comeuppance — scant reassurance indeed. *Turcaret,* which offers no palliative except the passage of time, remains permanently unsettling.

Sex, greed, and bad manners are eternal, and eternally linked. *Turcaret* may be a ruthless play, but it is not sour. Greed pixillates the characters; the genial amorality which suffuses the piece is close to the black comedy of the British playwright Joe Orton. As a portrait of the getting and the spending, *Turcaret* is as current and as risible as the Donald Trump, Leona Helmsley, Ivan Boesky, or Robert Maxwell sagas. Lesage, who furnished dozens of plays for the populist fair audiences, was not a brilliant wordsmith like Molière or Marivaux, but his cast of crass opportunists is well served by his blunt dialogue. If all of the characters are moved by the same matter, and if money makes people talk funny, then the challenge is to develop a patois of venality that accommodates all of the classes and castes represented, and to exploit all of the tonal shifts that occur when the lower orders overreach themselves or when the titled characters are duped into vulgarity.

It's very painful to switch philosophies! — *The Triumph of Love*

Although he was rediscovered, play by play, from the 1920s through the 1950s, Pierre Carlin de Marivaux's original status as a *méconnu* in the French canon has more to do with his refusal to promote himself in his own time than it does with any hidden virtue in his work. He never presumed. He was a private man in a hysterically public century. After Louis XIV died in 1715, the grandson who succeeded him, seven-year-old Louis XV, could hardly command the divinity or the respect of the great Sun King. More than a sigh of relief, the seven years of the French Regency, the period during which Marivaux began his career, was the last cloudless debauch of feudal France. The eighteenth-century exploration of individual *sensibility* (a dread buzzword of the age) is a healthy, skeptical *embourgeoisement* of culture. For the first third of the century, characters of "sensibility" and "morality" walked onstage from the outside. The plays surrounding them evolved much more slowly; if Regency writers were happy to drop baroque pretence, they were loath to throw over Boileau's prescription completely. For his part, Marivaux neither drew on fixed character types nor offered satiric portraits nor imitated the classical theater of crisis; he wrote characters and situations that *developed*. The very titles of his plays display movement — not *The Miser, The Imaginary Invalid, The Knight à la Mode, The Liar, The Gambler,* but *The Surprise of Love, The Dandy Corrected, Harlequin Refined By Love, The Triumph of Love*. And for much of his theatrical career, he carried out his dramaturgy of language and love without the Comédie-Française.

Marivaux's most public statement about the purpose of his literary art is "Je voudrais rendre les hommes plus sages et plus humains." Le Théâtre des Italiens, reinstated in 1716 by the scandalous Regent, had as its slogan "Castigat ridendo mores." Marivaux and Riccoboni's troupe, seeking to "make mankind wiser and more human," seeking to "punish customs with laughter," had an entire culture to reprove, a culture bearing its own device, and it is fitting that Voltaire, Marivaux's eternal gadfly, should have penned it.

> I love luxury, and even softness,
> I love all pleasures, and arts of every kind,
> Cleanliness, taste, and every adornment,
> All men of honor feel exactly as I.

The most important thought in this quatrain, taken from the poem "The Worldly Man," is "arts of every kind." Voltaire is slyly including *artifice* of every kind, deception, self-deception, the gestures that speak civility but mask a monster. Marivaux and the Italiens didn't crusade to tear down the posture of the worldly man, built as it was along the domesticated, asymmetrical curves and surfaces of the rococo, but they did manage, subtly in some collaborations, overtly in others, to reveal that the worldly man's stance was as much an illusion as the other fictions that order rational existence.

Marivaux's first comedy to be staged, the one-act fairy play *Harlequin Refined by Love* (1720), contains the germ of all his thematic preoccupations, as well as his dramaturgical technique. In the first scene, ten lines into Marivaux's dramatic career, Trivelin, the Fairy's factotum, exhorts his bored mistress to demand less *glory* in order to experience more *pleasure*, which is as plain a shift from the baroque to the rococo as can be found. The characters, the locale, and the *lazzi* may be Italian, but the title of the play promises a sentimental education. Harlequin would rather gorge himself than woo the smitten Fairy, but when he spots the shepherdess Silvia, it's love at first sight: after a prolonged piece of business about a bee on his nose, he picks up a handkerchief, looks at her, and a commedia clown is forever transformed. Suddenly he speaks naturally, *nobly,* and the play begins to demonstrate the value of discourse offered and withheld. Enraged to discover Harlequin speaking the language of love, the Fairy vows to kill Silvia. The play ends happily, as it must, but not before Harlequin has learned to dissemble his feelings, learned the power of silence, and learned how to lie and to swear to his own advantage. In other words, he has learned how to be human.

Marivaux once wrote, "I have spied in the human heart all the different niches where Love can hide when it is afraid to show itself, and each one of my comedies has for its object to make Love come out from of its niche." The positive moral of *Harlequin Refined by Love* is that the power of love makes men eloquent, sensitive, diplomatic, reasoning, and civilized. This principle will never leave Marivaux—he will re-examine, with growing profundity, the obverse consequences of silence, diplomacy, and linguistic deceptions in his novels and later plays, whether they are philosophic comedies, heroic comedies, bourgeois dramas, or the love comedies for which he is most celebrated. Intent on dramatizing all the metaphysical modulations of love, Marivaux and his renovation— or re-invention—of the love comedy prompted Voltaire to complain that Marivaux knew every byway of love, but missed the main highway.

If entertainment was the sine qua non of commedia dell'arte, then love was its engine. As soon as the archetypal ancestors of Riccoboni's contract players fell in love, the play took off—thence the duels, the jealousies, the rivals, the parents. In a commedia scenario, however, the characters never stop to consider their emotional situation; one never hears, "I don't know where I'm at," or, "boy, what has love done to me?" They immediately set about removing their multiple obstacles. Marivaux's modest yet enduring dramatic revolution is to make self-reflection both the substance and the sole obstacle of his theater. In his greatest plays, he begins with a heroine of superior reasoning who falls in love on sight without knowing it. Against her judgment and her will, she must overcome an agonizing process of self-deception. A Marivaux plot is loose, easy, a geometric series of expected entrances and exits. The traditionally irascible fathers and scheming mothers are models of liberality who gently smile at the foibles of their daughters. Wise servants fall in love with alacrity and then push their poky masters along. Marivaux's dramaturgy allows his audience to see more than his wrongheaded characters. As with Chekhov, we wait for them to catch up to their self-delusions.

"I don't know where I'm at" ("Je ne sais où je suis") is the hinge. As Brady points out in his *Love in the Theater of Marivaux,* his heroes and heroines admit this when they are conflicted between the person and the persona, between the individual conscience and the social role or masks they inhabit, masks that are regulated by duties to family, social status, wealth, and a highly refined *amour propre.* The Other attacks their self-fortified citadel of reason and vanity. A crisis of identity develops, and the self fluctuates between social conditioning and individual need. Since Marivaux is not a playwright to advocate a repudiation of society, his characters are in a bind. The person must connect to the persona; moments of deceit and self-deception are adjudicated by the use of stratagems and tests. When the masks fall, the self is permitted to see clear into its heart. Love is declared, and the play falls silent.

Yet Marivaux's presentation of love isn't always a gentle movement to conjugal silence. Characters are as often manipulated out of love, and several of his finest works have plangently unresolved questions at the final curtain. The title of Marivaux's third comedy (and his personal favorite), *Double Infidelities,* gives the play away at the start; the audience is alerted not to watch for the outcome, but rather to study the dual progressions of falling out of love and falling in love again. Pitting the court against the country, the Prince and Flaminia *will* the dissolution of the pastoral love between Silvia and Harlequin in order to gain them for themselves. Several critics, including Anouilh (who uses Marivaux's *False Confidences* as the play-within-the-play in *The Rehearsal*), have detected the hand of a cruel manipulator in this metaphysician of the heart, going so far as to brand him a forerunner to Laclos.

The Triumph of Love, less well known than *Double Infidelities,* also features a willful manipulator at its quickening heart: Princess Léonide. Or rather Princess Léonide, who is also Phocion, who is also Aspasie. Actually, there are two different Aspasies, endowing the leading actress with a total of four distinct identities to portray. In toto Princess Léonide is the brainiest, as well as the most diabolical female in Marivaux's theater. A patent flair for dishonesty and an overt penchant for cruelty made her a woman too problematically powerful for eighteenth-century theatrical convention, yet make her a fascinating heroine more than two hundred years later. In terms of *vraisemblance,* contemporary critics found her swaggering demeanor more in keeping with a romanesque adventuress than the Spartan princess she is. Her cross-dressing and the resulting androgynous erotics in her scenes with a confused prince were, at best, a telling violation of *bienséance.* Marivaux himself conceded in his preface to the play that the initial reception of *The Triumph of Love* was "bizarre."

The philosopher Hermocrate and his maiden sister Léontine have taken to the woods to escape a frivolous, unreasoning, lovestruck society. They have raised Agis, a royal foundling, to scorn love and its distaff inspiration. Princess Léonide has glimpsed Agis reading in a forest and fallen in love with him. He also happens to be the rightful heir to the throne upon which she sits. Her aim is to win his love at any cost and, not incidentally, restore him to power. Unlike most Marivaux heroines, Léonide is in love before the play begins and is well beyond being derailed by its exquisite divagations. She knows how to manipulate love and its powers to her advantage; her stratagem is the quicksilver improvisation of her four identities. In the first two acts she seduces the three hermits in dazzling turns. As Phocion, the comely young scholar seeking hermitage for her philosophic aspirations, she appeals to the long-dormant vanity of the aging Léontine. Hermocrate, with his "advanced" powers of reason, discovers "Phocion's" true sex immediately, but instead of revealing her royal identity, she assumes another female guise, that of Aspasie, a Portia-like casuist who trusses up the philosopher with his own logic. And after the defenseless Agis has two itchy, homoerotic encounters with young lord Phocion, she reveals a second Aspasie to him, an utter gamine who, ostensibly seeking his protection, exploits his sexual naiveté nonetheless. Is the true Princess Léonide any one of these assumed characters? Or is she the woman, who, when reporting her progress with Agis to her maidservant, says, "Two more interviews and he'll be cooked clean through"? Or is Léonide the haughty princess who threatens to put her rustic henchmen in prison for their greed?

Love proves itself more powerful than reason, but its lesson is a harsh one for the pair of siblings, who gradually awaken to the force of love like children groping for speech. "It's very painful to switch philosophies!" Hermocrate cries out to Agis when he confesses he has been wrong about love all along. He and Léontine have a touching scene at the end of Act II, in which they wonder aloud whether they were hasty to quit society. Haltingly they sound each other's warming hearts. When each tells the other, abashed, that they are not too old for romance and are even . . . *attractive*, Marivaux achieves an unsentimental, Chekhovian pathos. Hurled into passion's chasm in their twilight years, love has made them human, and that is a wonderful, terrible thing.

The ancient laws of comedy cannot provide a triple wedding for four people, but Marivaux unties his plot in the third act with scant regard for awakened sensibilities. After revealing her ruse, Léonide tells Hermocrate and Léontine that they deserve to be humiliated, and she walks out with Prince Agis. The kingdom is restored; the servants have been paid; but the jilted pair are destroyed by change, by the revelation that they are prey to human emotion just like everyone else. Like Flaminia is *Double Infidelities*, Princess Léonide is a dangerous force. What Marivaux has done, and it is no less astonishing for being simple, is to combine the role of the dewy ingenue with the nervy confidante. Léonide revels in her role-playing and is thrilled to debase the hapless philosopher and his bluestocking sister. She has mastered all of Marivaux's languages — male, female, seductive, sophistic, high-born, and low — and has absorbed all the stratagems of his dramaturgy.

Long before Rousseau, Marivaux upheld the rights of the individual to develop as a human being; he always allowed his characters the space and the opportunity to recognize themselves, to know themselves, and to proceed from there. And in that most aesthetically lachrymose and scientifically providential of centuries, he did it without tears, long-lost siblings, hearts melting all over the boards, or degenerate verse. When love triumphs over reason three times in *The Triumph of Love*, Marivaux the moralist is at cross-purposes with Marivaux the psychologist. That there are as many victims as victors in love when the curtain falls propels the play out of its original rococo context and places Marivaux firmly in our century.

In translating *The Triumph of Love*, it seemed most essential to capture all of the exuberant shifts in diction, not only as Léonide spins in and out of each separate identity for every new entrance of a suitor, but also the fluctuations that constantly occur within the scenes, when each of the lovers (the Princess included) slip in or out of discursive attitudes when they feel uncomfortable with their dawning emotions. Far more than the situation or the characters, the tonal incongruities and collisions in the language — a character in its own right in Marivaux — provide the thrust for an actable English translation. Lady Léontine, for example, becomes quite grand, almost comically dainty, when Phocion tickles a vanity she thought she'd suppressed. Yet as soon as she imagines her actions are observed, a horrid self-consciousness helps her regain her initial hauteur. And the merest intimation of the physical aspect of love gives all of the hermits verbal fidgets. Hermocrate, for his part, tries to reason, deflect, bluster, insult, and finally whine his way out of loving Aspasie before his inevitable comic submission.

The loser pays for dinner. — *Eating Crow*

The ancient authors knew that the essential comic urges are food, sex, and money. In France, the commedia dell'arte and the fair theaters kept these urges indecorously alive at the same time as Louis XIV's splendid century of cultural centralization attempted to subdue them or suppress them altogether. Lesage, as we have seen, reclaimed money in all its glorious specificity for the stage; Marivaux, along with Richardson and Rousseau, was one of the great eighteenth-century estheticians of foreplay—he ultimately must share responsibility for such deathless sentiments as, "I love you, but I'm not *in* love with you." In plays like *The Italian Straw Hat, The Piggy Bank, Monsieur Perrichon's Trip,* and the hitherto untranslated *La Chasse aux corbeaux,* Eugène Labiche, writing for the nineteenth century, dramatizes food, along with sex and money, for the triumphant, and triumphantly complacent French bourgeoisie. The observation is not intended facetiously: The Second Empire (1852–1870) was one of the most voracious and omnivorous societies Europe has ever seen. Consumption was its central fact and metaphor. From 1838 to 1876, Labiche fed more than 175 farces to an audience ravenous for formula.

It is beyond the scope of this introduction to detail how the theater was transformed by the French Revolution and by France's subsequent spasmodic experiments with democracy. By mid-century, a dichotomy still existed between the Comédie-Française, which, in the face of changing political and aesthetic ideology, continued its somnolent trajectory, and the dozens of boulevard theaters, which earlier in the century had traded most heavily in melodrama based on Pixérécourt's model. By the time Labiche started writing, the boulevard theaters specialized in *vaudevilles* and the *haute comédie* or literary comedy. Vaudeville, an elastic form that combined loosely linked scenes with satiric couplets sung to popular airs, had been the chief draw at the fair theaters since the early eighteenth century (Lesage wrote dozens of them). By the mid-nineteenth century, Scribe, developing and perfecting his well-made play out of the vaudeville form — "great effects from small things: that is my science" — had begun to downplay the sung portion of the evening in favor of a tightly wound plot built on coincidence, terrible secrets, and *coups de théâtre*. Scribe is followed by Augier and Dumas fils, who interlard the artificial conventions of the well-made play with pietistic commentary about social ills and the necessity of maintaining the integrity of the family.

Despite his enormous success, Labiche was never satisfied with being simply a *vaudevilliste*. He had devoted himself to a genre which was held in low repute by academicians who reproached it for its total lack of literary ambitions and for its overly colloquial dialogue. He wanted to write a more tasteful comedy of manners or character, plays in which the author indicts society for its faults and vices, exalts forsaken values, and proposes a moral. Labiche wrote that the Théâtre du Palais-Royal (the boulevard theater which premiered most of his work) "will have done me a great wrong if it has taken the scattered comic elements I possess in my brain and exhausted them on the farce. I've always hoped and dreamed of writing a play for the Comédie-Française. The instant a suitable subject comes into my head, I will jump on it."

Like *Turcaret*, and similar to Augier's play *The Money Question* (the original source for the epigram "Business is other people's money"), *Eating Crow*, a play of which Labiche was very proud, demonstrates that, in a world divided between the takers and the taken, the need for money will make people do anything. Its tone differs from Lesage to the degree that there is no need to conceal the fiscal motive — the values that Lesage satirized have been accepted wholesale. Labiche's characters assume from the outset that everyone is on the make.

In order to marry Clotilde Renaudier, the woman he loves, Albert de Criqueville, a penniless dandy with only a bachelor's degree to commend him, needs to raise a hundred thousand francs and, in a new comic requirement, a well-paying job. He is about to throw himself into the Seine one winter morning when he overhears a chance reading of La Fontaine's "The Fox and the Crow," the famous fable whose lesson is, "Every flatterer lives at the expense of the one who listens to him." Armed with this maxim, he and a bootblack named Antoine, whose fortune Criqueville promises to make, decide to make a science out of La Fontaine and start hunting crow. The shooting gallery includes bureaucrats, tailors, humpbacks, skinflinted capitalists, paralegals, boulevard peacocks, dowagers, short-order cooks, and the English. His strategy —

flatter til they fall — nets him a suit, cigars, expensive lunches, and tickets to the races. But, pressing further for the serious money, he discovers that the monied class closes ranks when threatened, and that it is more to his advantage to make himself *feared* than loved. After attempting to calumniate Flavigny, a railroad minister who has refused him a job, Criqueville has an opportunity to destroy his reputation. Instead, he takes the high road and behaves so nobly toward Flavigny that he gains a post in his administration. It is Flavigny who supplies the hastily conceived moral of the play: "The best way to succeed is a little heart and a lot of work."

In Labiche's time, it was considered bad form (and bad business) to go against the prevailing morals of the stage; a play like *Eating Crow* contains two apparent lessons: "In order to succeed, make yourself feared," and, in an ironic tip of the hat to moral tradition, "to succeed, a little heart plus a lot of work." Labiche, angling for a genteel literary success, may have thought he was being sincere when he has Flavigny draw that second ethical conclusion. If so, he was only fooling himself. Criqueville may have been industrious, but his activities were dishonest. His refusal to destroy Flavigny in the *scene à faire* may display a little heart, but it is also a calculated risk that happened to pay off. "A little heart and a lot of work" is as bald a prerogative for capitalism as one can find in nineteenth-century drama. Do as Flavigny says, not as Criqueville does. The disappointing reception of *Eating Crow* in its own day may stem in part from an audience that, accustomed to a more antic and unsparing Labiche, could not take Criqueville's moral conversion at face value. Today we know better, and the play can be enjoyed for what it is, a vulgar tear through the streets of Paris.

Labiche's mastery of Scribean formula can be illustrated by the pattern of dramatic reversals, increasing in speed and intensity, that Criqueville undergoes. His fortunes start at the bottom, but by the end of the first act, he has gained entrance into the tailor's home; at the end of Act II, he is splendidly attired and about to lunch at someone else's expense. In Act III, which takes place at the glittering Café de Paris, he is fed and lodged in an acquaintance's empty carriage; he experiences his first obstacle when he discovers that his brand-new best friend Montdouillard is his rival for the hand of Clotilde. In Act IV, he undergoes two rapid negative reversals: Flavigny turns him down for a job, and Montdouillard refuses to give him loan shares at cost. He temporarily regroups with the hump-backed Saint-Putois, but then again loses his chance for gainful employment. Then comes the news that the announcement of Montdouillard's nuptials are to be held the very next day. Criqueville's fortunes are at their lowest point, and he contemplates the Seine again as the fourth act ends. In the final act, Criqueville honorably burns the written evidence against Flavigny that has just conveniently fallen into his hands — pure Scribe — and wins the job. Montdouillard suspects that Criqueville has started a rival corporation, merges with his nonexistent business, and gives him the money in stocks. All that is left is the girl, but Labiche dashes Criqueville's hopes by giving Clotilde to Montdouillard. Yet, in the final, shamelessly contrived yet deliciously satisfying *coup de théâtre*, Clotilde's father, endowed with a singular sense of smell, recognizes Montdouillard as the sexual reprobate he has been hunting down for the entire play. All true to the aim of *vaudeville*, which is to get the girl's father, who said no at the top of the show, to say yes at the final curtain.

Eating Crow endures, but not in accordance to Labiche's ambitions for it. *Eating Crow* is a funny, accidentally incisive critique of *surfeit*. The dandy Montdouillard's suite of twenty-three ostentatious waistcoats is not only a very funny running gag, it offers a visual image of a grossly expanding society in which the stomach serves as a bank. The eating contest in Act III between the Englishman and the disguised Antoine (as hungry a clown as Arlecchino ever was), in which the loser pays for dinner — or eat until you explode — is a living demonstration of what the market will bear. When the Englishman discovers, however, with whom he has been at table, the contest is called off for crossing class lines. The play treats moral, social, and financial turnover. The gift of a two-franc cigar is immediately made worthless next to a five-franc cigar, which is topped by a ten-franc cigar three lines later. Hard specie circulates in *Turcaret;* in Labiche, the point is what money can buy. We are a long way from Corneille's unadorned classical locus; *Eating Crow* presents Paris as a clotted Balzacian boutique where its citizens, unbound by honor or love or duty, do not have intelligent discussions about art or scientific positivism — they talk *things*. The conduct of life (and theater) now requires a wealth of props: cigars, gloves, stoves, pianos, dogs, waistcoats, canes, nankeen jackets, crystal, race horses, hacks, cushions, newspapers, letters, and toilet water. And, as for the groaning board, *marrons glacés, andouillettes,* cream horns, beefsteaks, chicken with olives, mayonnaise, cabbage, stew, champagne, and absinthe all make an appearance. The only commodity to remain offstage is Clotilde, whose hymen is the greatest stage property of them all; she refuses to appear, even at the comic conclusion, the announcement of her wedding to the enterprising Criqueville. Labiche is wise to leave her in the wings—if set into motion, she might prove either too true a product of a mercenary world to be good, or too good to be true.

A majority of the scrambling characters in the play are from elsewhere—Picardy, the Auvergne, Soissons. One-third of Paris's population in the Second Empire, like the heroes in Balzac and Stendhal, were rustics up from the country, desperately trying to make their fortunes and lose the taint of the provinces. The humble sausages sizzling in the stove in the middle of the tailor's salon, a meal that Criqueville and Antoine would kill for at the end of Act I, will no longer pass muster in Act II when a more refined opportunity arises. In this society, there will always be something bigger, something more to have, a new material imperative. There will never be enough. It is no coincidence that Catiche the cook, who arrives in Paris the moment the play begins, only knows how to make an omelette. With each subsequent stage cross she makes, Catiche is seen toting groceries required for increasingly labor-intensive—and to her, frivolous—recipes. An omelette, no more than water and eggs, is a subsistence food, adequate nourishment in the country. Labiche asks: Whither the egg? At work in the play is a liminal nostalgia for the things left behind, values discarded and displaced, for the simple values that France set aside once it shifted to steam. Antoine does eat too much against the Englishman (and, incidentally, doesn't have to spring for the meal), but he is not ashamed to admit it. Criqueville, on the other hand, has schemed his way back into the system, implicitly asking the question: When you trade up, what do you trade away?

The critic Hippolyte Parigot wrote, "There are two remedies for the dyspepsia afflicting the end of this century: Vichy (the spa) and Labiche. Vichy doesn't always succeed. Labiche takes immediate effect." Labiche's success in his own time and his continued influence more than a hundred years after his death can be attributed to his comic verve. Labiche's theater is not literary; given his prodigious output, how much attention could he lavish upon any one piece? *Eating Crow* is, after all, one of six farces he premiered in 1853. Unlike the works of Augier or Dumas fils, whose brilliant tirades and speeches of justification, subject to ephemeral literary fashions, have been gathering dust in libraries for decades, Labiche's style is utterly a spoken one, a familiar, utilitarian, pedestrian French. Set speeches only appear to heighten the infrequent psychological situation, and, except for fox and crow references, imagery seldom dresses a comic situation. He refrains from puns, a reflex for most *vaudevillistes* of the period, but knows the value of comic repetition and riposte. Coarse at times but never vulgar, Labiche's characters speak a sprightly dialogue of daily life in a self-important capital. The syntax is highly simplified — subordinate clauses and logical connections are a rare occasion; we are a long way from the classical convention in which dramatic characters are endowed with the immediate means to speak their minds fully and accurately. Labiche's world has no time to ponder; the Second Empire, an era in which even the carriage drivers are dabbling in stock splits, is teeming with *activity*. A page of Labiche is scattered with ellipses and dashes, acting as a blueprint for the process of dramatic thought.

The most striking aspect of Labiche's dramaturgical style is a preponderant, nearly obsessive use of asides. A corollary to political democracy is a theatrical democracy in which no one individual has to idly stand by for the confidences and exposition of his superiors. Labiche is democratic with his asides; secondary and tertiary characters of all classes are given equal opportunity to display their duplicitous natures. Lacking classical friends and confidants to whom they can handily reveal their hidden motives, Labiche's characters turn again and again to the audience, a complicit audience of well-fed individuals, an audience just like them. Labiche's reliance on the aside reveals the egocentrism of individuals completely occupied with themselves. Some indispensable asides serve as plot points, but in addition to these, there are far more asides — the brief flash of a fallen mask — devoted to revealing the true feelings cloaked beneath the fulsome compliment.

Translating Labiche presents a completely different challenge from translating the court playwrights. The gauntlet that Molière throws down is to be funny. Lesage sets his characters on one another and lets them flay one another with a lapidary wit that provokes ironic laughter from an audience of ostensible moral superiors. The tonal filigrees and psychological fits that Marivaux's lovers endure elicit a gentler, knowing laughter of recognition, and an appreciation of a highly literate style. It is easy for a translator to wander afield from Marivaux's and Lesage's comic interests and betray them with too heavy or too obvious a hand. Labiche uses comic methods closer to our own. Criqueville's opening suicide monologue is meant to be performed like stand-up comedy. Working without formal or thematic constraints, Labiche uses punch lines, running gags, absurd non sequiturs, and one-liners designed to demolish an audience with the business, indeed the science, of laughter. Chuckles do not obtain in Labiche's theater, so betraying him in translation and production means not going for the big laughs.

If euphony and flourish are the guiding principles to translating Marivaux's rhetorical inventions, and if tooling lines to character is the best strategy with which to animate Lesage's mordant portrait gallery, it is essential, when translating Labiche, to concentrate on rhythm. His characters, all charming surface, don't speechify and don't psychologize. They aren't even particularly good listeners; they top one another, undercut one another in focus-stealing asides. This is a comedy of rim-shot salvos; their lines are meant to build and detonate with an economy that is easy to recognize but difficult to duplicate. Not only should they sound funny when taken singly, they have to sound right in sequences of two and three. Ideally, an audience will be laughing at the sound of the rhythm even before the sense of the joke lands, so the translator has to rebuild a French machine to English expectations and expostulations.

I

TURCARET

IN THE ORIGINAL EDITION of Turcaret, *published in 1709 by Pierre Ribou, the play was preceded and followed by a critical dialogue. Asmodeus, the eponymous Devil on Two Sticks, and his eager pupil Don Cléofas had first appeared two years earlier in Lesage's highly popular novel of manners.*

A Critique of the Play
Turcaret
by the Devil on Two Sticks

ASMODEUS. Since my magician has set me free again, I'm going to take you all over the world, and every day I promise to grant you the objects of your wishes.

CLÉOFAS. You weren't kidding when you said we'd go at a great pace, in spite of how crippled you are; just now we were in Madrid. I only had to wish to be in Paris, and here we are. My God, Lord Asmodeus, it's a pleasure to travel with you.

ASMODEUS. Is that so?

CLÉOFAS. But where have you taken me? We're on top of a theater; I see the sets, the loges, the parterre—we must be at the Comédie-Française.

ASMODEUS. You guessed it. They're just about to perform a new play that I wanted to amuse you with. While we wait for it to start, we can converse without anyone seeing or hearing us.

CLÉOFAS. What a beautiful gathering—all women!

ASMODEUS. There would have been even more of them except for the shows at the fair. Most women nowadays rush there in a frenzy. I for one am delighted to see them adopt the taste of their lackeys and their grooms. That's why I'm opposed to the Comédie-Française. Every day I inspire new chicaneries for the fairground actors. I'm the one who furnished them with their Swiss.[1]

CLÉOFAS. What do you mean by your *Swiss?*

ASMODEUS. I'll explain that another time. Let's just look at what's in front of us. See how hard it is to get a seat? Do you know why there's a

1. Le Suisse was a character of Italian origins who appeared in fairground plays speaking a nonsense, pidgin mixture of German and French.

crowd? Today is the premiere of a comedy about a businessman. People love to laugh at the expense of those who make them cry.

CLÉOFAS. You mean to say that businessmen are all—

ASMODEUS. There are some extremely honorable businessmen. I will admit that their number isn't very great, but there are some who have actually made their fortunes without straying from principles of honor and integrity, and with whom the nobles of the robe and the sword deign to align themselves. The playwright respects them; he would be wrong to confuse them with the others. There are honest people in every profession. I even know some commissioners and court clerks with a conscience.

CLÉOFAS. Then this play shouldn't offend the honorable businesspeople.

ASMODEUS. Just as *Tartuffe*, which you read, doesn't offend the truly pious. Why on earth would businessmen be offended to see a sot or a knave from their ranks on the stage? His part doesn't represent the whole. If they were offended, they'd be acting with more delicacy than all the courtiers and lawyers, who are delighted to see all the ignorant and corruptible marquesses and judges on stage.

CLÉOFAS. I'm curious to know how the play will be received. Do me a favor and tell me in advance.

ASMODEUS. I thought I told you that devils can't predict the future. But even if we could, I'm sure we could never predict whether a play will succeed or fail. That's completely unfathomable.

CLÉOFAS. No doubt the author and the actors flatter themselves that it will succeed.

ASMODEUS. On the contrary, the actors have a low opinion of it, and their forebodings, while not infallible, were more than enough to frighten the author, who has gone and hidden himself in the third balcony. To make matters worse, a cashier and a stockbroker who've heard all about the play have just sat down next to him, and they're tearing it apart mercilessly. Fortunately for him, he's so deaf he can't hear half of what they're saying.[2]

CLÉOFAS. I should think there'd be a lot of cashiers and stockbrokers in the audience.

ASMODEUS. I see only gangs of bookkeepers and rival authors down there, hissers and booers all primed to react.

CLÉOFAS. Doesn't the playwright have any supporters?

ASMODEUS. Of course. All of his friends and his friends' friends are here. What's more, they've stationed several police grenadiers in the orches-

2. By 1709 Lesage was nearly deaf and used an ear trumpet.

tra to keep the bookkeepers in line—I wouldn't want to give my response to the play in front of them. But the actors have appeared; let's be quiet and listen. You know enough French to judge the play. After the parterre has reached its verdict, we'll either reverse or confirm their decision.

❀ ❀ ❀

TURCARET

First presented by the Comédie-Française on 14 February 1709

Cast
in order of appearance

MARINE, maid to the Baroness
THE BARONESS, a young widow and coquette
FRONTIN, valet to the Chevalier
FLAMAND, valet to Turcaret
TURCARET, a tax farmer in love with the Baroness
THE CHEVALIER, a dandy
LISETTE, maid to the Baroness
THE MARQUESS, a dandy
RAFLE, a usurer
FURET, a rogue
JASMIN, lackey to the Baroness
MADAME JACOB, a dealer in secondhand merchandise and Turcaret's sister
MADAME TURCARET, Turcaret's wife

Setting: The private rooms of the Baroness in Paris.

Act I

MARINE. And still another six hundred francs yesterday!

BARONESS. I won't put up with your reproaches.

MARINE. And I will not be silenced. Madame, your conduct is intolerable.

BARONESS. Marine!

MARINE. You've tried my patience to the limit.

BARONESS. What do you want me to do? Am I the kind of woman to economize?

MARINE. That would be asking too much, but it's clear—to me, if not to you—that soon you'll be forced to.

BARONESS. What do you mean?

MARINE. You are the widow of a Belgian colonel killed in Flanders last year. Now you've already eaten through what little money he left you on his departure; there was nothing left but the furniture, which you would have had to sell if lady luck hadn't thrown Turcaret the tax farmer your way. Am I right, Madame?

BARONESS. I won't contradict you.

MARINE. Now this Turcaret, a fairly unpleasant man, whom you fairly dislike despite your intentions to marry him—

BARONESS. Now wait—it is he who intends to marry me—

MARINE. He's not exactly rushing to the altar, is he?

BARONESS. Marine!

MARINE. Though I must say it's no hardship if you get a whopping present from him every day in the meantime. I've nothing against that; you're managing that front nicely, but I will tell you, what I won't put up with is how you've fallen for this measly chevalier-about-town, who is squandering everything you've made off the tax farmer. On himself! What do you intend to do with him?

BARONESS. I shall retain him for a friend. Is one not permitted to have friends?

MARINE. Sure, as long as you can make use of him in a pinch. You could even marry this one in case you miss out on Turcaret—he's not one of those knights sworn to celibacy in defense of Malta—he wages his campaigns at the card table; he's the original jack of diamonds.

BARONESS. I find him an extremely honorable man.

MARINE. With those passionate pouts of his, his soothing tone, his simpering face, I think he's a great actor. And the proof of that is Frontin, his valet Frontin, has never said the slightest thing to me against him.

BARONESS. An admirable prejudice, I must say. Your conclusion, then?

MARINE. That the master and his servant are two scoundrels in cahoots to swindle you, and even though you're old enough to know better, you're letting yourself get taken in by their game. I will grant you that in your widowed state, the Chevalier was the first man to pay you any attention. Rudely. And this show of sincerity has him so firmly rooted in this household that he now spends your purse as if it were his own.

BARONESS. It is true that I was sensitive to the first favors of the Chevalier. I admit that I ought to have sounded the depths of his feelings before revealing my own to him. I will even go so far as to admit that you are perhaps right to upbraid me for all that I've done for him financially.

MARINE. Of course I'm right. And I won't stop reminding you of that fact until you've shown him the door.

BARONESS. And if I don't?

MARINE. Oh, Monsieur Turcaret will find out whom you've wanted to "retain for a friend," and, I tell you, it won't be pretty. The Chevalier won't sit well with him. He'll stop with the presents, he'll never marry you, and then you'll be reduced to marrying the Chevalier, which would be a disaster.

BARONESS. You've thought this through, Marine. Your reflections are judicious, and I should profit from your thinking.

MARINE. You damn well better. Look at the future. Think of a solid marriage. Reap the benefits of Turcaret while you wait for him to marry you. If he doesn't come through, well, the world will talk, but at least in compensation you'll have property, and money in the bank, jewels, fat notes of credit, dividends in perpetuity. Then, someday, some capricious or restless gentleman will come along and rehabilitate your reputation with an honorable alliance.

BARONESS. You're absolutely right, Marine; I shall break with the Chevalier. He'll only ruin me in the end.

MARINE. It's the only course to take. Keep your hooks in Turcaret, then either marry him or destroy him. It'll be *your* choice to make. You'll skim enough of his fortune to cut a brilliant figure in society with. They can talk all they want, but you'll outlast the gossip, you'll outlast the slander. Eventually the world will get used to confusing you with women of quality.

BARONESS. [*Dramatically.*] My resolution is made; I shall banish the Chevalier from my heart. No longer shall I bolster his fortunes. No longer shall I repair his losses. He shall receive nothing further from me.

MARINE. Here comes Frontin. Test your resolve. Give him the ice.

BARONESS. I shall.

[FRONTIN *enters*.]

FRONTIN. I come on behalf of my master, as well as on my own behalf, to wish you good day.

BARONESS. [*Coldly.*] I am obliged to you, Frontin.

FRONTIN. And does Mademoiselle Marine also wish for me to take the liberty of greeting her?

MARINE. Good day and get lost.

FRONTIN. [*Presenting a note to the* BARONESS.] This message, which Monsieur the Chevalier has written, will inform my lady of a certain mishap—

MARINE. [*To the* BARONESS.] Don't accept it.

BARONESS. Accepting it is no compromise. Let's just find out what has happened.

MARINE. It killed the cat.

BARONESS. [*Reading.*] "I have just received the portrait of a countess. I send it forthwith and renounce her for you, although, my dear Baroness, you must not compensate me for the sacrifice. So preoccupied, so enthralled by your charms am I that I haven't the liberty to be unfaithful to you. Pardon me, my adorèd one, if I speak no further of this to you. My soul is utterly despondent. I have lost all of my money. Frontin will tell you the rest. Your Chevalier."

MARINE. If he's lost all his money, what rest is there to tell?

FRONTIN. Allow me. In addition to the six hundred francs that my lady had the goodness to lend him yesterday, and his small amount of pocket money, he pledged his word for nine thousand francs and lost. That is the rest. My master never wastes words in his notes.

BARONESS. Where is the portrait?

FRONTIN. Here it is.

BARONESS. He has never mentioned this countess to me before, Frontin.

FRONTIN. Oh my lady, we made the conquest without thinking. We won her—met her—the other day at cards.

MARINE. The Countess of Canasta.

FRONTIN. It was she who provoked my master. For a laugh he responded to her affectations. But she took the matter too seriously. She sent us the portrait only this morning. We don't even know her name.

MARINE. I'll bet she's some old maid from Normandy, whose family chips in to keep her in an attic here—and the furniture comes and goes on what she wins.

FRONTIN. [*To* MARINE.] Of that we are also quite ignorant.

MARINE. You are? You two aren't the kind to make fiscally foolish sacrifices. You know the price of everything.

FRONTIN. [*To the* BARONESS.] Do you know, my lady, that last night my master very nearly made his eternal farewell? When we came home, he threw himself into an armchair and began to recall the unlucky cards

Fate dealt him, all the while seasoning his reflections with startling epithets and apostrophes.

BARONESS. You have seen this countess in person, Frontin. Is she prettier than her likeness?

FRONTIN. No madame. Hers is not, as you can see, a regulated beauty. But she's piquant enough, oh lord, she's piquant enough. Now, first I wanted to let my master know that oaths were just so many wasted words, but then considering that lamentation is the only relief for a desperate gambler, I let him console himself.

BARONESS. [*Intent on the portrait.*] How old is she, Frontin?

FRONTIN. I couldn't possibly guess. Her paint is so fresh I might miss by twenty years.

MARINE. Then she's fifty at least.

FRONTIN. That may well be, since she looks thirty. Then my master, after driving himself to distraction, called for his pistols.

BARONESS. His pistols, did you hear that, Marine, his pistols!

MARINE. He won't kill himself, my lady, he won't kill himself.

FRONTIN. I refused him, so he drew his sword in a rage.

BARONESS. He's wounded himself! Marine, surely—

MARINE. No way. Frontin would have stopped him.

FRONTIN. That's right. Recklessly I threw myself upon him: "Monsieur," I said to him, "what do you think you're doing? You've exceeded the limits of suffering that a loss at cards entitles you to. If bad luck makes you rue the day, at the very least spare your life for the sake of your lovable Baroness—she's bailed you out of many a scrape. Rest assured"— and I only said this to appease his madness—"she wouldn't leave you in this one."

MARINE. [*Sotto voce.*] Slyboots.

FRONTIN. "It's only nine thousand francs," I said. "Turcaret has a broad back. He can carry the load just this once."

BARONESS. And then, Frontin?

FRONTIN. And then, my lady, at those words—for such is the power of hope—he let himself be disarmed like a child. He went to bed and fell right to sleep.

MARINE. The big baby.

FRONTIN. But when he woke up this morning, he felt anew his wracking torments. The portrait of the countess did nothing to dispel them. He sent me here immediately to have you decide his fate. What shall I tell him, my lady?

BARONESS. You will say to him, Frontin that he can always depend on me, and that, as I currently have no cash in hand. . . . [*She begins to remove her diamond ring.*]

MARINE. [*Restraining her.*] What are you doing?

BARONESS. [*Putting it back on.*] You will say that I am touched by his plight.

MARINE. And for my part, say I am deeply vexed by his misfortune.

FRONTIN. He'll be vexed all right. [*Aside.*] A plague upon the soubrette!

BARONESS. Say to him, Frontin, that I am sensitive to his pains.

MARINE. Say his afflictions affect me vividly, Frontin.

FRONTIN. If that is indeed the case, Madame, then never again will you see him. The disgrace he feels at being unable to meet his debts shall exile him forever. Nothing so dishonors the son of a good family. We leave at once by post.

BARONESS. By post, Marine!

MARINE. They couldn't make the fare.

FRONTIN. Adieu, my lady.

MARINE. Don't write.

BARONESS. [*Removing her diamond again.*] Wait, Frontin. [*To* MARINE.] I haven't the strength to abandon him. Here is a diamond worth fifteen thousand francs that Monsieur Turcaret gave me. Go pawn it and rescue your master from destitution.

FRONTIN. I go to call him back to life. I won't fail to give him a full account, Marine, of your enormous sympathy.

MARINE. Oh, the two of you—a couple of swells.

[FRONTIN *exits.*]

BARONESS. No harangues, if you please. Let's not get carried away.

MARINE. I assure you, my lady, I won't waste my breath. It shouldn't matter to me that it all goes out as fast as it comes in. They're your affairs, madame, they're your affairs.

BARONESS. I am more to pity than to blame—my actions are hardly those of a free will—I am ensnared by such tender longing, I can hardly resist.

MARINE. Tender longing? Do you think weakness looks good on you? Good God, you're in love like some fat housewife.

BARONESS. That is so unfair, Marine! At least let me be grateful to the Chevalier for making such a gallant sacrifice for me.

MARINE. It's a ludicrous sacrifice! You're so easy to dupe. Upon my life, that's some old family portrait. It's probably his grandmother.

BARONESS. [*Looking at the portrait.*] You know, I think I've seen this face before—and quite recently at that . . .

MARINE. Let me see. I think you're right. She's that colossus from the provinces we saw at the ball three days ago—remember, she was the one who begged every man there to remove her mask, and then nobody knew who she was when it came off.

BARONESS. She looked built to last.

MARINE. [*Returning the portrait.*] A little like Turcaret.

BARONESS. Be quiet, Marine. Here comes his lackey.

MARINE. Oh, the bearer of glad tidings. Look, he's holding something— the good news for today.

[FLAMAND *enters and presents a little box to the* BARONESS.]

FLAMAND. My lady, Monsieur Turcaret bids you to graciously accept this little token. Your servant, my lady.

MARINE. You are always welcome, Flamand. I much prefer seeing you to that sleazy Frontin.

BARONESS. [*Displaying the case.*] Look at the handiwork on this case; have you ever seen anything so delicate?

MARINE. Open it, open it. Something tells me the inside will be more ravishing than the outside.

BARONESS. [*Opening it.*] What do I see? A note of credit! This is serious.

MARINE. How serious?

BARONESS. Ninety thousand francs.

MARINE. Grave. [*Low.*] That covers the loss of three diamonds.

BARONESS. I spy another note.

MARINE. Also marked payee?

BARONESS. No, it's a poem Monsieur Turcaret has addressed to me.

MARINE. Does it rhyme?

BARONESS. [*Reading.*] "To Alice—a quatrain." I suppose I am Alice. He bids me in verse to accepts his chit in prose.

MARINE. I'm anxious to hear it—we've always done so well by his pretty prose.

BARONESS.

> Come cash this check, dearest Alice.
> Come send my soul to heaven.
> Render it sweet my heart, once callous.
> As sure as four and three make seven.

MARINE. A finely turned thought.

BARONESS. And so nobly expressed. Authors truly coin themselves in their works. Put the case into my writing desk.

[MARINE *exits.*]

BARONESS. I must give you something for your trouble, Flamand. [*She gives him some coins.*] I want you to drink to my health.

FLAMAND. I will, my lady, and not the cheap stuff, neither.

BARONESS. You flatter me.

FLAMAND. When I worked for that high counselor, I drank anything, but since I've been in Monsieur Turcaret's service, I've gotten dainty.

BARONESS. They say there is nothing like the home of a financier for finishing one's taste.

[MARINE *returns*.]

FLAMAND. My lord approaches, my lady, no, I guess he's already here.

[TURCARET *enters and* FLAMAND *exits*.]

BARONESS. I am delighted to see you, Monsieur Turcaret; it gives me an opportunity to praise you for that poem you sent me. Surely you realize it is the very latest in gallantry. Never has Voiture or Pavillon penned anything finer.

TURCARET. You're fooling me.

BARONESS. Most assuredly not.

TURCARET. Seriously, Madame, you think they're good?

BARONESS. The most thoughtful in the world.

MARINE. It even rhymes.

TURCARET. You know, it's the first poem I ever made.

BARONESS. You're fooling me.

TURCARET. And I didn't get any help from professional authors, like some people do.

BARONESS. I can tell. A professional writer wouldn't dream of expressing himself this way.

TURCARET. I wanted to find out whether I was capable of making up a poem. Love has ignited my talents.

BARONESS. Is there anything you're not capable of, Monsieur?

MARINE. Well I'd like to take a moment to praise your prose. It's worth at least as much as your verse.

TURCARET. It should—it's been countersigned by four county treasurers.

MARINE. That's better than a literary prize.

BARONESS. I don't approve of your prose in the least, sir. It makes me feel like quarreling with you.

TURCARET. How come?

BARONESS. Have you lost your mind, sending me a note of credit? Every day you commit some such folly.

TURCARET. Don't make fun of me.

BARONESS. How much is this paper worth? I was so angry with you, I didn't even bother to check the amount.

TURCARET. It's only ninety thousand francs.

BARONESS. Ninety thousand francs! I'm absolutely furious! If I thought it was that much, I would have sent it back to you on the spot.

TURCARET. No no.

BARONESS. Now that I do know, take it back.

TURCARET. But if you've accepted it, you can't give it back.

MARINE. [*Low.*] He's got that right.

BARONESS. Your motive is far more offensive than the amount.

TURCARET. Why?

BARONESS. By overwhelming me with gifts each day, it appears to me that you need to, shall we say, bribe me, in order to keep me in your thrall.

TURCARET. My lady, that is not at all the point I have in mind. What an idea!

BARONESS. You deceive yourself, sir. I do not love you any more for them.

TURCARET. [*To* MARINE.] How frank, how sincere she is.

BARONESS. I am touched by your zeal, moved by your attentions . . .

TURCARET. [*To* MARINE.] What an honest heart!

BARONESS. And by the simple delight of seeing you.

TURCARET. I am spellbound. . . . Adieu, spellbinding Alice.

BARONESS. Not leaving so soon?

TURCARET. Yes, my queen. I only dropped in on my way to a board meeting. I have to blackball some flat-footed nobody who wants to join the company. I'll come back as soon as I can tear myself away from business. [*He kisses her hand.*]

BARONESS. Would that you were already on your way—back.

MARINE. [*Curtsying.*] Adieu, Monsieur, I am your very humble servant.

TURCARET. Say, Marine, it's been a long time since I've given you anything. [*He gives her a a handful of silver.*] Here, I won't even count it.

MARINE. [*Accepting it.*] Then neither will I. Genteel is as genteel does. [TURCARET *exits.*]

BARONESS. He is quite satisfied with us, Marine.

MARINE. Let's keep it that way. He's the perfect mark for coquettes—pots of money, open-fisted, and stupid.

BARONESS. My training has been put to excellent use.

MARINE. Yes, but here come Frick and Frack—they make up for him. [*The* CHEVALIER *and* FRONTIN *enter.*]

CHEVALIER. I have come to express my most profound gratitude, my lady. Without your assistance, I would have violated the gambler's creed. My word would have lost all credit, and I would have been shunned by good society.

BARONESS. I am thrilled to have granted you this pleasure.

CHEVALIER. How incomparably delicious it is to have one's honor bailed out by the very object of one's love.

MARINE. [*Aside*.] He's tender and impassioned—refusing him anything is a tall order.

CHEVALIER. Good day to you, Marine. [*To the* BARONESS.] I also bear thanks to Marine. Frontin told me how impressed she was with my suffering.

MARINE. Oh yes, mercy me—I was very impressed with how much it cost us!

BARONESS. Silence, Marine. You and your freakish outbursts.

CHEVALIER. No, let her continue. I love honest and sincere people.

MARINE. And I loathe those who are neither.

CHEVALIER. Distemper makes you so witty, Marine. These brilliant retorts quite slay me. I want you to know that what I bear for you are feelings of true friendship. And I wish to give you proof of them. [*He feigns going through his pockets*.] Remind me of this moment, Frontin, the very next time I win.

FRONTIN. [*To* MARINE.] His word is like a blank check.

MARINE. I don't need his money, as long as he hasn't come to plunder ours.

BARONESS. Watch what you're saying, Marine.

MARINE. It's highway robbery.

BARONESS. You lack respect.

CHEVALIER. No need to take her seriously.

MARINE. I can control myself no longer, Madame. I won't stand idly by and watch this joker deceive you while you deceive Monsieur Turcaret.

BARONESS. Marine!

MARINE. It's ridiculous to have it all go in one hand and right out the other! Is that any way to behave? We bear the shame and they bear the profit—away!

BARONESS. Now you've gone too far. I'll stand no more of this.

MARINE. Nor will I.

BARONESS. I'll discharge you.

MARINE. You can't fire me—I quit! I won't have it said of me that I helped ruin a financier and didn't come out ahead on the deal.

BARONESS. Out of my sight, hussy! And don't come back except to settle the household accounts.

MARINE. I'll settle them with Monsieur Turcaret, thank you very much; and if he's got brains enough to believe me, you'll be settling this hash together.

[MARINE *exits*.]

CHEVALIER. She is, I'll admit, an impertinent creature. You had every right to discharge her.

FRONTIN. Every right, my lady. That was no servant—that was a mother.

BARONESS. A mother superior stationed at my ears.

FRONTIN. She had no business giving you all that advice. She would have ruined you in the end.

BARONESS. I've wanted to be rid of her for some time, but I don't trust new faces.

CHEVALIER. It would, however, be unpleasant if, in the first flush of her anger, she went and gave Turcaret certain inconvenient notions.

FRONTIN. And she won't miss a trick. Chambermaids are like religious bigots—they perform acts of charity only for spite.

BARONESS. What have we to worry about? I don't fear her. I have a mind and Turcaret hasn't. I don't like him, and he's besotted with me. I can convince him that throwing Marine out is but another one of my virtues. But I feel we have to do more than get rid of her—what we need is to carry out a master plan, a plan that has just occurred to me.

CHEVALIER. And what is that plan, gracious lady?

BARONESS. Monsieur Turcaret's lackey, Flamand, is such an idiot, such a complete boob, that he'll never be of the slightest use to us. I'd like to put someone crafty in his place—one of those superior genius types fashioned specifically to govern mediocre minds, a genius who can be kept in perpetually profitable situations.

FRONTIN. A superior genius—you rang, madame?

CHEVALIER. Frontin would indeed be useful to us placed in the bosom of our public treasurer.

BARONESS. I should love to stuff him there.

CHEVALIER. He'd give excellent service, would he not?

FRONTIN. I'm jealous you thought of it first. Upon my honor, Monsieur Turcaret shall be jerked all over the map.

BARONESS. He's just presented me with a note of credit for ninety thousand francs. I'd like it changed into hard currency, but I don't know anyone who can do that. I must ask you, my dear, to undertake this transaction for me. I'll give you the note—you redeem my diamond, which I shall be glad to have back—and then give me the balance of the note.

FRONTIN. All completely above board, my lady.

CHEVALIER. I'll waste no time. You shall have the money without delay.

BARONESS. Just let me fetch the note.

[*The* BARONESS *exits.*]

FRONTIN. Ninety thousand! A great windfall from one great lady. I'd have to be very lucky to find any more like her. But just between us, for a coquette I find her a trifle too trusting.

CHEVALIER. I know what you mean.

FRONTIN. This more than compensates for giving up that crazy old countess this morning.

CHEVALIER. I should say so.

FRONTIN. The Baroness is convinced that you've lost nine thousand francs at cards and that her diamond is in hock; are you going to return her ring with the remainder of the note?

CHEVALIER. Of course. What do you take me for?

FRONTIN. You mean all of it, without skimming off any incidental, out-of-pocket expenses?

CHEVALIER. I shall take great pains to return all of it.

FRONTIN. I don't know, you have these little moments of integrity—I never know when to expect them.

CHEVALIER. I would never consider dumping her so cheaply. Who do you think I am?

FRONTIN. Oh, I do beg your pardon—I judged you too rashly. I was afraid you were going to do things only halfway.

CHEVALIER. I would never walk until after Turcaret went belly-up.

FRONTIN. Oh, after his annihilation—

CHEVALIER. I court the coquette to ruin the financier.

FRONTIN. Now that's my master's voice.

CHEVALIER. Shhh, here comes the Baroness.

[*The* BARONESS *re-enters.*]

BARONESS. Hurry, my liege, hurry; cash this note without delay and return my ring as soon as you can.

CHEVALIER. Sooner! Frontin will bring it. Before I take leave of you, allow me, enchanted as I am by your bountiful conduct, to make known to you my—

BARONESS. No, I forbid you to speak of it.

CHEVALIER. You show such restraint for a heart as welcoming as mine.

BARONESS. No goodbyes, dear one, for I know we shall meet again presently.

CHEVALIER. I could not leave you without so sweet a hope.

[*They exit separately.*]

FRONTIN. I do admire the train of life; we pluck a coquette; the coquette devours the businessman; the businessman fleeces the rest of us—it makes for a deliciously deceitful food chain.

Act II

[FRONTIN *hands the* BARONESS *her diamond.*]

FRONTIN. Here is your diamond, quick as a bunny. The pawnbroker placed it in my hands as soon as he saw that dazzling note of credit, which he's decided to retail with a good bit of interest. I left my master there, but he's coming to give you the balance of the note.

BARONESS. I'm finally rid of Marine. I thought she was merely bluffing, but she actually meant to carry out her threat—she just left. Therefore, Frontin, I am in need of a new chambermaid. I charge you with procuring one.

FRONTIN. I have the very thing you want. She's a demure young miss, as obliging as can be. Your household could be in any state of undress and she'd never bat an eyelash.

BARONESS. I love that kind. You know her personally?

FRONTIN. So personally, we are practically related.

BARONESS. That is to say she is trustworthy.

FRONTIN. As trustworthy as I am. She is under my tutelage. I keep track of her wages and her earnings, and I take care to furnish her overhead.

BARONESS. Is she currently hired out to anyone?

FRONTIN. No, she left her last situation a few days ago.

BARONESS. Why was that?

FRONTIN. She was working for very retiring people. A married couple who loved each other. You could die of boredom in a place like that.

BARONESS. Where has she been staying?

FRONTIN. With a charitable old prude who lets rooms to unemployed ladies' maids to find out what's going on in the better families.

BARONESS. I'd like her to start today. I simply cannot do without a maid.

FRONTIN. I'll send her to you, madame—I'll fetch her myself, in fact. You'll be very pleased with her. I haven't spoken of half her talents. She sings and plays all sorts of instruments—ravishingly.

BARONESS. She sounds like a very accomplished young lady, Frontin.

FRONTIN. I'll stand behind my guarantee. I'm preparing her for a career at the Opéra, but she needs to ripen in the world a bit—the Opéra requires finished pieces.

BARONESS. I cannot wait to meet her.

[FRONTIN *exits.*]

BARONESS. She will be a great amusement for me. Marine vexed me with her sermons; this new girl can entertain me with song. [*She sees* TURCARET.] Oh, no, here comes Turcaret—looking rather unhinged. Marine must have gotten hold of him.

[TURCARET *enters, out of breath.*]

TURCARET. I don't know where to begin with you, you—false heart!

BARONESS. Marine got hold of him.

TURCARET. I've had news of you, you adder, I've had all the news. I've been given a list of your treacheries, and of your moral misconduct.

BARONESS. A lovely start, sir—and such polished terms.

TURCARET. Let me speak. I want to confront you with the truth. Marine told me all about you. That handsome chevalier who comes here night and day—and it did look fishy to me—is not your cousin, as you led me to believe. You were planning on marrying him after you'd left me in the lurch, me, after I'd made your fortune.

BARONESS. I, sir, I love the Chevalier?

TURCARET. Marine was very convincing. She says that dandy goes out in society only because you've given him all of the trinkets I gave you.

BARONESS. What a nasty piece of goods Marine was. And was that all she told you, sir?

TURCARET. Don't talk back to me, you puff adder! You should be ashamed! Don't you talk back! [*Pause.*] Say something. For instance, what's become of that diamond I gave you the other day? I want to see it— show it to me right now, show it to me.

BARONESS. If you are going to adopt that tone, sir, I don't feel I need show it to you.

TURCARET. Oh, and what the hell kind of tone do you suggest I adopt? And don't think I'm going to let you off with just some noise here. Don't think I'm enough of a sot to dump you without a fight. I'm leaving marks of my resentment. I'm an honest gentleman; I love on good faith; my designs were legitimate; I don't fear scandal, not me. You're not dealing with some pious nancy here, believe you me!

[TURCARET *goes into her bedroom and begins to break things.*]

BARONESS. No, I'm dealing with a lunatic, a man possessed. Oh, go ahead, be my guest, do as you wish; I won't stand in your way. [*Crashes are heard.*] He's gone out of his mind—Monsieur Turcaret, Monsieur Turcaret, I'll make you atone for this fit . . .

TURCARET. [*Returning.*] Well, that feels better. I broke the big mirror and the most expensive figurines.

BARONESS. Why not break them all and finish what you began, Monsieur?

TURCARET. I'll finish when it pleases me to, Madame. I'll teach you to play me for a fool. Now, as per that note of credit that I sent you this morning—hand it over.

BARONESS. Hand it over? To you. And suppose I gave that to the Chevalier, too?

TURCARET. No surprise there.

BARONESS. You are absolutely raving. I pity you.

TURCARET. I don't believe this. Instead of throwing yourself at my knees and begging my forgiveness, you insist that I'm in the wrong.

BARONESS. You are.

TURCARET. How about, just for fun, persuading me of it?

BARONESS. I might, if you were in a state to listen to reason.

TURCARET. Oh, and what would you say then, traitress?

BARONESS. What a snit you're in! I shall say nothing to you, sir.

TURCARET. [*Out of breath.*] Speak, madame, speak. I'll hold my temper.

BARONESS. Listen to me then. All of these absurd conjectures that you have just made are based on a false report that Marine—

TURCARET. A false report! For Christ's sake, it's not—

BARONESS. Do not swear, sir. Do not interrupt me; pretend that you've held your temper.

TURCARET. I'll shut up.

BARONESS. Do you happen to know why I just let Marine go?

TURCARET. Yes. For having taken my best interests to heart.

BARONESS. On the contrary. It's because she reproached me incessantly for feeling love for you. "Is there anything more ridiculous," she'd say from morn to midnight, "than to see the widow of a colonel daydream about this Monsieur Turcaret, ill-born, unfeeling, a man of the most vulgar appearance—"

TURCARET. You can stop right there. Marine is an insolent wench.

BARONESS. "—when you can choose a husband among two dozen suitors of illustrious rank; when you withhold your consent even to the most ardent entreaties of a Marquess who worships you and his entire family—are you so feeble-minded to sacrifice everything to this Monsieur Turcaret?"

TURCARET. This isn't possible.

BARONESS. I don't claim to make a merit of my preference, Monsieur. The Marquess in question is a young nobleman, extremely attractive in his person, but whose deportment and mores don't suit me in the slightest. He occasionally calls on me here with my cousin the Chevalier, who is his friend. I discovered that he purchased Marine's confidence; that is why I sent her packing, I might add. In revenge, she has sold you— with a generous markup—a thousand falsehoods, and you are foolish enough to place your faith in them. Didn't you take a moment to reflect that there before you was the testimony of a highly disgruntled servant, not to mention that, if I had had anything with which to be reproached, then would I have been so impolitic as to dismiss a maid whose indiscretions I might have to fear? Such reasoning did not, pray tell, spring naturally to mind?

TURCARET. It did not, my lady, but I . . .

BARONESS. But, but, you are in the wrong. So she said, did she not, among her host of calumnies, that I no longer had the large diamond which you placed on my finger in jest the other day and forced me to accept?

TURCARET. She swore to me that you gave it this morning to the Chevalier, who is as much your cousin as the boogieman.

BARONESS. If I were to show that very diamond this very moment, what would you say?

TURCARET. Well, I'd say—but you can't.

BARONESS. Might this be the stone in question? Do you recognize it, Monsieur? So you see how much credence to lend to certain domestic reports.

TURCARET. That Marine is a great big hussy. I recognize my injustice. Forgive me, madame, for abusing your character.

BARONESS. I will not. You and your tantrums are beneath excuse.

TURCARET. I admit it.

BARONESS. How could you let yourself be so easily swayed against a woman who loves you so tenderly?

TURCARET. I'm so unhappy.

BARONESS. Admit that you are a very weak man.

TURCARET. I am a very weak man.

BARONESS. An outright dupe.

TURCARET. An outright dupe. Oh Marine, that jailbird Marine! You cannot imagine all the filthy lies she told me. She said that you and the Chevalier think of me as your cash cow, and that if I'd given you everything for tomorrow today, you'd have the door slammed in my face.

BARONESS. Bitch.

TURCARET. I'm not making it up—she said it like it was established fact.

BARONESS. But believing her was your failing.

TURCARET. Yes, Madame, I gave into it like a complete idiot. What was I thinking?

BARONESS. Do you intend to repent for your gullibility?

TURCARET. [*Throwing himself to his knees.*] I beg a thousand pardons. I'll pay for everything.

BARONESS. You are forgiven. Raise yourself, sir. I imagine you could only be less jealous if you loved me less. The excess of the one passion allows me to overlook the violence of the other.

TURCARET. What bounty! Bounty to the beast!

BARONESS. How could you believe for an instant that my heart would hesitate between you and the Chevalier?

TURCARET. It's not a question of belief. It's fear.

BARONESS. What can one do to allay that fear?

TURCARET. Send him far away. *Please*. Let me help you; I know how to do it.

BARONESS. How is it done?

TURCARET. I'll farm him out, give him a branch office in the provinces.

BARONESS. A branch office.

TURCARET. It's just my way of removing obstacles. I can't count the number of cousins, uncles, and husbands I've set up as branch managers. I sent one all the way to Canada once.

BARONESS. Please recall that the Chevalier, my cousin, is a nobleman: certain forms of employment are unsuitable for a man of his birth. Without having you go to all the trouble of banishing him from Paris, let me instead give you my oath that there isn't a man in the world who could cause you less worry.

TURCARET. [*Grunts.*] You're choking me with joy. You've related all this to me in such a natural manner that I'm completely persuaded. Goodbye, my one, my only, my goddess. I shall repair the mess I just made in there. That big mirror had a flaw in it anyway—and those china figurines were pretty cheap.

BARONESS. Too true.

TURCARET. I'm going to get you some more.

BARONESS. You see how much your follies cost?

TURCARET. Pin money! I didn't break more than nine thousand francs' worth.

[*He starts to go; she stops him.*]

BARONESS. Wait, sir. Before you go, I must request a favor of you.

TURCARET. Anything—give me your orders, my lady.

BARONESS. If you hold me in esteem, please find a clerkship for your lackey Flamand. I've conceived a great liking for that boy.

TURCARET. If I thought he had a head for figures, I'd have already pushed him in that direction. But he's half-witted, and that's not good for business.

BARONESS. So give him a job that won't be difficult to manage.

TURCARET. It's as good as done—he starts today.

BARONESS. That's not all. Let me give you Frontin in his stead—he's been lackey to the Chevalier, my cousin. He's a very sharp fellow.

TURCARET. I will take him, Madame, and Flamand will be made a clerk.

[FRONTIN *enters*.]

FRONTIN. [*To the* BARONESS.] My lady, the young lady I mentioned earlier will be arriving soon.

BARONESS. [*To* TURCARET.] Monsieur, here is the valet I'd like to give you.

TURCARET. He appears so innocent.

BARONESS. You are so gifted with physiognomies.

TURCARET. My glance is inevitable. [*To* FRONTIN.] Come here, my boy. Tell me something, have you any principles?

FRONTIN. Which principles do you mean?

TURCARET. Business principles. That is to say, do you know anything about frauds—how to prevent them—how to promote them?

FRONTIN. Not yet, sir, but I am a quick study.

TURCARET. You know arithmetic, don't you? Do you know single-entry bookkeeping?

FRONTIN. Oh yes, sir, I can even enter something twice. I know both kinds of handwriting, and can switch back and forth.

TURCARET. A round hand?

FRONTIN. A round hand, and also an oblique hand.

TURCARET. What do you mean by oblique?

FRONTIN. You know, crooked. Uh, a handwriting that you know . . . a handwriting that isn't legitimate.

TURCARET. [*To the* BARONESS.] He means a bastard hand.

FRONTIN. Just the word I was looking for.

TURCARET. What simplicity. This boy, madame, is but a seedling.

BARONESS. One who will flower in your greenhouse.

TURCARET. Of course he will, oh, of course he will. A brilliant mind isn't necessary for a brilliant career in tax finance. No sense being held back by intelligence. Outside of myself and perhaps two or three of my peers, it's all just middle management. You just have to master the lingo and get used to the routine—he'll be a made man in no time. We have so many clients—we endeavor to take the best that world has to offer. There's our science in a nutshell.

BARONESS. And a useful one at that.

TURCARET. Kid, you're mine. I'll put you on the payroll right now.

FRONTIN. Then I shall look upon you as my new mentor. But first I must fulfill one final duty as lackey for Monsieur the Chevalier. He wishes for you and for the Baroness, his cousin, to dine here this evening.

TURCARET. A decent spread?

FRONTIN. I'm going to order aspics of all dimensions from Fouquet's, along with eighty bottles of champagne, and, to enliven the digestion, there will be voices and instruments.

BARONESS. Music, Frontin?

FRONTIN. At such a pitch, my lady, that I've been told to order a hundred bottles of sauterne to drown the orchestra with.

BARONESS. A hundred bottles!

FRONTIN. That's not much—there'll be eight strings, four Italians, three divas, and two enormous tenors.

TURCARET. Sounds fancy—a real catered affair.

FRONTIN. When Monsieur the Chevalier gives one of his dinners, it's all finger bowls, lobster bisque, and pickle forks.

TURCARET. I'm sold.

FRONTIN. It seems he has the backing of a contractor's purse.

BARONESS. [*To* TURCARET.] He means to say that he does things in the grand manner.

TURCARET. On with the show. I think to ice the cake, what say I run to the jeweller's and round you up something spangly—

BARONESS. Show some moderation, I beg of you. Don't rush into the sort of expense that—

TURCARET. [*Interrupting her.*] Fie, my lady, fie! Stop with such niggardly piffle. I leave you, my queen.

BARONESS. Do not dawdle, dearest. I await your return with great impatience.

[TURCARET *exits.*]

BARONESS. Here you are, on the high road to fortune.

FRONTIN. Yes, my lady, and in a position that won't interfere with your own projects.

BARONESS. Now is the time to allow your superior genius his greatest sphere . . .

FRONTIN. I shall endeavor my utmost to prove him to you.

BARONESS. When will you bring me my new maid?

FRONTIN. I expect her any moment.

BARONESS. Let me know when she gets here.

[*The* BARONESS *exits into her chamber.*]

FRONTIN. Courage, Frontin! Fortune calls, my friend. The conduit of the coquette has led you to the tycoon's lair. What joy! And such a glittering view! I fancy that everything I touch will turn to gold. And here is my pupil.

[LISETTE *enters.*]

FRONTIN. How welcome you are, Lisette. Impatience greets your arrival in this house.

LISETTE. That's a good sign. [*Looking around.*] Nice place.

FRONTIN. I've brought you up to date on everything that's been happening—and everything that needs to happen—you have only to take your part in the score. Just remember to be tirelessly obliging.

LISETTE. You told me that.

FRONTIN. Endlessly flatter the Baroness's infatuation with the Chevalier.

LISETTE. Stop with these pointless reminders.

FRONTIN. [*Spotting the* CHEVALIER.] Here he comes.

LISETTE. I haven't met him yet. Oh Frontin, he's very . . . well-made.

FRONTIN. You can't be poorly constructed and expect to capture a coquette.

[*The* CHEVALIER *enters but does not see* LISETTE.]

CHEVALIER. I've come to tell you—[*Sees her.*]—what have we here? Who is this shiny bauble?

FRONTIN. Marine's replacement—I have given Lisette to my lady.

CHEVALIER. A friend of yours, doubtless?

FRONTIN. We've known each other a very long time. You could say I am her guarantor.

CHEVALIER. A most delicious guarantee. Upon my word, she is enticing . . . as for you, Frontin, I have a bone to pick.

FRONTIN. What?

CHEVALIER. A large bone to pick. You have been privy to all of my affairs, and yet I see you've hidden yours. You are not a sincere friend.

FRONTIN. I didn't want to—

CHEVALIER. [*Interrupting.*] A confidence is made to be shared. Why have you kept such a beautiful discovery a mystery to me?

FRONTIN. Sir, I was afraid . . .

CHEVALIER. Of what?

FRONTIN. Of . . . the hell with it—you can figure it out.

CHEVALIER. [*Aside.*] The sneak. Where did he unearth this pretty face? [*To* FRONTIN.] Frontin, dear Frontin, your taste is so fine and discriminating when choosing for yourself—why save your bad taste for friends? Oh, what a fetching tableau, what an adorable nymph.

LISETTE. [*Aside.*] These young lords are so polished.

CHEVALIER. No, I've never seen anything as resplendent as this creature.

LISETTE. [*Aside.*] His expressions give me goosebumps! It's no wonder society dames are hot for them.

CHEVALIER. Let's swap, Frontin. Yield this girl to me, and I'll let you have my agèd countess.

FRONTIN. No sir, my inclinations are those of a commoner. I'm satisfied with just Lisette — I've given her my pledge.

CHEVALIER. Then you can boast of being the happiest of nobodies. . . . [*To* LISETTE.] But you, delicious Lisette, you deserve —

LISETTE. Enough sweet talk, Monsieur. I'm going to greet my new mistress, who hasn't met me yet; if you like, you can continue this line of conversation in front of her.

[LISETTE *exits into the* BARONESS*'s room.*]

CHEVALIER. Frontin, this is serious. I haven't brought the balance of the Baroness's money from the note.

FRONTIN. That's bad.

CHEVALIER. I went to look for a moneylender who's helped me in the past, but he left Paris. Certain transactions sprang up to hasten his departure, so I'm putting you in charge.

FRONTIN. Why me?

CHEVALIER. Didn't you tell me once that you knew an exchange broker who loaned money on the spot?

FRONTIN. Yes, but what are you going to tell the Baroness? If you tell her you still have the note, then she'll figure out we never pawned her diamond; and even she knows that a moneylender doesn't give something for nothing.

CHEVALIER. You're right. Tell her that I cashed it in, but I left it at my house and you'll bring it to her tomorrow morning. In the meantime, go to your broker and take the money you get there home. I'll wait for you there right after I've spoken to her.

[*He goes into the* BARONESS*'s chamber.*]

FRONTIN. God help me, I don't lack for work. First to the caterer, from there to the loan shark, from the loan shark home, then back here to meet Turcaret. Give me the life of action. But patience — after the period of exhaustion, after the time of toil and tribulation, I shall arrive at the era of prosperity. What satisfaction then — what peace of mind then, what total peace. Only my conscience will be at war.

Act III

BARONESS. Well, Frontin, have you ordered the feast? Will supper be sumptuous?

FRONTIN. Lisette can tell you how royally I entertain out of my own pockets, so you can imagine what I can come up with on someone else's tab.

LISETTE. It's true, my lady. He does one proud.

FRONTIN. The Chevalier is expecting me. I'm going to bring him up to date on this evening's arrangements; and then I'll come back to take possession of my new master, Monsieur Turcaret.

[FRONTIN *exits*.]

LISETTE. Frontin is a man of merit, my lady.

BARONESS. It would appear that you don't lack for merit yourself, Lisette.

LISETTE. He's got a lot of know-how.

BARONESS. I find you no less crafty.

LISETTE. I hope, my lady, my little talents will prove useful to you.

BARONESS. I have one caution: I don't want to be flattered.

LISETTE. Flattery is my enemy.

BARONESS. When I consult you on private matters, above all, be sincere.

LISETTE. I won't fail to.

BARONESS. I find that you have been too obliging thus far.

LISETTE. I have?

BARONESS. Yes. You don't combat my feelings for the Chevalier enough.

LISETTE. Why fight them? They're so defensible.

BARONESS. The Chevalier appears worthy of my tenderness.

LISETTE. I share your opinion.

BARONESS. His passion for me is constant and true.

LISETTE. Such a faithful and sincere chevalier. There aren't many like him out there these days.

BARONESS. Why, this very morning he rejected a countess for me.

LISETTE. A countess!

BARONESS. To be honest, she was not in her first youth.

LISETTE. But that only ennobles the sacrifice. I know a thing or two about men. It costs them more to give up an old lady than any other kind.

BARONESS. He just delivered the balance of a note I entrusted to him. I find him so high-minded.

LISETTE. Principled to a fault.

BARONESS. A man of integrity, scruples . . .

LISETTE. But, but, here is a chevalier unique to his species!

BARONESS. Let us be quiet. I hear the tread of Turcaret.

[TURCARET *enters*.]

TURCARET. I'm here. . . . [*Sees* LISETTE.] You have a new chambermaid.

BARONESS. Yes, Monsieur. What do you think?

TURCARET. She'd do after a long sea voyage. We'll have to get acquainted.

LISETTE. At your leisure, Monsieur.

BARONESS. Lisette, you know we've a dinner to prepare for: see to it that the table is properly set and the room is lit.

[LISETTE *exits*.]

TURCARET. She looks like a very sensible girl.

BARONESS. One who has your interests at heart.

TURCARET. I'll be grateful to her for that. Let's see, I just bought you thirty thousand francs worth of mirrors, figurines, and occasional tables. Their taste is exquisite—I picked 'em out myself.

BARONESS. Your knowledge is universal.

TURCARET. I know it all, but one thing I especially know is real estate. Wait til, wait til you see the mansion I'm going to have built for you.

BARONESS. What? You're building a mansion?

TURCARET. For you. I've already bought the property—it's four acres, six rods, nine fathoms, three feet, and eleven square inches—isn't that a lovely spread? The construction will be magnificent; I'd tear it down two or three times over rather than miss even the slightest little detail. I mean, I'm not building some tinpot castle here. I'm not having the industry make fun of me!

BARONESS. They wouldn't dare.

TURCARET. [*Seeing someone enter.*] Who's this guy?

BARONESS. [*Low to* TURCARET.] It's the young marquess I told you about, the one whose suit Marine championed. I ought to forbid his visits— they give me not the slightest pleasure.

MARQUESS. [*Not seeing* TURCARET.] The Chevalier is simply nowhere to be found.

TURCARET. [*Aside.*] It's the Marquess de la Tribaudière. Shit.

MARQUESS. I've been looking for him for two days now. [*Sees* TURCARET.] It can't be—yes—no, it isn't—it is Monsieur Turcaret. [*To the* BARONESS.] What is this man doing here, madame? Do you know who he is? Don't tell me you do business with him—he'll ruin you, for Christ's sake!

BARONESS. Monsieur Marquess—

MARQUESS. He'll drain you dry, he'll skin you alive! He's the most bloodthirsty of leeches—he sells silver at the price of gold!

TURCARET. [*Aside.*] I'd have done better to leave.

BARONESS. You are mistaken, my lord. Monsieur Turcaret passes in society as a man of means and honor.

MARQUESS. So he does: he covets the means of men and the honor of women. That is his reputation.

TURCARET. Most honorable Marquess, what a joker! [*To the* BARONESS.] What a wag, what a wag.

BARONESS. He is either teasing, or he is merely ill-informed.

MARQUESS. Ill-informed! My lady, there is no one better informed to warn you about this marauding miscreant. Why, he's wearing something of mine right now.

TURCARET. Something of yours? I would take an oath to the contrary, sir.

MARQUESS. Legally you are in the right. Given the nature of our agreement, I suppose the diamond is yours. I let the term expire.

BARONESS. Why don't the two of you explain the meaning of this riddle to me?

TURCARET. It's no riddle at all; I don't know what he's talking about.

MARQUESS. He's right, it's all very clear, no riddle at all. Fifteen months ago I needed money. I had a stone worth twenty-five thousand francs. I was told to go to Turcaret. Monsieur Turcaret sent me to one of his agents, to a certain Monsieur Ra . . . Ra . . . Rafle. He runs Turcaret's pawnshop. Good Monsieur Rafle lent me 56,600 francs on my ring. He stipulated a fixed date for me to reclaim it. As a spirit of exactitude is not native to me, the date passed, and my diamond was lost.

TURCARET. My dear Marquess, my dear Marquess, do not tar me with the same brush as Rafle, I beg of you. We are not in the same league — he's a petty grifter whom I dismissed from my organization. If he made a bad deal with you, I suggest you take your case to court. I don't know anything about your diamond; I've never handled it. I've never even seen it.

MARQUESS. It passed to me from my aunt, a most beautiful brilliant — of a clarity, a cut, and a size very nearly like . . . [*Sees the* BARONESS*'s ring.*] that one, my lady. Apparently you have a certain arrangement of a personal nature with Monsieur Turcaret?

BARONESS. Another mistake, Monsieur. I bought it from a woman who peddles trinkets secondhand.

MARQUESS. And to that I reply, what goes around comes around. Monsieur Turcaret has secondhand peddlers in his empire, and, it is said, even in his family.

TURCARET. That's below the belt!

BARONESS. Do not insult my guest, dear Marquess.

MARQUESS. That is not my aim. I am far too much in his service to insult him, although he treats me very harshly. We enjoyed a close relationship at one time. He was, after all, my grandfather's lackey. He carried me in his arms; we played together all the time. We hardly left each other's side. The ingrate has forgotten it all.

TURCARET. I do remember, but the past is past, and I only live in the present.

BARONESS. Let us please change the subject. You are looking for the Chevalier?

MARQUESS. Here, there, and everywhere, my lady: in the theaters, the bars, the casinos, the dance halls. The rake is making progress—he's become a libertine.

BARONESS. I shall rebuke him for it.

MARQUESS. Go to, my lady. I am beyond redemption myself. I lead a life of regulated dissipation; I'm always at the table—I run tabs all over town; everyone knows my old aunt is going to cash in soon, and I'm obviously well-disposed to gorge on her inheritance.

BARONESS. Not a bad risk.

MARQUESS. Not for a usurer. Am I right, Monsieur Turcaret? My aunt, however, is bent on correcting me. And to delude her into believing that my conduct is already under reconstruction, I intend to visit her in my present rational state. She'll faint dead away—having only seen me drunk.

BARONESS. I must confess it is a novelty to find you otherwise. You've been excessively sober this evening.

MARQUESS. Yesterday I dined with three of the most beautiful women in Paris. We drank until dawn, and then I went home to have a little nap in order to greet Auntie on an empty stomach. Adieu, my adorable pet. Tell the Chevalier he should show himself to his friends more often. Lend him out sometimes or I'll have no choice but to keep coming back. Adieu, Turcaret. I bear you no rancor. [*Extending his hand.*] Let us renew our former friendship. But be sure to tell that craven agent of yours, Monsieur Rafle, to treat me more humanely the next time I am in need.

[*The* MARQUESS *exits.*]

TURCARET. Friend of yours? He's a lunatic—the most outrageous liar I've ever met.

BARONESS. And that's saying a lot.

TURCARET. How I suffered during that conversation.

BARONESS. So I gathered.

TURCARET. I don't care for outright dishonesty. In fact, I was so shocked when he said those things I just didn't have the strength to respond to them. Didn't you notice?

BARONESS. You turned the other cheek.

TURCARET. Me, a usurer! What slander!

BARONESS. I believe that the slander is more Monsieur Rafle's concern.

TURCARET. Is it a crime for people to lend money on collateral? Better to lend on collateral than on character, I say.

BARONESS. Of course.

TURCARET. To say, right to my face, that I had been his grandfather's lackey. Nothing could be further from the truth. I have never, never, never been anything more than his . . . overseer.

BARONESS. Even if it were true, to prick you with it now, after so long! The debt has been retired.

TURCARET. Absolutely.

BARONESS. You are far too rooted in my heart for this sort of tittle tattle to make any impression on me.

TURCARET. You do me too much honor.

BARONESS. You are a man of great honor.

TURCARET. You're joking.

BARONESS. A man of true honor.

TURCARET. Oh, stop.

BARONESS. You've aped the grace and manners of the high-born far too well for anyone to suspect you're not.

[FLAMAND enters.]

FLAMAND. Sire . . .

TURCARET. What do you want?

FLAMAND. He is downstairs what asks for you.

TURCARET. Who?

FLAMAND. That man that you know . . . there, that monsieur . . . monsieur . . . thing.

TURCARET. Monsieur thing!

FLAMAND. The clerk you make love to.

TURCARET. What?

FLAMAND. The one who, whenever he comes to see you, you make everyone else go away and nobody is allowed to listen.

TURCARET. Monsieur Rafle.

FLAMAND. It is completely that him, sire, it himself.

TURCARET. Have him wait there. I'll come down.

BARONESS. Didn't you say you had dismissed him?

TURCARET. That must be why he's here. He's looking to finagle his way back in. He's a good enough sort at heart, really, a man I can rely on. I'll go and see what he wants.

BARONESS. Oh, no, no. You can talk here. I want you to feel completely at home. [To FLAMAND.] Have him come up, Flamand.

[FLAMAND exits.]

TURCARET. You are so genteel.

BARONESS. I won't spoil your meeting. Don't forget the favor I asked you concerning Flamand.

TURCARET. It's already been taken care of, my dear.

[The BARONESS goes into her chamber. RAFLE enters.]

TURCARET. What's this all about, Rafle? Why'd you come here? When I'm visiting ladies in their private apartments, I haven't come to do business.

RAFLE. The gravity of this particular piece of business should excuse my intrusion.

TURCARET. All right, what's so important?

RAFLE. May I speak freely?

TURCARET. You may. I am the master here. Speak already.

[RAFLE *pulls a sheaf of papers from his pocket and looks in his dossier.*]

RAFLE. First, this child of good family to whom we lent nine thousand francs last year at an interest rate of 200 percent—as per your instructions—finds he cannot repay. On the brink of delinquency, he has spilled the entire affair to his uncle, a chief district judge, who, in concert with the entire family, is currently bent on destroying you.

TURCARET. Let the whole pack of deadbeats just try! I don't scare so easy.

RAFLE. [*Consulting his dossier.*] That cashier you backed who just went bankrupt for 1,800,000 francs—

TURCARET. What? But I ordered him to—dammit! I know how to get a hold of him.

RAFLE. But they're filing suit against you. This is a pressing matter.

TURCARET. I'll take care of it. I've taken steps—it'll blow over by tomorrow.

RAFLE. I'm afraid tomorrow may be too late.

TURCARET. You're one nervous nellie—why don't you just get on board, Rafle? Did you go see that young man I set up on rue Quincampoix?

RAFLE. Yes, sir. He'd be happy to lend you the twenty thousand out of his net, provided he gets a seat in the company, and that you'll bail him out should he get caught red-handed.

TURCARET. Now there's a lad with grit—fair enough. Tell him that I'll cover his butt no matter what. Is there anything else?

RAFLE. [*Looking at his dossier.*] Do you remember a tall spindly fellow who gave you two thousand francs two months ago so that he could be made a branch manager in Valognes?

TURCARET. Well?

RAFLE. Calamity has befallen him.

TURCARET. Well, what?

RAFLE. His good faith has been abused. Someone stole fifteen thousand francs from him. He was just too good.

TURCARET. Too good, too good! Why the hell did he want to get into the business? I'll give him too good!

RAFLE. He's written an extremely touching letter in which he beseeches you to take pity on him—

TURCARET. A waste of paper.

RAFLE. Imploring you not to remove him from the office.

TURCARET. His ass is already out the door! The post returns to me, and I'll resell it to somebody else.

RAFLE. I thought you might.

TURCARET. I mean, who am I working for here? The people? Am I supposed to go against my own interests? If I did, the company should have my head on a platter!

RAFLE. I wrote him back, telling him he could in no way depend on you.

TURCARET. Good work, Rafle.

RAFLE. [*Looking at his dossier.*] Are you interested in acquiring, at seven percent, five thousand francs from a decent locksmith I know—they're his life savings.

TURCARET. Sure, sure, that sounds good. I will do him the honor of taking his money. Go round him up. I'll be home in fifteen minutes. Have him bring it in hard currency. Go, go.

[RAFLE *starts to leave, then comes back.*]

RAFLE. I almost forgot the main reason I'm here. I didn't write it down.

TURCARET. And what is the main reason?

RAFLE. Madame Turcaret is in Paris.

TURCARET. [*Sotto voce.*] Lower your voice, Rafle, lower your voice.

RAFLE. [*Low.*] I ran into her yesterday in a carriage with some young lord whose face is somewhat familiar to me—

TURCARET. [*Low.*] You didn't speak to her, did you?

RAFLE. [*Low.*] No. But this morning she sent word. She made me promise not to tell you anything, only that you owe her fifteen months' back pension to keep her in the country. She won't leave Paris until she's been paid off.

TURCARET. For the love of Christ! We have to get rid of that battle-ax. Give her the locksmith's five thousand right away, but she has to clear out tomorrow!

RAFLE. I'll go bring the locksmith to your house.

TURCARET. I'll meet you there.

[RAFLE *exits.*]

TURCARET. It'd be a catastrophe if that beast took it into her head to come poking around. I would definitely lose face with the Baroness, since I told her I was a widower.

[LISETTE *enters.*]

LISETTE. My lady wishes to know whether Monsieur is still conducting business?

TURCARET. My flunkies can't settle anything without checking with the boss first.

[FRONTIN *enters.*]

FRONTIN. I am enchanted, sir, to find you engaged in conversation with this charming young lady. Despite my own personal interest in her, I would not dream of disturbing your encounter.

TURCARET. You're not butting in. Come here, Frontin, I regard you as my man in all matters. Help me win the esteem of the young lady.

LISETTE. I admire you already far more than I can say.

FRONTIN. I don't know which lucky star you were born under, sir, but everybody just has a natural infirmity for you.

TURCARET. It doesn't come from the stars—it comes from manners.

LISETTE. Yours are so exquisite, so prepossessing, so mannered.

TURCARET. How would you know?

LISETTE. Since I've been here, I've heard nothing but from my mistress.

TURCARET. All good, I hope.

FRONTIN. She loves you so tenderly, she is incapable of concealing her passion. Lisette can tell you.

LISETTE. It is you he ought to believe, Monsieur Frontin.

FRONTIN. No, I myself don't fully understand all that I know on the subject. What gets me is the absolute excess of her passion, when really, if the truth be told, Monsieur Turcaret hasn't done all that he might to deserve it.

TURCARET. Wha—what do you mean by that?

FRONTIN. I've seen you, sir, twenty times over, neglect certain essential details.

TURCARET. The hell I have! I have nothing on that score to reproach myself with, nothing, do you hear?

LISETTE. Of course not. I am certain that Monsieur is not the kind of man who would allow even the slightest occasion to please the woman he loves to pass him by. It is precisely through these trifling details that a man earns his lady's affections.

FRONTIN. Nevertheless, Monsieur doesn't deserve it as thoroughly as I might wish.

TURCARET. Explain yourself.

FRONTIN. You won't find it unseemly for a good and faithful servant to take the liberty to speak to you with his frank and open heart?

TURCARET. What do I pay you for? Speak.

FRONTIN. You don't respond enough to the love that the Baroness bears for you.

TURCARET. I don't respond to it!

FRONTIN. No, Monsieur, you don't. You be the judge, Lisette. Monsieur, for all his courtly strategies, still makes crucial lapses in his attentions.

TURCARET. What do you mean by lapses?

FRONTIN. Oh, a certain thoughtlessness, a certain negligence . . .

TURCARET. And? And?

FRONTIN. I mean, isn't it the tiniest bit shameful, for example—in a certain sort of way—that you still haven't thought of presenting the Baroness with a carriage?

LISETTE. No carriage? Pardon me, sir, I didn't know. Why, your book-keepers do as well by their lady friends.

TURCARET. She's free to use mine whenever she feels like it. What's the difference?

FRONTIN. But sir, to have a carriage of one's own versus being obliged to borrow a friend's is a difference of the most telling sort.

LISETTE. Monsieur, you're too much in the know not to know these things; women are more sensitive to the vanity of having a carriage than to the pleasure of using it.

TURCARET. Well if you put it that way . . .

FRONTIN. Our girl here is extremely quick-witted.

TURCARET. You're not as dumb as I took you for either, Frontin.

FRONTIN. Oh, sir, since being in your employ, I feel myself getting smarter by the minute. I know I'll profit so much from you.

TURCARET. It's all up to you.

FRONTIN. I promise to apply myself. Now, I'd give the Baroness a great big carriage, gorgeously upholstered, with all the trimmings and trappings.

TURCARET. She shall have one. Your arguments have persuaded me.

FRONTIN. I knew it was just an oversight on your part.

TURCARET. I'll go right now and order it.

FRONTIN. Good heavens no, sir. You absolutely cannot touch the matter. It wouldn't look proper if it were known in society that you gave a carriage to the Baroness.

TURCARET. It's my money, isn't it?

FRONTIN. You need a loyal but disinterested middleman. I know a couple of saddlers who don't know that I'm in your service. If you like, I can arrange . . .

TURCARET. You appear well-versed in these things. I'm willing to place myself in your hands. [*Giving him his purse.*] Here's eighteen hundred francs—pocket money—you can use them as a down payment.

FRONTIN. Never fear, sir. As for the horses, I have a cousin once removed who is a great horse trader. He can provide you with an excellent team.

TURCARET. Cheap?

FRONTIN. He will sell them in good conscience.

TURCARET. Sure, the conscience of a horse trader!

FRONTIN. I can answer for him as well as for myself.

TURCARET. In that case, he's hired.

FRONTIN. Another lapse of attention—

TURCARET. [*Interrupting.*] You can take a hike with your lapses of attention! Are you out to ruin me? Tell the Baroness that I had to close on a deal back at the office.

[TURCARET *exits.*]

FRONTIN. Not a bad start.

LISETTE. Not for the Baroness, no, but what about us?

FRONTIN. Well, we keep these eighteen hundred francs for starters. I'll make that much on the carriage. Put them away—they'll be the foundation of our joint account.

LISETTE. We'll have to build quickly on the foundation because, I warn you, my mind has been taking a moral turn of late.

FRONTIN. What do you mean?

LISETTE. I'm getting tired of being a lady's maid.

FRONTIN. You want to be a lady?

LISETTE. Don't make fun of me. The air one breathes in a house frequented by big shots runs counter to humility: since I've been here, ambitious ideas keep popping into my head. Hurry, Frontin, and swag the loot; because otherwise, no matter what our little understanding has been— well, all I can say is that the first fop who's loaded that comes along to court me—

FRONTIN. Give me time to enrich myself.

LISETTE. I'll grant you three years—that should be enough for a man with cunning.

FRONTIN. More than enough, my princess. In order to meet your requirements, I shall spare no one and no thing. *And,* if I should fail in my mission, it won't be for any lapses of attention.

[FRONTIN *exits.*]

LISETTE. I can't help loving that Frontin. He's my very own chevalier, mine alone. And at the rate he's going, I have a sneaking suspicion that I will become a woman of quality sometime soon.

Act IV

CHEVALIER. What are you doing here? Didn't you tell me you'd be going back to your exchange broker? Shouldn't you have found him by now?

FRONTIN. Excuse me, sir, but he was low on funds; he didn't have the whole amount on him. He told me to come back tonight. You can have the note if you like.

CHEVALIER. Keep it—what do you want me to do with it? Is the Baroness in her room? What's she doing?

FRONTIN. She and Lisette are discussing a carriage that I'm ordering for her, as well as a country house she wants to rent until I can get Turcaret to buy it outright.

CHEVALIER. A carriage? A country house? What madness!

FRONTIN. It's Turcaret's treat.

CHEVALIER. What wisdom.

FRONTIN. There's just one teensy bagatelle that's bothering her.

CHEVALIER. What is that?

FRONTIN. The house in the country needs furnishing. She doesn't know how to hit Turcaret up for it—the superior genius she's placed in his service is on the case.

CHEVALIER. How do you plan to wheedle that out of him?

FRONTIN. I'm tracking down a shady acquaintance from the old days who can help us pull in the ten thousand we need to set up housekeeping with.

CHEVALIER. Have you thought this all through?

FRONTIN. Do you need to ask? Thinking things through is my forte. A forged document . . . a false summons. It's all up here with my genius.

CHEVALIER. I advise you to be careful, Frontin. Turcaret knows his business.

FRONTIN. My old friend knows it better than Turcaret. He has the craftiest, the most intelligent handwriting . . .

CHEVALIER. Well observed and duly noted.

FRONTIN. His writings have nearly landed him in several stately institutions.

CHEVALIER. Say no more.

FRONTIN. My machine will be ready to roll as soon as I track him down. Farewell. Here comes the Marquess—he's been looking for you.

[FRONTIN *exits and the* MARQUESS *enters.*]

MARQUESS. For the love of Christ, there you are! You've made yourself scarce. I've been looking for you these past forty-eight hours. I need some advice concerning an affair of the heart.

CHEVALIER. You? How long have you been embroiled?

MARQUESS. Four days . . . at most.

CHEVALIER. And you've only just now come to tell me about it! You're becoming downright discreet.

MARQUESS. If I thought I had sunk to discretion, I might as well join a temperance movement. You know me — an affair of the heart occasions but the faintest of murmurs. I made this conquest by purest chance; I'm sticking with it solely for amusement; I shall cast it off out of caprice or, maybe, just maybe, I'll come up with a justification.

CHEVALIER. What a tender liaison.

MARQUESS. Well it just doesn't do to have life's pleasures occupy us too seriously. *I* fret over nothing. She gave me her portrait; I lost it. Any other gentleman would hang himself over it. [*Gestures to illustrate.*] I care about it this much.

CHEVALIER. Yes, but women stand in line for that sort of abuse. Tell me — who is the lady in question?

MARQUESS. A woman of quality, a provincial countess, so she claims.

CHEVALIER. You sleep all day and drink all night; when did you find time to wage your campaign?

MARQUESS. I believe there is always time at the masquerade balls for such happy opportunities.

CHEVALIER. You met her at a ball then.

MARQUESS. Exactly. I went the other evening, warmed by wine — quite combusted, if you must know. Nothing could hinder me; I aroused some pretty masks at first, then I beheld a waist, a bosom, a turn of the hips. . . . I accost, I beg, I plead, I press, I force an unmasking — I behold a vision . . .

CHEVALIER. Young?

MARQUESS. Rather old.

CHEVALIER. Yet beautiful.

MARQUESS. Not too beautiful.

CHEVALIER. I see Love hasn't exactly blinded you.

MARQUESS. I do only justice to my beloved.

CHEVALIER. She's witty at least?

MARQUESS. Oh, as for wit, she's a marvel. What a fluxion of thoughts! What an imagination! She regaled me with scads of charmingly extravagant anecdotes.

CHEVALIER. What was the result of the conversation?

MARQUESS. I escorted her home with her retinue; I offered her my services, and the old fool accepted them.

CHEVALIER. Have you seen her since?

MARQUESS. The next night, when I got up, I presented myself at her rooming house.

CHEVALIER. Rooming house?

MARQUESS. Rooming house.

CHEVALIER. Rooming house.

MARQUESS. Rooming house.

CHEVALIER. And?

MARQUESS. And . . . more vivacious conversation, fresh follies, tender protestations on my part, vivid rejoinders on hers. The day before yesterday she gave me that cursèd portrait that I lost. I haven't seen her since. She's expecting me today, but I frankly don't know what to do. Will I go? Won't I go? What is your counsel?

CHEVALIER. Not going would be impolite.

MARQUESS. Yes, but going would make me look almost . . . zealous. We can't have that. The juncture is critical. To show this much interest— that's chasing after a woman, which is so bourgeois, don't you think?

CHEVALIER. In order to advise you, I would have to meet her.

MARQUESS. A rendezvous can be arranged. Perhaps you and the Baroness might come to dinner this evening.

CHEVALIER. We're giving a dinner here tonight.

MARQUESS. I shall bring my conquest.

CHEVALIER. But the Baroness . . .

MARQUESS. Oh, she and the Baroness will get along famously! It's a splendid idea for them to get to know each other; then we'll be able to double.

CHEVALIER. Won't your countess object to appearing with you, tête-à-tête, in a private home?

MARQUESS. Object? My countess isn't objectionable in the least; she's someone who really knows how to have a good time—she's completely transcended all the prejudices of her upbringing.

CHEVALIER. Really? Bring her along—she sounds like fun.

MARQUESS. She will win you over completely. A lively woman with such dainty manners. Petulant, absentminded, dizzy, dissipated, and always dusted with snuff. No one would take her for a woman from the provinces.

CHEVALIER. What a captivating portrait you paint! I cannot wait to meet the likeness.

MARQUESS. I shall go round her up. No good-byes.

CHEVALIER. Ever your servant.

[*The* MARQUESS *exits and the* BARONESS *enters.*]

BARONESS. What are you doing here all alone? I thought I heard the Marquess's voice.

CHEVALIER. He left this very instant. [*He laughs.*]

BARONESS. What are you laughing at?

CHEVALIER. He's smitten with a countess from the provinces who lives in a rooming house.

BARONESS. A rooming house?

CHEVALIER. A rooming house. He's gone to bring her here to dinner. She'll be another act for the party.

BARONESS. What? Are you saying you invited them to dine with us?

CHEVALIER. The more the merrier. We must besot Monsieur Turcaret with spectacle.

BARONESS. He won't find having the Marquess to dine entertaining; you don't know that they know each other, indeed, dislike one another intensely—there was a horrible scene between them here only—

CHEVALIER. [*Interrupting.*] The pleasures of the table repair all injury. They couldn't be so ill-disposed toward one another as to be beyond reconciliation. Let me be in charge of that—put your faith in me. Turcaret is a boor—

BARONESS. Shut up, I think he's here. I hope he didn't hear you.

[TURCARET *enters.*]

CHEVALIER. [*Kissing* TURCARET.] Might Monsieur Turcaret permit one to kiss him, and permit one to demonstrate in advance the vivid pleasure that one shall soon enjoy to be beside him, glass in hand?

TURCARET. The pleasure of that vividness . . . sir, will be . . . very, uh . . . even. The honor that I receive from one part . . . joined to . . . the satisfaction that . . . one gets from another . . . part of madame, makes in truth, that . . . I assure you . . . that . . . I am extremely easy with that part.

BARONESS. Sir, you are engaged in compliments that only embarrass the Chevalier, and I fear neither of you will conclude.

CHEVALIER. My cousin is right. Let us do away with ceremony and think only of enjoying ourselves. Do you like music?

TURCARET. Shit, yes, I subscribe to the opera.

CHEVALIER. Opera is the predominant passion of all the right people.

TURCARET. Mine, too.

CHEVALIER. Music stirs the passions.

TURCARET. And how! A beautiful voice, backed by a trumpet, throws me right into a sweet reverie.

BARONESS. What refined taste you have.

CHEVALIER. He's definitive. And what an ass I have been not to have thought of a trumpet. [*He starts to exit.*] If your taste runs to brass, I'll go right now and send word for . . .

TURCARET. I wouldn't hear of it, dear Monsieur Chevalier—I mean, one little trumpet . . .

BARONESS. [*Low to* TURCARET.] Let him go.

[*The* CHEVALIER *exits.*]

BARONESS. And now we can be alone together, and I can have you all to myself. Let us spare ourselves the unwelcome presence of intruders.

TURCARET. You love me far beyond my worth, my lady.

BARONESS. Who could not love you? The Chevalier, my cousin, has always had a fondness for you . . .

TURCARET. I owe him a lot.

BARONESS. His scrupulous attention to every detail that might please you tonight . . .

TURCARET. He seems like a really great guy . . .

[LISETTE *enters.*]

BARONESS. What is it, Lisette?

LISETTE. There's a man here dressed in dark gray and an old wig. His clothes smell. [*Low.*] The furniture for the country house.

BARONESS. Gracious! Have him enter, if you please.

[FURET *and* FRONTIN *enter.*]

FURET. Which of the two of you, my good women, is the mistress of the house?

BARONESS. I am she. What do you wish?

FURET. I will not respond until I have previously given myself the honor of saluting you, you, madame, and all the honorable company, with all due and requisite respect.

TURCARET. Here's an original.

LISETTE. Without so much ado, sir, tell us previously that you are who?

FURET. I am a bailiff, at your service, and I am called Monsieur Furet.

BARONESS. A bailiff, in my house!

FRONTIN. What effrontery!

TURCARET. [*To the* BARONESS.] My lady, would you like me to toss this boob out the window? He's not the first scoundrel to—

FURET. Do it gently, sir. Honest bailiffs like myself are not usually exposed to such adventures. I administer my little administration in such an obliging fashion that persons of true quality find it an honor to receive a summons from me. [*Removing a paper from his pocket.*] And here's one that I will have, if you please, the honor, with your permission, sir, that I will have the honor of presenting, with all due respect, to madame . . . with your consent, sir.

BARONESS. A summons for me? [*To* LISETTE.] See what it says, Lisette.

LISETTE. I can only read love letters . . . you look at it, Frontin.

FRONTIN. I'm still developing my head for business.

FURET. It is a question of a debt that the deceased Baron Porcandorf, your husband—

BARONESS. He's dead—it's no affair of mine—I closed our joint account.

TURCARET. If that's true, then he can't get anything out of you.

FURET. Begging your pardon, sir, the act, having been countersigned by madame—

TURCARET. It's been countersigned? Oh.

FURET. And in a most elegant hand, I might add. There is a repayment schedule attached; shall I read you the terms? It's all right here in the summons.

TURCARET. [*Grudgingly.*] Let's hear whether it's been drawn up right.

FURET. [*After putting on spectacles.*] "As witnessed by, etcetera, being present in their full persons, the most high and mighty Lord Georges-Guillaume de Porcandorf and Lady Agnès-Hildégonde de la Dolin-villière, his spouse, duly authorized and bonded by him for the purposes of this transaction; the aforementioned have recognized a debt to Aloysius-Jérôme Poussif, merchant to horses, in the sum of thirty thousand francs . . .

BARONESS. Thirty thousand francs!

LISETTE. O cursèd bondage!

FURET. . . . for a carriage and train furnished by the said Poussif consist-ing of a dozen mules, fifteen chestnut horses from the Auvergne, three Norman nags, all equipped with manes, tails, and ears, fully garnished with harness, saddles, bridles, and halters . . .

LISETTE. [*Interrupting.*] Bridles and halters! Why should a woman have to pay for that kind of frippery?

TURCARET. Don't interrupt . . . [*To* FURET.] Finish, my good man.

FURET. . . . against payment of said thirty thousand francs, the aforemen-tioned debtors have impounded, attached, and generally mortgaged all goods present and to come, renouncing all said rights to division or discussion, and for the execution of the present act, have elected as their domicile the house of Innocent Blaise le Juste, former solicitor of the Châtelet, residing at rue Bout du Monde. Made and passed, et cetera . . ."

FRONTIN. Is this transaction on the up and up?

TURCARET. There's nothing there I would correct, except the amount.

FURET. The amount, sir, is beyond correction. I find it exceedingly clear.

TURCARET. [*To the* BARONESS.] This is bad news.

BARONESS. What do you mean, bad news? Is just signing my name seriously going to cost me thirty thousand francs?

LISETTE. This is what comes of being too obedient to your husband. Will womankind never correct this character flaw?

BARONESS. What injustice! [*To* TURCARET.] Is there any way to countersue this act, Monsieur Turcaret?

TURCARET. From all appearances — no. If you hadn't expressly given up your rights to division and discussion in the document, we could have outfoxed this Poussif.

BARONESS. Since you condemn me for my actions, I see that I must steel myself to pay it. I shall not countermand your decision.

FRONTIN. [*Low to* TURCARET.] See how she defers to your judgment.

BARONESS. How too, too, inconvenient. This will upset the project I was planning for a certain note of credit you are aware of.

LISETTE. Let us pay up, my lady. We don't want to file suit against the good advice of Monsieur Turcaret.

BARONESS. Heaven forfend! Why, I'd sooner sell my jewels and my furniture.

FRONTIN. [*Low to* TURCARET.] Sell her furniture, her jewels — and all on account of a dead man's mules. My poor lady!

TURCARET. You will sell nothing, Madame. I will eat the debt. I shall make it my business.

BARONESS. Do not sport with me, sir. I shall simply cash in this note.

TURCARET. Use it for something else.

BARONESS. Sir, the nobility of your offer pains me more than the debt itself.

TURCARET. Let us speak no more of it. I shall aright this mess this very instant.

FRONTIN. What a beautiful soul! [*To* FURET.] Come with us, Monsieur Furet — you shall be paid in full.

BARONESS. [*To* TURCARET.] Do not tarry, dear heart. Think of those who await your return.

TURCARET. I'll square this away in two shakes and return in time for the first course.

[TURCARET, FRONTIN, *and* FURET *exit*.]

LISETTE. That was some swindle those two pulled. Have you ever seen such a big fat dupe?

BARONESS. Almost too big, Lisette.

LISETTE. He walked into the trap almost before they set it.

BARONESS. Do you know, I'm beginning to feel sorry for him?

LISETTE. Let's not pity the pitiless! Compassion is wasted on a shark like him.

BARONESS. Even so, I'm starting to have my doubts . . .

LISETTE. Stifle them.

BARONESS. Regrets even . . .

LISETTE. This is no time to start that, my lady. When all is said and done, the regret you may feel for having ruined a businessman would be nothing compared to the regret you'd feel for having missed the opportunity.

[JASMIN *enters.*]

JASMIN. A lady is here from Madame Dorimène.

BARONESS. Dorimène must be proposing some sort of outing . . . send her in, Jasmin.

[MADAME JACOB *enters.*]

MADAME JACOB. Salutations. I ask your pardon my lady for the liberty I'm taking here. I sell items of a secondhand nature. I've had the occasional honor of selling lace, pomades, and all manner of unmentionables to Lady Dorimène. I sent word to her that I'd gotten a deal for her, but she's not flush at present, if you know what I'm saying and I think you do, and so she told me you might wish to avail yourself of this particular item.

BARONESS. What is it?

MADAME JACOB. It's a headpiece—a jeweled tiara worth 4,500 francs. Belongs to a tax collector's wife in Lille. Only wore it twice. Now she thinks it's tacky and wants to unload.

BARONESS. I suppose it wouldn't hurt me to see it.

MADAME JACOB. I'll bring it by as soon as it comes in, make you a nice price.

LISETTE. You won't stand to lose; my mistress is generous.

MADAME JACOB. I've got room to haggle; selling rags isn't my only line of work, believe me. I work a lot of different streets.

BARONESS. I am certain you do.

MADAME JACOB. I mean really, if I didn't have other resources to fall back on, I couldn't have raised my children as honestly as I have. I have a husband, mind you. But he's only good for enlarging the family, not supporting it.

LISETTE. Lots of husbands do just the opposite.

BARONESS. What else is it that you do, Madame Jacob, to provide for your family?

MADAME JACOB. I'm a marriage broker. *Legitimate* marriages only; they don't yield as much as other kinds of arrangements, but at least I can sleep easy at night. Not four months ago I married a young musketeer to the widow of a government revenuer. A perfect match—every day it's open house—they're eating his inheritance in high style, I tell you.

BARONESS. So the pair fell out well together.

MADAME JACOB. I stand behind the product. All of my marriages are happy. [*To the* BARONESS.] And if my lady happened to be in the market for a husband, I have an excellent prospect.

LISETTE. She's full of bargains today, my lady.

MADAME JACOB. He's a gentleman from Limousin. Excellent material—a prince. The woman who gets him could lead him by the nose.

BARONESS. Society hasn't fatigued me enough to want to get married again.

LISETTE. Well I'm ready to enroll, Madame Jacob.

MADAME JACOB. I have just the man in mind. A big burly salesman—he's made his pile and now he's looking for a pretty wife.

LISETTE. He'll do.

BARONESS. You must be wealthy, Madame Jacob.

MADAME JACOB. Don't I wish, my lady. I cut a poor figure in Paris when I should be a high roller, having as I do a tycoon for a brother.

BARONESS. You have a brother in finance?

MADAME JACOB. High finance, as high as it gets. [*Pause.*] All right, since you force it out of me, I am the sister of Monsieur Turcaret. You've heard of him, right?

BARONESS. You're Monsieur Turcaret's sister!

MADAME JACOB. On both his father's and his mother's side.

LISETTE. Monsieur Turcaret is your brother, Madame Jacob?

MADAME JACOB. Is there an echo in here? Yes, my brother, my own brother, and it's made me no greater lady because of it. . . . You two look pretty squeezed about this. No doubt it's because he makes his big sister scrounge for a living.

LISETTE. You took the words right out of my mouth.

MADAME JACOB. You ain't heard the half of it—he's forbidden me to set foot in his house. *And* the skinflint doesn't even have the decency to give my husband a job.

BARONESS. This cries out for vengeance.

LISETTE. What a rotten kid brother.

MADAME JACOB. A rotten brother and a rotten husband. He tossed his wife right out of the house.

BARONESS. Perhaps it was a bad match.

MADAME JACOB. Was? Is! My sister-in-law lives in the country. They have no truck with each other.

BARONESS. Monsieur Turcaret isn't a widower?

MADAME JACOB. You bet your life he's not. He and his wife separated ten
years ago. And to keep her out of Paris, he pays her a pension to stay
in Valognes.

BARONESS. [*Low to* LISETTE.] Lisette?

LISETTE. [*Low to* BARONESS.] What a scumbag.

MADAME JACOB. God'll make him pay for it sooner or later, you can lay
money on it. Somebody else was telling me today that there's been a
crisis in the company.

BARONESS. A company crisis?

MADAME JACOB. Surprise, surprise. He's been leching after every woman
but his own for years. As soon as he falls in love with one, he throws
all his money down the toilet. The man's a sieve.

LISETTE. [*Low.*] Who would know better than us?

MADAME JACOB. I don't know who his current attachment is, but there's
always some chippy fleecing him—he thinks he has them under control, because he promises to marry them. What a half-wit—*wenn der
Putz shteht, ligt der Seichel in drerd,* I always say.

LISETTE. What does that mean?

MADAME JACOB. "You can't win an argument with a hard-on."

BARONESS. That's entirely—

MADAME JACOB. What do I care? He deserves ruin, the shit deserves it.
If I knew who his present cookie-do was, I'd tell her to hit him for all
he's worth, gnaw him, swallow him whole—wouldn't you?

LISETTE. I wouldn't waste a second, Madame Jacob.

MADAME JACOB. Sorry to bend your ears with my problems, but when I
stop to think about it, I get so wound up, I can't stop talking. Adieu,
my lady. As soon as the headpiece comes in, I'll bring it right over.

BARONESS. No hurry, good woman, no hurry at all.

[MADAME JACOB *exits.*]

BARONESS. Well . . . Lisette?

LISETTE. Well . . . my lady?

BARONESS. Would you have ever guessed that Monsieur Turcaret had a
sister who peddled door to door?

LISETTE. Would you have ever guessed he had a wife living in the country?

BARONESS. The beast! He lied to me! He promised me he was a widower.

LISETTE. The old goat. [*Looking at the* BARONESS.] What is it? What's
wrong? What's this pitiful face you're making? You're taking this too
hard—you're acting like you were seriously in love with Turcaret.

BARONESS. I don't love him, but when a woman loses the opportunity to

marry a man, doesn't it call for some token sorrow at least? The cad!
He has a wife! I have to break with him—I'll bar the door.

LISETTE. Not so fast, my lady, the interest of your fortune dictates that you
demolish him first. Let's go and smash open his strongbox, let's seize
his banknotes, let's put him to the fire and the sword; let's turn him
back into Madame Jacob's little brother—let's make him so pitifully
miserable that he'll start to take pity on others—even his wife!

Act V

LISETTE. [*Alone.*] What a set-up. Frontin and I already have 1,800 francs,
and Furet's false summons will bring in at least that much. If we keep
piecing together enough of these little sums, we'll wind up with quite
a nest egg.

[*The* BARONESS *enters.*]

BARONESS. It seems to me that Monsieur Turcaret should have returned
by now.

LISETTE. Some new piece of business must have turned up.

[FLAMAND *enters, no longer in livery.* LISETTE *doesn't recognize him at first.*]

LISETTE. What does this guy want?

BARONESS. Who let him in without notice?

FLAMAND. No harm done, my lady—it's me.

LISETTE. It's Flamand, Flamand out of livery with a sword at his side.
What a metamorphosis.

FLAMAND. Shush, mademoiselle, shush. One must not, if you please, call
me plain old Flamand. I am no longer Monsieur Turcaret's lackey, no.
He has found me a good position, yes. I am presently in finance, oh yes,
and by this act, I must be called Monsieur Flamand, do you understand?

LISETTE. Quite. Now that you've become a clerk, you won't be treated
like a lackey anymore.

FLAMAND. It is to my lady that I owe my gratitude—I have come expressly to thank her. She is a good lady, who showed such goodness
toward me to have had me given a good commission that will net me
nine hundred good francs a year, and which is in a good location to
boot, that is to say, in Falaise, which is such a good city, and where
there are, it is said, such good people.

LISETTE. There's a lot of good to be said for that, Monsieur Flamand.

FLAMAND. I'm doorman-in-chief for the gate of Guibrai. I'll have the keys
and will have the right to let people in and out as I please. I've been
told it's a good right to have.

LISETTE. Good God.

FLAMAND. And the beauty part is that this office blesses all who've held it — everyone gets rich from it. They say Monsieur Turcaret got his start this way.

BARONESS. How glorious for you, Monsieur Flamand, to follow in the steps of your master!

LISETTE. And we commend you, for your own good, to be as honest as he is.

FLAMAND. I promise to send you little presents from time to time, my lady.

BARONESS. I ask nothing of you, my poor Flamand.

FLAMAND. I know how clerks are supposed to treat the ladies who find work for them. But I am afraid of getting fired; in the business world, you have to watch out for that, you know.

LISETTE. We know.

FLAMAND. Like, for instance, the clerk that they fired today to make room for me got the job through a certain lady that Monsieur Turcaret is no longer hot for. Take care, my lady, that the same thing doesn't happen to me.

BARONESS. I shall give it all of my attention, Monsieur Flamand.

FLAMAND. I bid you to always please Monsieur Turcaret, my lady.

BARONESS. Since the matter is of such import to you, I shall do my utmost to fulfill it.

FLAMAND. Always slap on enough rouge to excite him.

LISETTE. Go, doorman-in-chief, hence to the gate of Guibrai! We know what we have to do. . . . We don't need your advice. . . . You're such a moron — don't ever change. This is me talking, that's right, do you understand?

[FLAMAND *is pushed out the door.*]

BARONESS. That was the most appalling . . .

LISETTE. You'd think having been a lackey for so long would have wised up his manners.

[JASMIN *enters.*]

JASMIN. Monsieur the Marquess has arrived with a large lady.

BARONESS. The gorgeous conquest. I'm curious to see her.

LISETTE. So am I, my lady, so am I — she's already made quite a picture in my mind.

[*The* MARQUESS *and* MADAME TURCARET *enter.*]

MARQUESS. I come, my charming Baroness, to present to you a most attractive woman, the wittiest, most gallant, and amusing personage in my acquaintance. The number of sterling qualities common to the both of you should unite you in a bond of mutual esteem and amity.

BARONESS. Toward this union I am most disposed. [*Low, to* LISETTE.] She's the original of the Chevalier's portrait.

MADAME TURCARET. I fear, my lady, that you might soon lose these fine and fancy feelings for me. A person of high, indeed, brilliant society, such as yourself, will find scant amusement in the commerce of a woman up from the country.

BARONESS. But you haven't at all a provincial air, madame: our most fashionable women haven't manners any more agreeable than yours.

MARQUESS. For God's sake, no! I'm something of an expert, madame, and you must certainly agree that, in seeing this form and this face, that I am the lord with the best taste in all of France.

MADAME TURCARET. You are too gallant, my lord Marquess. I could consent, without a speck of vanity, to such flattery in the country, where I do shine. There I am the height of all the fashions—the moment they're invented, they're sent to me. Why, I can boast of being the first woman in the city of Valognes to wear tights!

LISETTE. Bring on the regiment.

BARONESS. How delightful to serve as a model for a community like that!

MADAME TURCARET. I set that town on its ear! I have assembled the cream of our youth and made a little Paris of them within my borders.

MARQUESS. A little Paris, you say! Did you know that it takes three months in Valognes to polish off a courtier?

MADAME TURCARET. I don't live like a country lady. I am made for society. I couldn't bear to be cooped up in a château, so I reside in town, and I daresay that my house is practically a charm school for the younger set.

LISETTE. Lower Normandy Junior High.

MADAME TURCARET. We gamble; we gather for slander; we read the wittiest works fabricated in Cherbourg, Saint-Lô, and Coutances, which are as juicy as any works by Vire or Caen. I also arrange small floor shows and collation suppers. To tell you the truth, my cooks are unable to make stews of any sort, but they can barbecue meats to perfection— one more or one less turn of the spit and they'd be ruined.

MARQUESS. Spit turns are truly the cornerstone to good dining—gracious me, long live barbecue valognaise!

MADAME TURCARET. I often give costume balls, real refined and elegant-like. When it comes to knowing the art of the mask, Valognes ladies are the fanciest in the world; each one of us has a favorite disguise. Guess what mine is?

LISETTE. Madame disguises herself as Love, perhaps?

MADAME TURCARET. Oh, no, you're too kind.

BARONESS. You get yourself up as a goddess, I should think, or one of the Graces.

MADAME TURCARET. Guess again. [*Pause.*] As Venus, my dears, as Venus.

BARONESS. Venus! Well, madame, I'm sure no one could possibly recognize you in that disguise.

LISETTE. No one at all.

[*The* CHEVALIER *enters.*]

CHEVALIER. My lady, we shall soon hear the most ravishing concert. [*Sees* MADAME TURCARET, *aside.*] But what do I see?

MADAME TURCARET. [*Aside.*] O heavens!

BARONESS. [*Low, to* LISETTE.] I hadn't a doubt.

CHEVALIER. [*To the* MARQUESS.] Is this the woman you were describing to me, Marquess?

MARQUESS. Yes, this is my Countess. Why do you look surprised?

CHEVALIER. I wasn't expecting that Countess.

MADAME TURCARET. [*Aside.*] What a pickle.

MARQUESS. Explain yourself. Do you happen to know my Countess?

CHEVALIER. Know her? I have been courting her for a week.

MARQUESS. Oh, you infidel! You ingrate!

CHEVALIER. This very morning she blessed me with the gift of her portrait.

MARQUESS. What the deuce? Does she have portraits to give to everybody?

[MADAME JACOB *enters.*]

MADAME JACOB. My lady, here's the headpiece you wanted to take a gander at.

BARONESS. You've chosen an awkward moment—I have company.

MADAME JACOB. I beg your pardon, my lady. I'll come back some other time. [*Sees* MADAME TURCARET.] But Madame Turcaret! What is my sister-in-law doing here?

CHEVALIER. Madame Turcaret?

BARONESS. Madame Turcaret?

LISETTE. Madame Turcaret?

MARQUESS. That's entertainment.

MADAME JACOB. And by what happenstance, Madame, should I be meeting you in this house?

MADAME TURCARET. [*Aside.*] Brazen it out, girl. [*To* MADAME JACOB.] I am afraid you must mistake me for someone else. I do not know you, my dear.

MADAME JACOB. You don't know Madame Jacob? The hell you don't. Do you pretend not to know me because for the last ten years you've been separated from my brother who can't stand the sight of you? Is that why?

MARQUESS. What could you be thinking of, Madame Jacob—do you know you are speaking to a Countess?

MADAME JACOB. To a Countess! Aren't we grand? And in what location, pray tell, is her county?

MADAME TURCARET. You are an insolent woman, my dear.

MADAME JACOB. I'm insolent? Don't start with me, sister—if it's a question of mudslinging, I can sling it with the best!

MADAME TURCARET. I don't doubt that the daughter of a groom from Domfront would be accustomed to uncouth expressions.

MADAME JACOB. And proud of it! Now here is a woman so well brought up she reproaches me for my birth. You have apparently forgotten that your father, Monsieur Briochais, was a pastry chef in the village of Falaise. Keep it coming, Madame La Comtesse, oh, we go way back. . . . My brother will piss himself when he finds out you've come to Paris all decked out with a burlesque title. I wish he'd just walk right through that door.

CHEVALIER. Your wish is my command, my lady. Monsieur Turcaret is expected for dinner.

MADAME TURCARET. [*Aside*.] Aiieeeee!

MARQUESS. [*To* MADAME JACOB.] And you must also sup with us, Madame Jacob.

MADAME JACOB. I love family dinners.

MADAME TURCARET. It was a mistake to come here.

LISETTE. You don't mean that.

MADAME TURCARET. [*Attempting to leave*.] I'll just be going.

MARQUESS. [*Stopping her*.] You can't go until you've seen Monsieur Turcaret, if you please.

MADAME TURCARET. Do not detain me, Marquess, do not detain me.

MARQUESS. Lady Briochais, you shall remain.

CHEVALIER. Let her go.

MARQUESS. I shall do nothing of the kind. To punish her for having been a two-timing siren, I want to return her to her husband's care.

BARONESS. No, my lord, I beg of you, let her go.

MARQUESS. A useless entreaty, my dear. [*To* MADAME TURCARET.] All I can do for you, Madame, is permit you to disguise yourself as Venus. He won't recognize her then.

LISETTE. Speak of the devil, here he comes.

MADAME JACOB. This should be good.

MADAME TURCARET. O unhappy day!

BARONESS. Must we have this scene in my house?

MARQUESS. What a climax for me.

[TURCARET *enters.*]

TURCARET. I sent the bailiff away and put an end to the—[*Aside.*] Can I believe my eyes? My sister here! [*Sees* MADAME TURCARET.] Jesus, it's the missus!

MARQUESS. Here you are, in familiar territory, are you not, Monsieur Turcaret? [*Gesturing to* MADAME TURCARET.] Here is a ravishing Countess—I lie in her chains. You must make her acquaintance, and let us not forget Madame Jacob.

MADAME JACOB. Brother!

TURCARET. Sister! Who the hell let them in?

MARQUESS. You must thank me for that, Monsieur Turcaret. Embrace them, kiss these two cherished creatures. How moved he appears. Which is more touching—the call of the blood or the caterwaul of conjugal love?

TURCARET. [*Aside.*] I can't look at her. I will see an evil genie.

MADAME TURCARET. [*Aside.*] I cannot look at his face without shrieking.

MARQUESS. Don't hold back, my tender spouses—after ten years of separation, let the joy of your reunion burst forth.

BARONESS. You were not expecting to meet your wife here, so I can appreciate your embarassment. Why did you tell me you were a widower?

MARQUESS. She told me she was a widow.

BARONESS. Why have you deceived me? Speak!

TURCARET. I thought, madame . . . that in making you believe that. . . . I was thinking of being a widower so that you'd believe that I didn't have a wife. [*Aside.*] My mind is going; I don't know what I'm saying.

BARONESS. I have divined your thought, sir, and I pardon you for a deceit you must have believed necessary in order to gain my favor. I shall even press further; instead of drifting into meaningless reproach, I would like to effect a deep and lasting reconciliation between you and your wife.

TURCARET. Who, me? I pass. You don't know her. She's a demon. I'd rather live with the wife of Genghis Khan.

MADAME TURCARET. Oh, and you're a picnic, I suppose! I don't relish this any more than you do—less in fact. And I would never have to come to Paris to spoil your fun, I would have stayed put in the country if you had kept up with the payments to keep me there.

MARQUESS. To keep her in the country? Monsieur Turcaret, you are in the wrong. A woman of Madame Turcaret's size and caliber deserves to be paid a quarter in advance.

MADAME TURCARET. He owes me for five. And I'm not leaving until he pays me. I'll stay in Paris, go to every one of his mistresses and raise a great big stink. And I'm warning you, there's no place like the present.

TURCARET. Battle-ax!

MADAME TURCARET. I've got eyes, by God, I've got eyes; I know what's going on around here. My husband has always been the biggest stupe.

TURCARET. Witch! Cow! If I didn't respect the present company, why I'd—

MARQUESS. Don't let us stand in your way, Monsieur Turcaret. You are among friends; follow your heart's inclinations.

CHEVALIER. [*Getting between husband and wife.*] Monsieur!

BARONESS. Remember that you are in my house.

[JASMIN *enters.*]

JASMIN. [*To* TURCARET.] A carriage has just stopped at the door; two gentlemen who say they're your associates want to speak to you.

[JASMIN *exits.*]

TURCARET. I'll be right back—to teach you how to behave in a proper home!

[TURCARET *exits.*]

CHEVALIER. Calm your agitated state, Madame, so that Monsieur Turcaret will find you softened upon his return.

MADAME TURCARET. His ranting doesn't scare me.

BARONESS. We shall soften him in your favor.

MADAME TURCARET. I catch your drift, madame. You want me to reconcile with my husband so that I'll let him continue to keep you out of gratitude.

BARONESS. Your ire blinds you. My sole desire is the reunion of your two hearts. I yield Monsieur Turcaret to you. I wish never to see him again.

MADAME TURCARET. Yeah, well don't do me any favors.

MARQUESS. If my lady renounces the husband, I shall relinquish the wife. [*To the* CHEVALIER.] Come, my friend, it is your turn. It is indeed noble to master one's passions this way.

[FRONTIN *enters.*]

FRONTIN. O unforeseen calamity! O cruel disgrace!

CHEVALIER. What is the matter, Frontin?

FRONTIN. Monsieur Turcaret's partners have had his estate garnished for 1,800,000 francs—a cashier he co-signed with absconded with it! I just got here to warn him to flee, but alas, too late. His creditors have nabbed him.

MADAME JACOB. My little brother in the hands of his creditors! No matter how perverted or hard-hearted he is, I am moved by his misfortune. I'll extend all of my credit to him—I am his sister.

[MADAME JACOB *exits*.]

MADAME TURCARET. And I, I am going to find him and beat the shit out of him—I am his wife.

[MADAME TURCARET *exits*.]

FRONTIN. [*To the* CHEVALIER.] We had high hopes of ruining him, but the hand of justice beat us to the kill.

MARQUESS. Fine, fine, he has enough money to pull through.

FRONTIN. But they say he's pissed away an absolutely enormous fortune, although that is not my main concern right now. It was my terrific luck to be at his house when his partners came in and took over.

CHEVALIER. So?

FRONTIN. Sir, they also seized and searched me to see if by chance I had any assets or incriminating papers on me that would satisfy his creditors. They confiscated my lady's note of credit that you entrusted to me.

CHEVALIER. What?

FRONTIN. They also seized the other one, the note for ten thousand that Turcaret gave me to settle with Furet on the horse swindle. Furet had just handed it to me.

CHEVALIER. And why the hell didn't you just say that you were *my* servant, not his?

FRONTIN. Really, sir, I jumped on the opportunity. I said that I belonged to a man of breeding and distinction, but when they saw how much money I had on me, they said they didn't believe me.

CHEVALIER. My despair is boundless—it cannot be contained.

BARONESS. Stop posing. My eyes have been opened. You told me that you had the money for the note at your house. In effect my diamond was *not* pawned, and I realize now what I should think of the tearful narrative Frontin told me about your suffering last night. Oh, Chevalier, I would not have thought you capable of such conduct. I dismissed Marine because she wouldn't take your part—I shall get rid of Lisette because she has. Adieu. I never want to hear from you—or of you— again.

[*The* BARONESS *exits into her chamber*.]

MARQUESS. [*Laughing*.] My God, that's funny. You make me laugh. The situation is too damned funny. Let's go have a bite and tie one on.

FRONTIN. Shall I accompany you, sire?

CHEVALIER. Never offer yourself to my eyes again. I am giving you notice.

[*The* CHEVALIER *and the* MARQUESS *exit*.]

LISETTE. What about us, Frontin—whose part do we take now?

FRONTIN. I have a new one to propose: our own. Long live the superior genius, my child. My audacity has paid off royally. I wasn't searched.

LISETTE. You have the notes!

FRONTIN. Not only do I have them, I've cashed them in and socked them away in safe deposit! Forty thousand francs in one day. If, my lady and queen, if your ambition can contain itself to this modest fortune, we can beget an honest family.

LISETTE. You have my consent, sire.

FRONTIN. The reign of Turcaret has ended, and mine has begun.

✻ ✻ ✻

Conclusion to the Critique of
Turcaret
by the Devil on Two Sticks

ASMODEUS. Well then, Lord Cléofas! What did you think of the play? It
has succeeded in spite of the claques; all the laughter from the people
who gave themselves over to the spectacle drowned out the voices of
the bookkeepers and the authors.

CLÉOFAS. Yes, but I believe they're giving themselves free rein now to
make up for the silence they were forced to keep.

ASMODEUS. I don't doubt it; they're already clustering in groups in the
orchestra and spreading their venom. I can pick out three ringleaders
and three wits who are trying to drag several minor geniuses over to
their opinion; but I also see the friends of the author hard on their
heels. A huge argument—feelings are running high on both sides. Half
speak worse of the play than they think, and the others think less of it
than they are saying.

CLÉOFAS. So what faults are the critics finding in it?

ASMODEUS. A hundred thousand.

CLÉOFAS. What are they?

ASMODEUS. They're saying that all of the characters are vicious, and that
the author has painted their manners with too unsparing a brush.

CLÉOFAS. They're not entirely wrong at that; the manners struck me as
being a little too sharply drawn.

ASMODEUS. True, but I'm happy with them. The Baroness reminds me a
little of your Dona Thomasa.[3] I love to see my kind of heroine rule in
the theater, but I don't like seeing them punished in the dénouement—
that hurts. Fortunately a lot of French plays spare me such pain.

CLÉOFAS. I get you. You don't approve of the Baroness being deceived
in her expectations, and you don't approve of the Chevalier losing his
hopes or Turcaret's arrest. You want them all to be happy, because their
punishment is a lesson that harms your devilish interests.

ASMODEUS. Agreed, but at least in consolation, Lisette and Frontin are
well rewarded.

CLÉOFAS. Some reward! Won't Frontin's reign end just like Turcaret's?

ASMODEUS. You are very shrewd. What do you have to say about the
character of Turcaret?

3. Dona Thomasa was a female courtier who toyed with Don Cléofas's affections in *Le
Diable boiteux*.

CLÉOFAS. If businessmen really behave like I've heard, then he's a failure. Business has mysteries which weren't unveiled in the play.

ASMODEUS. May Satan forbid the revelation of those mysteries. The author tickled me simply by showing what customs my acolytes follow in order to earn the riches I acquire for them.

CLÉOFAS. Then your acolytes act differently from other businessmen.

ASMODEUS. It's easy to recognize my people. They enrich themselves by usury; after they get rich, they do it by another name. They squander their riches when they fall in love, and their loves finish either in flight or in prison.

CLÉOFAS. Then that was one of your friends onstage tonight. But tell me, Lord Asmodeus, what's that noise down in the orchestra?

ASMODEUS. It's a Spanish knight denouncing the barrenness of the plot.

CLÉOFAS. That's a very Spanish criticism. Unlike the French, we are for the most part unaccustomed to plays that are thinly plotted.

ASMODEUS. That's the customary defect of this sort of play; they aren't crowded with incident. The authors want the audience to focus its attention on the characters they depict, and they look upon overly composed plots as a distraction. I agree with your opinion, provided that the play is interesting otherwise.

CLÉOFAS. But this one isn't.

ASMODEUS. And that's its greatest flaw. It would have been perfect had the playwright known how to invite us to love his characters, but he didn't have the intelligence or skill for that. He took it into his head, and at the wrong moment, to render vice hateful. Nobody liked the Baroness, the Chevalier, or Turcaret. And that's not the way to write a successful comedy.

CLÉOFAS. But I still found it entertaining. It was a pleasure to see so many people laughing. I only saw one man and one woman who kept a straight face. They're still sitting there in their box. How pained they look.

ASMODEUS. You'll have to excuse them. It's a Turcaret with his Baroness. To make up for them, however, there was a lot of laughter in the neighboring box—legal professionals without a Turcaret in the firm. But the crowd has just left the house; let's go over to the fair and see some new faces.

CLÉOFAS. Fine with me, but first tell me who that pretty woman is over there, the one who looks so upset.

ASMODEUS. She's still in shock over the mirrors and the porcelain figures Turcaret smashed; perhaps the same kind of carnival took place in her house today.

2

THE TRIUMPH OF LOVE

Author's Preface

The fate of this play has been bizarre. I felt it capable of being either a total failure or a great success; a total failure because its subject was so peculiar, and consequently ran the risk of being badly received; a great success because I saw that, if its subject were grasped, it could give rise to much pleasure. I deceived myself, however. The play was, truth to tell, neither a failure nor a success. Everything can be reduced to the simple statement that it did not please. I speak only of its first performance; after that, it experienced yet another fate; so delighted were the new spectators who came to see it, it no longer seemed the same play; indeed, they were much surprised to hear of its initial reception. I won't report the praise they made of it, but I am not exaggerating; let the public stand guaranty for what I say. And there is still more. Four days after its première in Paris, it was performed at court. There is assuredly more wit and taste in that vicinity; the play pleased in excess of what is permissible for me to say. Why then wasn't it better received at the start? And why such success afterward? Should I venture that the first spectators were better judges than their successors? No, that would be unreasonable. I can only conclude that this difference of opinion ought to urge each to beware the other's judgment. When, in an affair of taste, a thoughtful man encounters others like him who don't share his sentiment, he must worry, it would seem to me, that he had less wit than he thought—and that is precisely what happened with this play. I'd like to believe that those who found it so delightful were perhaps mistaken. That is being quite modest, especially since I myself am not very far from finding it bad; but I also believe that those who disapproved of it could also be wrong. And so, in order to judge it fairly, I ask that one read it with attention, without regard to what anyone else has thought of it.

※ ※ ※

THE TRIUMPH OF LOVE

PIERRE CARLET DE MARIVAUX

First presented by the Comédiens Italiens on 12 March 1732

Cast
in order of appearance

LÉONIDE, under the alias of PHOCION
CORINE, under the alias of HERMIDAS
HARLEQUIN
DIMAS
AGIS
LÉONTINE
HERMOCRATE

Setting: The gardens of the philosopher Hermocrate in ancient Greece.

Act I

[PHOCION *and* HERMIDAS *enter.*]

PHOCION. Here we are—the gardens of Hermocrate the philosopher. I think.

HERMIDAS. But my lady, we don't know anyone here. We'll be thought rude for entering so boldly.

PHOCION. No, the gates were open, and we've simply come to speak to the master of the house. [*Pause.*] At last I have time to explain all you need to know.

HERMIDAS. Well, that makes me breathe easier. But Princess, grant me a favor: permit me to question you as *my* fancy suits.

PHOCION. As you wish.

HERMIDAS. You quit your court, you leave the city. You bid me to follow. We arrive at your country estate without a retinue.

PHOCION. That is correct.

HERMIDAS. You know I have learned to paint—for my own amusement. We are hardly in the country for a week when you produce two portraits and ask me to make copies of them in miniature. One, a man of fifty and the other, a woman of . . . let's round her off at forty-five. Both attractive enough.

PHOCION. If the truth be known, then—

HERMIDAS. No, I'm asking the questions. As soon as I finish copying the portraits, you suddenly announce that you're indisposed—you absolutely cannot be seen. Then you dress me up as a man, gussy yourself up in the same way and we leave incognito in your coach-and-four! Now you're calling yourself Phocion, and I am Hermidas—I might have picked my own name at least. After fifteen minutes on the road, we ditch the coach and here we are in the garden of Hermocrate, a man whose philosophy I don't think you've got much reason to get mixed up with.

PHOCION. More than you imagine, Corine.

HERMIDAS. So why the fake illness? And the copied portraits—who are the man and the woman? What about these outfits? What about Hermocrate's garden? What do you want with him? What do you want with me? Where are we going? What will become of us? Whence leads this? Tell me quick or I'll die!

PHOCION. Are you finished? Listen to me and please pay attention. [*Pause.*] As you know, I happen to rule over these lands by accident. I occupy the throne that my uncle Léonides, the great general, usurped from the king, Cléomenes. What you don't know is that once, when my uncle was away commanding his sovereign's troops, Cléomenes fell in love with Léonides's wife, my aunt. He abducted her. Léonides, in rage and pain, attacked Cléomenes with his own armies and imprisoned the guilty pair.

HERMIDAS. [*Interrupting.*] What about my needs?

PHOCION. After several years he died —

HERMIDAS. Who?

PHOCION. The king, Cléomenes. In prison. His wife —

HERMIDAS. Your aunt —

PHOCION. Right — died six months later, in childbirth, bequeathing a prince to this world. This heir was kept hidden from Léonides. My uncle died in turn, heirless, mourned by his people, who saw fit to have my father rule. I myself have acceded to this tainted throne.

HERMIDAS. Wonderful. But what the hell does this have to do with our breeches or the portraits? That's what I want to know.

PHOCION. Watch your mouth. This prince, who first drew breath in a prison cell, who was kidnapped at birth by an unknown hand, this prince unknown to my father and uncle, I have news of this prince!

HERMIDAS. May the heavens be praised. He's under your rule.

PHOCION. No, Corine. It is I who shall place myself under his.

HERMIDAS. You, my lady, you'll do nothing of the kind! I will never endure this — I swear it! [*Pause.*] What do you mean?

PHOCION. If you would but hear me out. For twelve years this prince has been in the care of the wise Hermocrate. Euphrosine, a relative of Cléomenes —

HERMIDAS. Who's Euphrosine?

PHOCION. Does it matter at this point? Don't interrupt me! Euphrosine, a relative of Cléomenes, sent him to Hermocrate to raise seven or eight years after he disappeared and . . .

HERMIDAS. And? AND?

PHOCION. And . . . that's all I know. I learned this from a servant who once worked for Hermocrate and his sister.

HERMIDAS. A servant! Listen, you'd better certify the tale before you go off half-cocked like this —

PHOCION. Certification is not what I'm after. [*Pause.*] I wanted first to see Agis. Yes, Corine, that is his name. Agis. I found out that he and Hermocrate take walks every day in the forest near my château. So I left the city and came straight here to see him. That wily servant led me to a young man reading in thick vegetation. [*Pause.*] Until that moment I had often heard people speak of Love. It was only a word to me. Imagine, Corine, imagine a collection, an assemblage of all that we find noble and attractive in the Graces — imagine that and you will

scarcely have begun to imagine all the charms to be found in the form
and features of Agis.

HERMIDAS. What I'm beginning to imagine is that this charm bracelet is
what's dragged us into the bush.

PHOCION. As I withdrew, Hermocrate appeared and stopped to ask me
whether the Princess took strolls in that forest. He didn't know who I
was. I told him, my heart pounding, that it was said she did walk in
those parts. Then I rushed home.

HERMIDAS. A strange encounter indeed.

PHOCION. Stranger still has been my behavior since I saw Agis. I feigned
illness so we could travel here. My name is Phocion so when I meet
Hermocrate, I can beg his permission to stay awhile and profit from
his wisdom. I'll talk to Agis and try to sway his heart to my ends. He
cannot discover my true identity, for I was born of a blood he must
revile. Before I can reveal myself, Love will have to shelter my charms
from his wrath. I know he hates me.

HERMIDAS. If you say so. But my lady, what if under this three-piece suit
Hermocrate recognizes a certain young lady he met trespassing in the
woods? You won't get within ten feet of the house.

PHOCION. I've thought of that, Corine. [*Darkly.*] Should he recognize me,
so much the worse for him. I've set a snare that all his science can't
keep him from falling into. I hope he won't force me to use it, but Love
and Justice are my inspiration. I only need two or three meetings with
Agis, and I'll do anything to obtain them—even debunk one measly
philosopher.

HERMIDAS. What about the sister? From the looks of her portrait, a prude
like that won't submit to the presence of a handsome stranger like
yourself.

PHOCION. So much the worse for her, too. If she blocks my path, I'll treat
her no better than her brother.

HERMIDAS. Trick them both . . . hmmmm. And resorting to deceit—twice
over—doesn't offend you?

PHOCION. [*An outburst.*] It disgusts me! Yet my motives are praiseworthy
and my mission is blameless. I must avenge myself upon Hermocrate
and his sister. Since Agis has been in their care, they've taught him to
loathe me! Without knowing me, without sounding the depths of my
soul, filled to the brim as it is with Heaven's virtues, they paint my
features in vile and hideous tints! Corine, they have mustered an army
of enemies for me to battle. Even now they're raising fresh troops!

[HERMIDAS *gives her a look.*]

PHOCION. I do not merit their calumny. Is it because I occupy a throne usurped? Look not to me as usurper, I say—the legitimate heir has yet to come forth—he's been kept hidden in this very garden. Oh, how they wrong me! Corine, I shall act without scruples! [*Pause.*] Now hang onto those portraits you made and don't ask questions. For the time being, just do as I do and don't act surprised. When you need to know more, I'll keep you abreast.

[HARLEQUIN *enters unseen.*]

HARLEQUIN. Who are those two?

HERMIDAS. This is a mighty piece of work, my lady—our sex—

HARLEQUIN. [*Surprising them.*] Aha! "My lady"? "Our sex"? Out with it, my good men, you're women!

PHOCION. Heavens above! Unmanned so quickly!

[*They attempt to escape.*]

HARLEQUIN. No no no—my sweet things, before you run off, we have to arrive at an understanding. I took you first for two scamps; oh how I mistook you. You are two scampi.

PHOCION. We're lost, Corine.

HERMIDAS. Let me handle this, my lady. Fear nothing. This man's face doesn't fool me—he looks quite manageable.

HARLEQUIN. I'm a man of honor, beyond all price. I'll admit I've never smuggled your sort of contraband through customs, but the merchandise stops here. I'll have the gates shut tight.

HERMIDAS. Well, don't let *me* stop you. You shall be the first to repent of the wrong you do us.

HARLEQUIN. Show me some repentance, and maybe I'll let you pass.

[PHOCION *gives him several pieces of gold.*]

PHOCION. Proof for starters, my friend. Now wouldn't you have been sorry to have lost that?

HARLEQUIN. You have a point, since I'm so happy to find it.

HERMIDAS. Still feel like making a scene?

HARLEQUIN. I'm only just beginning to feel like not making one.

PHOCION. [*Giving him some more coins.*] Repent further.

HARLEQUIN. Funny, my bad mood has been cut short all of a sudden. Well then, my ladies, have you anything to declare?

HERMIDAS. A bagatelle. My mistress saw Agis in the forest. One look and she couldn't help but rend her heart to him.

PHOCION. *Render.*

HERMIDAS. Same difference.

HARLEQUIN. Touching.

HERMIDAS. My mistress, who is rich, independent, and eligible, would like to make him sensitive to her feelings.

HARLEQUIN. Very touching.

HERMIDAS. As far as we know, the only way to tenderize him is to engage him in conversation and sleep in his—[PHOCION *coughs delicately.*]—house.

HARLEQUIN. You mean share in all his comforts?

HERMIDAS. I like that you're bright. Now my lady can't do that walking around here in her own sex, am I right? Hermocrate wouldn't allow it. Agis himself would flee, given his philosophic rearing.

HARLEQUIN. And how. Love in this house? The combined wisdom of Agis, Hermocrate, and Lady Léontine creates the most learned obstacle Love could ever dare to meet. [*Pause.*] Mine is the only wisdom with any breeding in it.

PHOCION. We could tell.

HERMIDAS. So you see why my lady has chosen this disguise? So you see how there's no harm done?

HARLEQUIN. I can think of nothing more reasonable. My lady fell in love, by the by, with Agis. What of it? Let each take what he can, say I. There are plenty of hearts to go around. Have courage, gracious mistress . . . I mean, person. I offer you my services. You have lost your heart—do your best to catch another's. I'd give mine up, if I could only find it.

PHOCION. Count on my pledge, sir, and you shall enjoy a fate all men might envy.

HERMIDAS. And don't forget—she's Phocion, and I'm Hermidas.

PHOCION. Above all, Agis is never to know who we are.

HARLEQUIN. Fear nothing, Lord Phocion—en garde, Comrade Hermidas—you see my gift for swordplay?

HERMIDAS. Shhhh . . . someone's coming.

[DIMAS, *the gardener, enters.*]

DIMAS. Who's that you're talking to, friend?

HARLEQUIN. Two personages.

DIMAS. Hell, I can see that, but who are they? What do they want?

PHOCION. I wish to see Lord Hermocrate.

DIMAS. This ain't the way to go about it; master said no one's allowed tromping through the flower beds, so just turn yourselves around, go on out the way you come in, and knock at the front gate.

PHOCION. I found the garden gate open; are strangers not permitted to make mistakes?

DIMAS. I don't give permission for any such of a thing. I never heard tell people could come in where they please—waltz through the gates—should have the decency to call the gardener, and beg his privilege—be nice to *him*.

HARLEQUIN. You are speaking to a rich and important person.

DIMAS. I can see he's rich. Me, I'm the gardener—he can go round front.

[AGIS *enters.*]

AGIS. Dimas, what are you railing about?

DIMAS. Youth, sir. These tree-tromping youths.

PHOCION. You have arrived, sir, in time to disencumber me. My only wish is to speak to Lord Hermocrate. I found the garden open. I found the gardener rude.

AGIS. Dimas, please notify Léontine that a visitor worthy of esteem, even yours, wishes to speak to Hermocrate. [DIMAS *exits.*] I ask your complete pardon, good sir, for this rustic welcome. Hermocrate will also wish to make his excuses to someone whose physiognomy and bearing command respect.

HARLEQUIN. They're a *pair* of pretty faces.

PHOCION. If I have been handled brusquely, your courtesies repair everything. And if my physiognomy, whereof you speak, inclines you to wish me well, then my features have never given better service.

AGIS. Although it has only been a moment since we met, I assure you that one could not be more favorably inclined toward someone than I am for you.

HARLEQUIN. Looks to me like we'll have four pretty inclinations between us.

HERMIDAS. Why don't we take a walk and discuss ours?

[HERMIDAS *and* HARLEQUIN *exit.*]

AGIS. Sir, may I ask for whom I declare friendship?

PHOCION. Someone who willingly swears eternal friendship in return.

AGIS. I fear making a friend whom I might soon lose.

PHOCION. Sir, if it were up to me, we would never lose one another.

[*Pause.*]

AGIS. What do you want with Hermocrate?

PHOCION. His reputation brought me here. I was seeking his permission to spend some time in his company. Now, after meeting you, my motive is far more pressing. I wish to gaze at you as long as it is possibly . . . possible.

AGIS. And then what?

PHOCION. And then I don't know. That will be in your hands. I shall consult only you.

AGIS. Then I advise you not to lose sight of me.

PHOCION. Then we shall always remain together.

AGIS. I wish it with all my heart.

HARLEQUIN. [*To* HERMIDAS.] *My* mistress is advancing, and it looks like she's got her heavy carriage on today.

[LÉONTINE *and* DIMAS *enter.*]

DIMAS. Look milady, there's the strange squire. That other one is his train.

LÉONTINE. I have been informed, sir, that you ask to speak to my brother. He is not here at present. Might you confide in me?

PHOCION. I have a favor to ask, Madame, one you yourself could grant.

LÉONTINE. Explain yourself, sir.

PHOCION. My name is Phocion, Madame. The name is perhaps known to you. My father, whom I lost several years ago, placed it in some repute.

LÉONTINE. Proceed.

PHOCION. Alone and independent am I, travelling to school my heart, instruct my wit—

DIMAS. And shake the fruit off the trees.

LÉONTINE. You may go, Dimas.

[DIMAS *exits.*]

PHOCION. My travels take me to men whose knowledge and virtue distinguish them from all others of my sex. Some of these illustrious gentlemen have allowed me to live awhile with them. I was hoping that wise Hermocrate would not refuse me this honor.

LÉONTINE. To look at you, sir, you seem worthy of such virtuous hospitality—from others. It is impossible for Hermocrate to extend such an honor. Important reasons—you know them, Agis—prevent it. Allow me to reveal them to you.

HARLEQUIN. Hold on. I can keep one of them in my room.

AGIS. We don't lack for rooms.

LÉONTINE. No. But you know better than anyone why it cannot be permitted, Agis. We've made it our law never to share our retreat with anyone.

AGIS. Surely it would not violate our law to make an exception for a friend of virtue.

LÉONTINE. I cannot alter the law.

HARLEQUIN. [*Aside.*] Tough as old boots!

PHOCION. Madame, I see that you are inflexible to my laudable intentions.

LÉONTINE. Yes, despite myself.

AGIS. Hermocrate shall amend this legislation.

LÉONTINE. I remain firm. As I am certain of his firmness.

PHOCION. [*Aside to* HERMIDAS.] I shift to Plan B. [*Aloud.*] Madame, I withdraw my suit. But might I ask for a private audience with you?

LÉONTINE. Further entreaties are useless, sir; you shall only annoy me. However, if you insist upon it, I consent.

PHOCION. I do insist. Please withdraw for a moment.

[AGIS *exits*.]

PHOCION. [*Aside*.] May Love see fit to smile upon my stratagem. [*Aloud*.] Since you are unable to grant my wish, Madame, I shall press no further. Yet perhaps you will favor another. Might you decide my future peace of mind?

LÉONTINE. My advice, sir, is to wait for Hermocrate; he is the better choice for consultation.

PHOCION. No. In this instance you are my preference. I need reasoning that is compassionate. I need a heart whose severity is tempered with indulgence. Such a sweet hybrid flowers among your sex, not mine, so please hear me out; I call upon your prunish—your prudent reservoir of . . . goodness.

LÉONTINE. I know not what prompted your remarks, but your rank begs attention. Do speak. I listen.

PHOCION. Several days ago, while traveling in these parts, I espied a lady on her constitutional. She did not see me. [*Sigh*.] Shall I paint her portrait for you? Her size is majestic—without being large. Never have I seen such a divine countenance—why it is the only face in the world where one could witness the most tender charms wedded to the most imposingly modest and austere air. How could one not fall in love with her—however fearfully? She is young, but not in youth's first folly—that age disappoints me. No, she is of that truly lovable age, that age that dare not name its number, that age when one enjoys all that one is, no more, no less—the age at which the soul, undissipated, adds a dazzling ray of finesse to beauty.

LÉONTINE. I don't know of whom you speak. Such a woman as you describe is not in my acquaintance unless your portrait has been retouched.

PHOCION. The likeness resting in my heart is a thousand times greater than that which I have painted for you, my lady. I was just passing through, but the sight of this wondrous *sylph* transfixed me. She was speaking to someone. From time to time she smiled, and I perceived in her gestures, which belied her grave and modest bearing, an ineffable sweetness and generosity.

LÉONTINE. [*Aside*.] Who on earth is he describing?

PHOCION. She withdrew. When I inquired after her, I learned she was the sister of a famous, respected man.

LÉONTINE. [*Aside*.] What is happening to me?

PHOCION. She is completely unmarried, living in retreat with him. Like all sublimely virtuous souls, she prefers innocent repose to the wicked tumult of the world. Upon learning this, my reason followed my heart's example and gave itself to her forever.

LÉONTINE. [*Moved.*] I can listen to you no further. I don't know what love is. I could not advise you on a matter I do not understand.

PHOCION. Pray, let me finish, and may the word "love" not offend you. If I love, if I worship her lovable countenance, it is because my soul is in sympathy with all the beauties of her soul.

LÉONTINE. Let me take leave of you. I am expected within.

PHOCION. I am done, Madame. Filled as I am with such heartfelt emotion, I swear to love her all of my life. [*Carefully.*] Which means I promise to consecrate all my days in service of Virtue. I must talk to her brother and obtain his permission to stay. And then I plan to use submissive love, industrious respect, and tender homage to prove my boundless passion for her.

LÉONTINE. [*Aside.*] How do I escape such a snare?

PHOCION. I wished to present myself to her brother. Instead I found her and tried vainly to win her support. She slammed the gates on my heart. And now, in my wretched state, I only have recourse to you, my lady. I throw myself at your feet. O, pity me!

[PHOCION *falls to her knees.*]

LÉONTINE. What are you doing?

PHOCION. I beseech your advice and help with her.

LÉONTINE. After what I've just heard, I'll have to ask the gods.

PHOCION. The counsel of the gods rests in your heart. Trust their noble instructions.

LÉONTINE. In my heart? O heavens, you want me to consult the enemy of tranquillity?

PHOCION. How could a noble action upset your tranquillity?

LÉONTINE. Phocion, you claim to revere virtue. Is coming to surprise it reverent?

PHOCION. Is adoring it surprising it?

[*Pause.*]

LÉONTINE. What are your intentions?

PHOCION. I consecrate my life to you. Don't block my passage. Grant me several days in your midst — that is my sole desire. If you agree to this, Hermocrate will.

LÉONTINE. Keep you here? You, who love me?

PHOCION. What is wrong with a love that only increases my respect?

LÉONTINE. Can a virtuous heart demand that which it is not? Do you want me to lose my heart? What did you come here for, Phocion? What you propose is inconceivable to my being! What an adventure!

Must my reason perish in flames? I who have never loved—must I love you? The time is late for me to become sensitive. You are young and attractive; I am neither one nor the other.

PHOCION. What a strange response.

LÉONTINE. I admit that a small share of beauty befell me, and Nature imparted some of her charms upon my person. But I have always scorned these things. Perhaps you make me regret that. [*Pause.*] I am ashamed. I have them no more, or the little that remains will soon fade.

PHOCION. You cannot convince my eyes that what they see is not there.

LÉONTINE. I am no longer what I was.

PHOCION. All true souls share the same birthdate. [*Pause.*] You know what I ask; you know I shall press Hermocrate on this point. If you don't favor my wishes, I'll simply—and in great pain, mind you—DIE!

LÉONTINE. I don't know what to do. Hermocrate is coming. I will help you.

[HERMOCRATE *enters with* AGIS *and* HARLEQUIN.]

HERMOCRATE. Is this the young man in question?

HARLEQUIN. I saw him first. And I made sure to give him all your best wishes in advance.

LÉONTINE. [*Rapidly, as if one breath.*] Hermocrate, you see before you the son of illustrious Phocion whose esteem for *you* brings him hither. He loves wisdom, travels for instruction; several of your peers have had the pleasure of taking him in; he desires the same welcome from us; he begs with an eagerness that merits approval; I promised to do my utmost in his favor; I do so, and doing so, I leave you now.

[LÉONTINE *rushes off.*]

AGIS. If my desire is worthy of consideration, I concur with Léontine, good lord, and leave.

[AGIS *rushes off.*]

HARLEQUIN. As for me, my voice will outshout them both.

HERMOCRATE. [*Examining* PHOCION.] What do I see?

PHOCION. I bless their noble intercessions on my behalf. Good lord, please recognize my deep respect for you.

[PHOCION *bows.*]

HERMOCRATE. I thank you, sir, for all honor you do me. As for recognition, permit me to say that a disciple such as you does not appear to need a master such as I. Nevertheless, I would like to question you. [*To* HARLEQUIN.] Privately. [*To* HARLEQUIN.] You. Go.

[HARLEQUIN *exits.*]

HERMOCRATE. Either I am mistaken or you are not unknown to me. Sir.

PHOCION. Me? Sir?

HERMOCRATE. I have some suspicions which crave enlightenment.

PHOCION. What are these suspicions?

HERMOCRATE. First, you are not called Phocion.

PHOCION. I'm not?

HERMOCRATE. The man whose name you assume is currently in Athens, or so a letter from Mermicide informs me.

PHOCION. Phocion is a common name.

HERMOCRATE. An alias is the least of your falsehoods.

PHOCION. [*Aside.*] He remembers the forest.

HERMOCRATE. Second, that attire does not suit you. Admit it. I've seen you somewhere before, my lady.

PHOCION. [*Feigning surprise.*] You speak the truth, sir.

HERMOCRATE. Yes. You blushed in front of me.

PHOCION. If I blush, I do so unjustly. I disavow such an action. My disguise cloaks no nefarious design.

HERMOCRATE. I see behind the deception, and there is nothing praiseworthy about it. It does nothing but discredit your sex. The idea to come here and steal my pupil Agis, to lure him into danger, to throw his heart into deadly disorder — this plan, it seems to me, ought to give you plenty to blush about, young lady.

PHOCION. Who? Agis? You mean that boy just now? That is your suspicion? How could you of all men make this outrageous accusation? *You?* The gods, who truly know my heart, should have spared me this abuse. No, my lord, I did not come here to upset Agis's heart. Your hands may have raised him; your lessons may have fortified him, but I wouldn't need a disguise to conquer his childish heart. If I loved *him*, why I'd only have to look at him to woo and win. [*Pause.*] I look elsewhere, I seek someone more difficult to surprise. My eyes are powerless before this man; my charms are impotent — I cannot count on them as a resource — they would not please. So I hide them in manly raiment.

HERMOCRATE. If you're not thinking of Agis, what is the connection between your infatuation and your proposed sojourn here?

PHOCION. Agis! Agis! Always Agis! Do not mention him again. I repeat, I think not on him. Do you need incontestable proof of that? My sex is not too proud to offer it. My pride is nobler than yours — you wait and see. But if it is still a question of suspicions . . . the one I love, shall he give me his hand? Here is mine. [*Pause.*] Agis isn't here to accept my offer.

HERMOCRATE. To whom is it addressed?

PHOCION. Naming Hermocrate is but gilding the lily.

HERMOCRATE. Me?

PHOCION. You have been duly instructed.

HERMOCRATE. [*Disconcerted.*] So I have. Me, the object of someone's heart?

PHOCION. Listen to me. Allow me to justify my oath.

HERMOCRATE. All justification is useless. Fear not my philosophy, but am I made to be loved? You attack a solitary and untamed soul. Love is a stranger to me. My severity needs must rebuff your youth and charm. My heart can do nothing for yours.

PHOCION. I don't ask it to share my feelings. I have no hope for that. But let me finish. I told you that I loved you—no, let me speak.

HERMOCRATE. My eminent reason forbids me from hearing more of this.

PHOCION. But my glory and my honor—which I just compromised, by the way—force me to continue. I only aspire to appear worthy to you. There is nothing dangerous about me—except my now-humiliated charms, and the weakness of my sex, which you scorn.

HERMOCRATE. Your sex I prefer to ignore altogether.

PHOCION. Yes, my lord, I love you, but do not deceive yourself. This is no common penchant. I tell you that I love you, because I need confusion in order to say it, because confusion will perhaps cure me, because I need to blush out my weakness to conquer it. I don't say I love you to make you love me back. I do it so you can teach me not to love you anymore. Hate love, scorn love—I gladly consent—just teach me to be like you. Teach me to banish you from my heart. Forbid the attraction I feel for you. I don't demand your love—I *crave* it. Kill my craving!

HERMOCRATE. My lady, here is my prescription. I do not want to love you, period. [*Pause.*] May my indifference cure you; may it end a discourse poisonous to all who hear it.

PHOCION. Indifference! I might have known you'd reduce me to indifference! Is that how you respond to my courage in exposing my feelings to you? The wise man, the famous sage, the celebrated scholar, is he a kingdom unto himself?

HERMOCRATE. I am not . . . that . . . my lady.

PHOCION. So be it! But grant me time enough to discover your faults. Let me finish! Men speak of you everywhere. Your renown is widespread.

HERMOCRATE. Now it is I who blush.

PHOCION. Excuse the heart that delights in praising its love. [*Pause.*] My name is Aspasie, and I have lived, like you, in solitude. I was mistress of my fate, ignorant of Love, scornful of all men who tried to kindle it in me.

HERMOCRATE. Listening degrades me.

PHOCION. I was in my customary state when I first met you, when we were both walking. I did not know who you were at first; my thoughts were private. Yet, one look at you and I was moved—my heart cried out, "Hermocrate, Hermocrate."

HERMOCRATE. In the name of the virtue you say you cherish, Aspasie, please come to a point. I can bear no more of this story.

PHOCION. The tale seems frivolous to you—but believe me, the need to recover my reason is not.

HERMOCRATE. The need to recover mine is even greater. As blunt as I am, I still have eyes, you still have charms, and you say you love me.

PHOCION. I? Charms? My lord, do you spy them? Or are you afraid to feel them?

HERMOCRATE. I cannot expose myself.

PHOCION. If you avoid me, it follows that you fear them. You don't love me yet, but you fear loving me. More than enough for now. Hermocrate, you will love me.

HERMOCRATE. My answers are coming out wrong.

PHOCION. Oh my lord, let's go find Lady Léontine. I wish, as you know, to reside here awhile.

[DIMAS enters as PHOCION starts to exit.] You can tell me later what you have decided about my stay.

HERMOCRATE. Proceed Aspasie, I'll follow. [*She is gone.*] I got lost in that conversation. Come here Dimas—you see that young man ahead of me? I charge you to observe him carefully—follow him as closely as you can—check to see whether he seeks out Agis, understand? You know I admire your zeal—the best way for you to prove your worth is to follow my instructions. Exactly.

DIMAS. Said and done, milord. I'll report any news. Later if not sooner.

[HERMOCRATE *exits.*]

DIMAS. Maybe never.

Act II

[DIMAS *and* HARLEQUIN *appear on opposite sides of the stage.*]

DIMAS. Hey!

HARLEQUIN. Ho!

DIMAS. Listen. I tell you since these new people showed up, there's no talking to you. You're always whispering off to the side with that squire's valet.

HARLEQUIN. That's my good breeding, friend. I love you no less even if I have dropped you.

DIMAS. Oh, so it's genteel to dishonor your old friend. Friendship's like wine: the older the better.

HARLEQUIN. A tasteful comparison; we'll drink to that whenever you want—on me.

DIMAS. Big spender. Shake the money tree, eh? You've come into some.

HARLEQUIN. Never you mind.

DIMAS. Squeakin' squirrel.

HARLEQUIN. I do not merit such abuse.

DIMAS. I know the guests been greasing your palm. I've got eyes—I saw you counting your share.

HARLEQUIN. [*Aside.*] He's right. Now he's counting on a share for himself.

DIMAS. [*Aside.*] Now I've nabbed him. [*Aloud.*] Listen up, friend. Master's got some rumpus in his reason.

HARLEQUIN. Did he see me count my share?

DIMAS. Worse, much worse! He has put my eyes on the whole affair. He's having me play fox to sniff out the thoughts of our two fine strangers on the sly, tail their intentions, you hear?

HARLEQUIN. And . . . friend fox?

DIMAS. I only tell my master.

HARLEQUIN. Pretty please.

DIMAS. First off, I have to tell him what these people really are.

HARLEQUIN. Watch what you're saying.

DIMAS. What's it to you? I keep no secrets from him.

HARLEQUIN. You know who they are then?

DIMAS. The plant and the root, my friend, the plant and the root.

HARLEQUIN. I thought I was the only one who knew—

DIMAS. You? You know nothing!

HARLEQUIN. Yes I do!

DIMAS. You can't—they're too tricky for you.

HARLEQUIN. Don't flatter yourself. They told me so themselves.

DIMAS. Told you what?

HARLEQUIN. That they're women.

DIMAS. They're what?

HARLEQUIN. Women. [*Pause.*] You didn't know?

DIMAS. I do now.

HARLEQUIN. Seed sower! Ill-mannered raker! Hedgehog—

DIMAS. Women? This is choice.

HARLEQUIN. I am such an ass.

DIMAS. Here's a tale with profit in it. This is prime. Here's the stuff of blackmail.

HARLEQUIN. You mean you'd cut my throat, Dimas?

DIMAS. What do I care? That's choice—women pulling stumps behind the gardener's back, and *I* found them. I'll prune 'em all.

HARLEQUIN. You've got a sweet tooth for money.

DIMAS. Damned if I don't. Whose money might that be, friend?

HARLEQUIN. I'll have my lady finance you and buy back my blunder. I promise.

DIMAS. I warn you; small farmers don't come cheap. Tell me, how much did you get off the lady? Small change?

HARLEQUIN. She gave me twenty pieces of gold.

DIMAS. Twenty gold pieces? She's a regular charitable institution! So why'd she come take cover?

HARLEQUIN. Agis took her heart for a walk.

DIMAS. Sweet of him.

HARLEQUIN. She disguised herself to ransack his.

DIMAS. Sweet of her. Well, it all spells booty to me. And that little Hermidas—is she—

HARLEQUIN. That's a heart *I'm* set to plunder.

DIMAS. She's not spoiling for you. Here they come. Have their species trot forward.

[PHOCION *and* HERMIDAS *enter.*]

HERMIDAS. [*To* PHOCION, *referring to* HARLEQUIN.] I can't talk to him now. He's with the gardener.

DIMAS. [*To* HARLEQUIN.] They won't come near me. Tell them I've been made abreast of their personages.

HARLEQUIN. [*To* PHOCION.] Fear not, good mistress, but I've been a chatterbox.

PHOCION. Good mistress? To whom do you refer, Harlequin?

DIMAS. Cut your corn, lady. I outfoxed him.

PHOCION. Quoi? Vous m'avez trahie? O justes cieux! Il faut me venger! Misérable! Scélérat! Lâche! Traître!

HARLEQUIN. I left no stone unturned.

DIMAS. I know your heart's bent, ma'am, and I know what you're set to do to Agis's.

PHOCION. Corine, my project has failed.

HERMIDAS. Don't be discouraged, my lady. Every general needs footsoldiers. We need only buy off the gardener too—am I right, Dimas?

DIMAS. Missy, I share your opinion completely.

HERMIDAS. Name your price.

DIMAS. You get what you pay for.

HARLEQUIN. He isn't worth a ducat.

PHOCION. [*Giving him some money.*] Is this advance enough to tide you

over, Dimas? If you keep quiet, you shall thank the heavens above —
forever—for your association in this adventure.

DIMAS. Silence is golden.

HARLEQUIN. And if I'd held my tongue, all that money would have landed
in my pocket. My wages are buying off that green-thumbed vulture.

PHOCION. Rejoice that I'll enrich the both of you. Earlier Hermocrate
seemed disposed to let me stay here, but I fear he's changed his mind —
right now he's trying my case with his sister and Agis, who both want
me to stay. Tell me the truth now: did you let anything slip out about
Agis in front of him? Conceal nothing from me.

HARLEQUIN. Upon my word, o great and beautiful mistress, the answer
is no. This false friend here is the only one who dragged anything out
of me.

HERMIDAS. Prudence should have cut your tongue in two.

PHOCION. If you said nothing, then I fear nothing. Corine will tell you
how far I've succeeded. Now that Dimas is on our side, divide the
work between them, Corine. It's a matter of wooing the dispositions
of brother and sister. Here comes Agis — go quickly! And make sure
Hermocrate doesn't find us together.

[*They exit and* AGIS *enters.*]

AGIS. Dear Phocion, I've been looking for you. I am worried that Hermocrate is not so disposed to grant your wish. I've never felt so annoyed
with him. His allegations are unreasonable, of all things. But Léontine also spoke most favorably of you. So don't be discouraged, dear
Phocion. I beseech you as your friend, keep pressing your suit. We can
convince him.

PHOCION. You "beseech" me, Agis? Does this mean you find my presence
here . . . not unpleasant?

AGIS. If you leave, I can expect only ennui.

PHOCION. Only you can keep me here.

AGIS. Then your heart shares my feelings?

PHOCION. A thousand times more than I can say.

AGIS. Pray, may I ask you for proof of that? This is the first time in my life
that I've savored the taste of friendship. You reap the first fruits of my
heart. [*Pause.*] Do not teach me the pain of severed friendship: stay.

PHOCION. Me teach you that, Agis? How could I do that without also
falling victim to it?

AGIS. How your response touches me! Listen. Do you remember you told
me that it was up to me to see you always? Here is what I have
imagined.

PHOCION. Tell me.

AGIS. I don't know how I can leave this house. Important reasons — you will know them someday — keep me here. But you, Phocion, you who are master of your destiny, wait for me here to decide my own. Promise me to stay nearby. You'll be alone, true, but we'll be together. Can the world offer anything sweeter than the intercourse of two virtuous, loving hearts?

PHOCION. I promise you, Agis, wherever you are, that is what I'll call the world.

AGIS. I'm so happy. The gods made sure I was born in calamity. Your promise, I feel, is the first of many favors they have in store for me.

PHOCION. I do have one worry. *Love* might soon intercede and alter our tender feelings. The pull of a friend holds nothing against the push of a mistress.

AGIS. Love, Phocion? You have yet to know me well. May the sky render your heart as loveproof as mine. My upbringing, my sentiments, my reason have all closed my heart to love. Why, when I stop to think of it, I hate the odious sex that goads men to love!

PHOCION. [*Seriously.*] That sex is an object of hate, Agis?

AGIS. I shall flee it all my life.

PHOCION. Sir, that oath alters everything between us. I promised you I would remain, but that is now no longer possible. Honor forbids me. And so I take my leave. I do not wish to fool you. The friendship you have pledged to me forbids such base knavery.

AGIS. Knavery? What are you talking about? Why this change? What did I say that could possibly upset you so?

PHOCION. True friends never lie to one another. I cannot lie to you. You spoke a moment ago of the pain of severed friendship. Soon I shall feel it.

AGIS. Sever our friendship?

PHOCION. You are still my friend, but I am no longer yours. [*Pause.*] I am but one of those objects hateful to you. Yes, a hateful object I!

AGIS. What?

PHOCION. My lord, my garb dupes you. It shelters an unlucky girl who escaped the persecution of Princess Léonide. My name is Aspasie. I am the last in an illustrious family. My inheritance has forced me to flee the land of my birth. The Princess wants to yoke me to one of her relatives. I loathe the beast in question. After my refusal, I learned that she was going to have me kidnapped. My only recourse against such violence was to run away in this disguise. I had heard of Hermocrate and his learned solitude. So I came here, seeking retreat — incognito. I met you; you offered me amity; I saw you were worthy of mine. I confide in you even as I speak—that is proof of my feeling. And despite your principled hate which now must overrule your friendship, I will never withdraw mine.

AGIS. I don't know what to think.

PHOCION. Then let me collect your thoughts for you. Adieu.

AGIS. No!

PHOCION. Hermocrate wishes me to go. You suffer my feminine presence painfully. My departure should satisfy you both. I'll go and seek gentlemen whose goodness *will* grant asylum to an unfortunate girl. [*She begins to leave.*]

AGIS. No, my lady, stop. . . . It's true your sex is dangerous—but the unfortunate are always respectable.

PHOCION. You hate me, sir.

[*She begins to leave.*]

AGIS. No, no, Aspasie. I must be sensitive to your piteous condition. If it's necessary, I'll force Hermocrate toward consenting to your stay. Your unhappiness commands me.

PHOCION. So you'll only be acting out of pity, I suppose. Oh, this has been a discouraging adventure. The young lord they picked out for me is looking better all the time. Maybe I should just run myself in to him.

AGIS. My lady, I don't advise it. The hand must follow the heart. So I've always heard tell. They say the unhappiest fate of all is a union with someone you don't love. Life becomes then an unbearable fabric of listless tissue. Virtue, in such cases, even as it defends us, crushes the soul. But maybe you feel you would willingly love the beast chosen for you.

PHOCION. No, my flight is proof of that!

AGIS. Take care then, that some secret fondness doesn't lead you to another man.

PHOCION. That cannot happen. I resemble you on this point. My heart has never been moved until now—when it felt such friendship for you. And if you don't retract your feeling, my heart need never feel anything else.

AGIS. [*Confused.*] Don't ever go near that evil princess again! [*Pause.*] I still feel as I did.

PHOCION. You still like me then?

AGIS. And forever, my lady. Even more now . . . since there's nothing to fear. Since we feel so . . . friendly, right: right? So like . . . that's all we . . . no doubt . . . and . . .

PHOCION and AGIS. [*Sighing.*] Ahhhh!

PHOCION. My lord, as a friend you are overwhelmingly worthy. [*Dreamy.*]

As a lover, you are only too qualified. [*Catching herself.*] I say that as a friend.

AGIS. I hope never to become a lover.

PHOCION. [*Crushed.*] No? [*Catching herself.*] Let's set love aside. It's dangerous even to speak of it.

AGIS. Right . . . uh . . . your servant Hermidas is looking for you. Hermocrate must be free now. Permit me to join him.

[AGIS *exits.* HARLEQUIN *and* HERMIDAS *enter.*]

HARLEQUIN. Have no fear, Lady Phocion, your conversation had three guards.

HERMIDAS. Hermocrate never turned up, but his sister is looking for you. She was asking Dimas where you'd gone to. She looks sad—evidently old stoneface won't budge.

PHOCION. He resists in vain! I'll sculpt him to my pleasure, or all the art of my sex is worthless.

HARLEQUIN. And does Lord Agis promise anything? Has his heart simmered enough?

PHOCION. Two more interviews and he'll be cooked clean through.

HERMIDAS. Seriously?

PHOCION. Yes, Corine. The gods have shown me Love's reward.

HARLEQUIN. [*To* HERMIDAS.] May they reward me, too.

HERMIDAS. Fresh! Shush, there's Léontine. Let's go.

PHOCION. Did you give Harlequin his instructions?

HERMIDAS. Of course, my lady.

HARLEQUIN. You'll be charmed with my learning.

[*They exit.* LÉONTINE *enters.*]

PHOCION. I was going to hunt for you, Madame. I know what has happened. Hermocrate has refused to give his word.

LÉONTINE. Yes, Phocion. My brother, with what looks to me like groundless . . . mulishness, has refused to make a decision. I know you are going to tell me to press harder, but I've come to tell you I'll do nothing of the kind.

PHOCION. Nothing of the kind, my dove?

LÉONTINE. NO! His refusal has called me back to reason.

PHOCION. You deem this a return to reason? This? Léontine, this isn't possible; leaving is a sacrifice my heart cannot make for you. Me leave you? Where shall I find the force to do so? Where have you left me? Look at my situation—I am calling upon your virtue now. I interrogate your virtue—let it be the judge between us. I am here with you; you know that I love you; you see me penetrated by the most tender passion, *you* inspired it, and *I* should leave? Oh, Léontine, ask me for my life, tear my heart to bits — my life, my heart, yours, they're yours, yours, yours! Don't ask the impossible.

LÉONTINE. [*Aside.*] What . . . vivid . . . fluctuations! [*Aloud, grandly.*] No, Phocion. Never have I felt more the necessitous obligation of your imminent departure.

PHOCION. Translation, please?

LÉONTINE. You must go. [*Pause.*] I wash my hands of this affair. O just heavens! Joined to the impetuousness of your heart, what would I become? Is it my obligation to uphold this swarm of passionate expressions that escape your lips? Must I always battle, always resist, and never win? Phocion, you want to inspire me to love, don't you? You don't want me to feel the pain of loving you, but that is what I feel. So go, I beg of you. Leave me in this horrific state.

PHOCION. Save me, Léontine. The thought of leaving you drives me mad. I don't know how to live without you; if I go, it is to fill the pockets of my despair. You see? I don't know what I'm saying anymore.

LÉONTINE. And because *you're* desolate, I have to love you? I like that very much — it's tyranny.

PHOCION. Do you hate me?

LÉONTINE. I should.

PHOCION. Then are the dispositions of your heart favorable?

LÉONTINE. I choose not to listen to them.

PHOCION. I suppose not. As for me, I cannot keep from following them —

LÉONTINE. [*Exasperated.*] Oh, shut up. I hear somebody.

[HARLEQUIN *enters and silently stands between them for a moment.*]

PHOCION. What is your servant doing, Madame?

HARLEQUIN. Since he doesn't know you, sir, Lord Hermocrate has ordered me to examine your conduct.

PHOCION. But as long as I am with Madame, my conduct needs no chaperone. Tell him to withdraw, Madame.

LÉONTINE. It is I who should make the withdrawal.

PHOCION. [*Whispered to* LÉONTINE.] If you go without promising to speak in my favor, I shall no longer speak from reason.

LÉONTINE. [*Moved.*] Good heavens, no! [*To* HARLEQUIN.] Hence, Harlequin. Your presence isn't necessary.

HARLEQUIN. Is too. You don't know who you're dealing with. This gentleman here isn't as wise as a wizened old girl like yourself. No, he wants to tart up your reason.

LÉONTINE. What do you mean, Harlequin?

HARLEQUIN. A little while ago, his valet — that sly piece — accosted me and asked: Is there any way we can be friends? Oh, with all my heart, says I—How happy you must be here—Not bad at all—Such honorable masters—Most admirable, says I—Your mistress is so attractive—She's divine—Tell me, has she had any suitors?—As many as she wanted—Has she any now?—As many as she wants—Does she feel like getting married?—What she feels like isn't my affair—Will she remain a maiden?—I can't vouch for that—Who courts her, who doesn't, who comes, does anyone come? And so and so, so I said, by the way is your master in love with her?—Shush, we hope to stay here. But we do have riches and passion enough for ten households and—

PHOCION. [*Cutting him off.*] Enough!

HARLEQUIN. [*To* LÉONTINE.] You see how worried he is now? He'll tell you the rest.

LÉONTINE. Hermidas was only . . . having fun with you. Isn't that right, Lord Phocion?

[PHOCION *doesn't respond.*]

HARLEQUIN. Aha! Aha! Cat got your tongue? Dear mistress, I see your heart is on vacation from your reason. Phocion is giving it the grand tour even as I speak. I'm going to make Hermocrate come to your defense.

[*He starts to exit.*]

LÉONTINE. Where are you going? Stop, Harlequin. I don't want him to know I've been made love to!

HARLEQUIN and PHOCION. You've been what?

LÉONTINE. I mean to say—I've been broached by love.

HARLEQUIN and PHOCION. Beg pardon?

LÉONTINE. Love has entered my vocabulary.

HARLEQUIN. [*Pause.*] Well if you've befriended the scamp, there's no need for me to cry "thief." How easily wisdom accommodates itself. Adieu, Madame. Never forget the discretion of your humble servant, who wishes you all the best, then shuts his trap.

[HARLEQUIN *exits.*]

PHOCION. Have no fear, my lady. I'll pay for his silence.

LÉONTINE. Blackmail! What next? This is some kind of dream. You see what you've exposed me to! Oh no, here comes somebody else.

[HERMIDAS *enters, carrying a portrait that she gives to* PHOCION.]

HERMIDAS. Here's what you asked for, sir. See if you're happy with it. It would be a much finer likeness if the subject had sat for me.

PHOCION. Why did you bring it to me in front of my lady? Let's see—ah yes, it is indeed her face. There is her noble, refined air, and all the fire of her eyes. Although it seems to me that her eyes are still more fiery than that.

LÉONTINE. [*Piqued.*] You speak apparently of a portrait.

HERMIDAS. Give it back, sir, and I'll make her eyes *burn*.

LÉONTINE. Might one see it before it's whisked away?

PHOCION. It is not finished, my lady.

LÉONTINE. Well, if you have your reasons for not revealing it, I won't insist.

PHOCION. [*Quickly.*] Here it is. You will give it back.

LÉONTINE. Who is this? It's me. What is this?

HERMIDAS. It's you.

PHOCION. I never want to lose sight of you. Your tiniest absence is agony. A moment is a lifetime. This portrait will temper the sickness. Now give it back.

LÉONTINE. I shouldn't, but so much love on your part stunts my courage.

PHOCION. [*Softly.*] My love doesn't inspire you the least little bit?

LÉONTINE. [*Her admission at last.*] Alas! I didn't want it to happen, but perhaps I shall never be the mistress of it.

PHOCION. Oh, you overwhelm me with joy!

LÉONTINE. Now that I love you, will my heart stop?

PHOCION. Don't promise me your heart, Léontine, tell me that I have it.

LÉONTINE. True, too true for words.

PHOCION. Then I can stay—and you'll talk to Hermocrate?

LÉONTINE. I need some time to resolve myself to our union.

HERMIDAS. Shhh, change the subject—Dimas is coming.

LÉONTINE. No one must see how my heart has been moved. Goodbye Phocion. Fear not. My brother will consent.

[LÉONTINE *exits and* DIMAS *enters.*]

DIMAS. The philosopher's grazing over this way, all dreamy-like. Give me the field, my lady. I'll clip him to your fancy!

PHOCION. Courage, Dimas! I'll come back when he's gone.

[PHOCION *exits and* HERMOCRATE *enters.*]

HERMOCRATE. Did you watch Phocion?

DIMAS. I was going to bring you up to date.

HERMOCRATE. So. You've discovered something. Is he often with Agis? Does he look for him?

DIMAS. Oh no. No, way I sees it, he's got another tree to graft.

HERMOCRATE. What does that mean?

DIMAS. Means you're a man of merit, a man with large dimensions.

HERMOCRATE. What does *that* mean?

DIMAS. Your wisdom, your virtue, and your face beg praise.

HERMOCRATE. Oh, and why such enthusiasm, from you of all people?

DIMAS. Me? I tells it like I hears it. And it's all sighing and anguish around here. Alas and alack and all that—how I love him, this man, this agreeable gent.

HERMOCRATE. I don't know who you're talking about.

DIMAS. You. And a boy who is a girl.

HERMOCRATE. No one fits that description here.

DIMAS. You know Phocion, right? Well, clothes make her man. The rest is pure girl.

HERMOCRATE. What are you raving about?

DIMAS. And she's full of attractions. You must be a happy pappy being the target of all those attractions. I heard 'em talking out loud and they said they was waiting for the most mortal man . . . no, the most perfect mortal to be found in the whole pack of mortal men—the mortal called Hermocrate.

HERMOCRATE. Who? Me?

DIMAS. After you, who? Listen to this.

HERMOCRATE. Say no more.

DIMAS. Looking only to obey you, a little while ago while I was chopping in the brush, I was spying on her and her Hermidas—who's a her too—I hopped that hedge all foxlike and came out another end. And I heard 'em gossiping. Phocion said straight off: Ah, Corine, this is what's what; no cures for me; I love him too much, this man, I don't know what to do or say—But my lady, have your beauty speak for you—Ha, this beauty is no money under the mattress, he still wants me to leave!—Patience, my lady—But where does all that wisdom and learning get him?

HERMOCRATE. Surely you paraphrase.

DIMAS. Hold on, I'm about done—but what does he say to you when you speak to him, my lady?—He scolds me, and I get all mad. He plays the wise man, I do the same. I pity you, he says. But here I am all changed, I say. But have you no shame, he says. Where does shame get me, says me. But your virtue, my lady? But my torment, my lord? What—virtues never get married—

HERMOCRATE. Enough, Dimas. Silence.

DIMAS. I think you better cure this girl child, master—why don't you fall sick for her too? Make her your wife. If you never pollinate, your family'll be so much dead wood. A crying shame that. Speakin' familiar and family-like now, when you get sick with Phocion, could you put in a good word for me with the chambermaid? I feel my own sickness coming on.

HERMOCRATE. Why not speak for yourself?

DIMAS. I know all the tunes, master. I just don't know the words.

HERMOCRATE. Be discreet, Dimas. I order you to be discreet. It would be embarrassing for the person in question if her situation were known. As for me, I'll set things straight when I see her.

[HERMOCRATE *exits with a loud groan.* PHOCION *enters.*]

PHOCION. So what does your master think, Dimas?

DIMAS. First, he seems disposed to keep you.

PHOCION. So far so good.

DIMAS. Then, on the other hand, he hasn't said that you can stay.

PHOCION. That doesn't follow.

DIMAS. He doesn't follow himself. [*Groans.*] That was his parting word on the subject. All that philosophy—he hasn't got an ounce of it left. Out the window and into the mulch.

PHOCION. A portrait just unbuckled his sister's prudence. I've got one left for him. All according to my original plan. Yet Agis is avoiding me. We haven't spoken since he found out I'm a woman. He talks to Corine, not me!

DIMAS. He's heading this way, miss. Could you take care to remember my fortune at the end of the story?

PHOCION. Consider it done.

DIMAS. Many thanks to ye.

[DIMAS *exits and* AGIS *enters.*]

AGIS. Aspasie, why do you flee when I approach?

PHOCION. Why do you flee when I approach?

AGIS. I am bothered by something.

PHOCION. What?

AGIS. There is a person that I love, well, I am ignorant as to whether I like her as a friend or love her as a. . . . Anyway, since I'm still an apprentice on the subject, I've come to ask you for instruction.

PHOCION. I think I know this person.

AGIS. You should have no difficulty. When you came here, you know I loved neither thing nor person.

PHOCION. Yes. And since my arrival, you've met only me.

AGIS. Draw your conclusion.

PHOCION. It is I. [*Pause.*] Or so it follows.

AGIS. [*Softly.*] It does follow. It is you, Aspasie. And so I ask you, "Where am I?"

PHOCION. First, tell me where I am, because I am in the same state for someone I love.

AGIS. For whom, Aspasie?

PHOCION. Whom? The reasons I drew to conclude that you love me—are they not common to both of us?

AGIS. It is true that you had never loved before you arrived.

PHOCION. Yes, and (A) I feel differently now. (B) I've met only you. The rest is clear.

AGIS. So, your heart pines for me, Aspasie.

PHOCION. How long you've been at the solution! Yet all this knowledge doesn't make us any wiser on the subject. We loved each other before we started worrying about it. Now that we do know, do we love each other the same way, or differently?

AGIS. If we were to tell each other what we feel, perhaps that would settle matters.

PHOCION. Let's see then. Was it painful for you to avoid me a little while ago?

AGIS. The pain was infinite.

PHOCION. Hmmm . . . that's a bad start. Were you avoiding me because your heart was troubled, because it was full of unspeakable feelings?

AGIS. There you have me. A perfect diagnosis.

PHOCION. Yes. There I have you, but I must warn you that your heart won't get better just because I took its pulse correctly. I still have your eyes to check.

AGIS. My eyes look at you with a pleasure that goes beyond spectacles! I would give my life for you. I would give a thousand if I had them.

PHOCION. It's useless to interrogate you further. It's love.

AGIS. Oh no!

PHOCION. Damning proof—love in your expression, love in your heart, love in your eyes, love as it should ever be.

AGIS. Love as it has never been before. [*Pause.*] Now that I've shown you what is in my heart, can I see yours?

PHOCION. Agis, that's so sweet. Really. [*Pause.*] No. My sex can speak all it wants on the subject of friendship. Of her love, not a word. Besides, you're too tender at this point, and too abashed, I fear, by your tenderness. If I told you my secret now, you might melt away, and where would I be?

AGIS. You spoke of my eyes. Yours seem to tell me that you are not indifferent to me.

PHOCION. Well, if my eyes do the talking, I'm beyond reproach. They voice my love for you.

AGIS. O merciful heavens above! Her sentiments match mine! The charms of her speech have thrown me into passion's chasm!

PHOCION. But there is more to love than this, Agis. One must have the liberty to say it to oneself, to put oneself in the state of always being able to say it freely, openly. Out loud. And Lord Hermocrate, who governs you . . .

AGIS. I respect and love him. Yet I feel already that a heart should have no governor. I'll have to see him before he speaks to you. He could send you away today, and we need time to plan.

[DIMAS *appears upstage and sings to halt their conversation.*]

PHOCION. Agis, go to him right away and come right back. I have some other things to tell you.

AGIS. And I you.

PHOCION. Go now—if we're seen too long together, I'll be discovered. Adieu.

AGIS. Lovely Aspasie, I take my leave. I promise you, never will Hermocrate feel so beleaguered.

[AGIS *exits.* DIMAS *comes downstage.*]

DIMAS. [*Rapidly to* PHOCION *as he exits.*] High time lover boy went— here comes the rival!

[HERMOCRATE *enters.*]

PHOCION. Finally you appear. The ennui and the solitude you left me in will not lessen my affection. Sadder, yes, but no less tender am I.

HERMOCRATE. Other affairs have occupied me, Aspasie. This is no longer a question of affection. Dimas knows who you are. [*No response.*] Need I say more? He overheard the secret of your heart. [*No response.*] Neither one of us can depend on his discretion. Your stay here is henceforth unfeasible—you would be terribly wronged. For your honor's sake, you must leave.

PHOCION. Leave, sir? You would send me away in such a condition? A thousand times more troubled than I was before I came? What have you done to cure me? Wonderful wise Hermocrate has brought me no virtuous assistance that I can speak of.

HERMOCRATE. May your affliction heal itself by what I tell you now. You thought me wise; I daresay you loved me for it. I am not wise at all. A true sage would hold himself responsible for your peace of mind. Do you know why I send you away? I am afraid that your secret will explode and damage the esteem that I am held in by others; this means I sacrifice you to my arrogant fear of not appearing virtuous. That way I won't have to worry whether I am or not. This makes me only a vain man for whom true wisdom is less important than the miserable, fraudulent *imitation* he makes of it! There you have me—the object of your love.

PHOCION. Oh, I've never loved him so much!

HERMOCRATE. What did you say?

PHOCION. My lord, is that your only weapon against me? You only increase my ardor and tenderness for you when you expose, with pitiless courage, your desire to cover your own. And you say you aren't wise! You astonish my reason with subtle proof to the contrary!

HERMOCRATE. Wait, my lady. Did you believe that I was susceptible to all the ravages Love wreaks in other men? The blackest soul, the most vulgar lovers, the maddest knaves and damsels, never feel the agitations that pierce my breast—worries, jealousies, ecstasies have swept through me! Do you recognize Hermocrate in this portrait I paint for you? The universe is full of people who resemble me now! Renounce your love, my lady, a love that any man chosen randomly deserves as much as I.

PHOCION. No, I repeat, if the gods themselves were susceptible, they would be just like Hermocrate! Never was he more noble, never more worthy of my love, and never my love more worthy of him. You spoke of my honor. I feel honorable to have created even the smallest ecstasy in you. Sir, I seek peace for my heart no more. The oath you made has restored peace in my heart's kingdom. You love me. I am tranquil.

HERMOCRATE. I have one last word for you then. If you don't leave, then I will reveal your secret. In doing so, I will dishonor myself. I dishonor the man you love, and this affront will reflect back on you.

PHOCION. Then I go. I go secure in my revenge. And since you love me, may my revenge fester in your heart. Enjoy the fruits, if you like, of your cruel reasoning. I came to ask you for defense against my love; you gave me no help except to vow you loved me in return; and now, *after* your sacred vow is made, you send me away! After a vow that redoubles my tenderness! Oh, how the gods will loathe this wisdom preserved at the expense of a young heart cruelly tricked, a confidence cruelly betrayed, and virtuous intentions ridiculed, indeed *victimized*, by your ferocious opinions!

[PHOCION *bursts into tears.*]

HERMOCRATE. Please cry in moderation, my lady—someone's coming.

PHOCION. Oh, first you decimate me, then you will me to silence.

HERMOCRATE. [*Seriously.*] You have moved me far more than you think—just don't blubber *now*.

[HARLEQUIN *runs in, pursued by* HERMIDAS.]

HERMIDAS. Give me that! It's not yours!

HARLEQUIN. Loyalty forbids me—I must warn my master.

HERMOCRATE. What's the meaning of all this?

HARLEQUIN. Foul play, Lord Hermocrate. An affair of consequence that only the devil and these characters here know about.

HERMOCRATE. Explain yourself.

HARLEQUIN. I just now discovered this young man here in the position of a scribe! Yes, you heard right, a scribe! He was daydreaming, shaking his head, admiring his work. I noticed alongside him a palette with gray, green, yellow, and white—he was dipping a plume into it. I crept up behind him to look at the original—but what do I find? This was no scribe! No scribe at all! No words, no speeches—he was writing down a *face!* [*Pause.*] This face, this face . . . was you, Lord Hermocrate.

HERMOCRATE. Me?

HARLEQUIN. Your own face, except smaller. Why the nose you walk around with is bigger than the entire miniature! Is it fair, I ask you, to shrink people's faces, to diminish the immense sweep and grandeur of their features? Look at yourself.

[*He gives* HERMOCRATE *the portrait.*]

HERMOCRATE. Well done, Harlequin. I'll discover the meaning of this.

HARLEQUIN. Just don't forget to have him paint in the other two-thirds of your face.

[HARLEQUIN *exits.*]

HERMOCRATE. Why have you painted me? What were you thinking?

HERMIDAS. I wanted to have the portrait of an illustrious man.

HERMOCRATE. You do me too much honor.

HERMIDAS. And I knew that this portrait would please a certain someone who could not ask for it herself.

HERMOCRATE. Who is this person?

HERMIDAS. My lord . . .

PHOCION. Silence, Corine.

HERMOCRATE. What do I hear? What are you saying, Aspasie?

PHOCION. No more questions. You make me blush.

HERMOCRATE. My composure is slipping away.

PHOCION. I don't know how to bear this last blow.

HERMOCRATE. And I . . . how this ordeal deranges me.

PHOCION. Corine, how could you let Harlequin surprise you?

HERMOCRATE. [*His admission.*] You have triumphed, Aspasie, you win, I surrender to you. You may have my portrait. It belongs to you.

PHOCION. I won't keep it unless your heart abandons it to me.

HERMOCRATE. Nothing in me shall prevent you from having it.

PHOCION. Then you must value mine. Here it is.

[*She gives him her portrait. He presses it to his lips.*]

HERMOCRATE. Do you find me humiliated enough? No more quarrels. [*He moves to kiss her.*]

HERMIDAS. I forgot your ears! Might Lord Hermocrate permit me to finish his likeness? It will only take a moment.

PHOCION. Do not refuse. We are alone.

HERMOCRATE. [*Pleading.*] Aspasie, do not expose me to any risks—someone might surprise us.

PHOCION. You said this is my moment of triumph. Let us savor it. Your eyes look at me with a tenderness and a humility that must be preserved. You never see your looks, my lord. You have no idea how fetching they are. Proceed, Corine.

HERMOCRATE. Hurry.

HERMIDAS. Tilt your head a bit, please.

HERMOCRATE. Oh, you have reduced me so.

PHOCION. Your heart doesn't blush at my reduction.

HERMIDAS. Raise your chin.

HERMOCRATE. Must I, Aspasie?

HERMIDAS. Now turn to the right. [*Pause.*] Turn.

HERMOCRATE. Please stop. Agis is coming. You may go, Hermidas.

[HERMIDAS *exits.* AGIS *enters.*]

AGIS. I've come to plead with you my lord. Allow Phocion to stay. Please.

HERMOCRATE. [*Worried.*] You wish him to stay, Agis?

AGIS. Nothing on earth would please me more. I swear to you I would be very angry if you made him leave.

HERMOCRATE. I had no idea that you were already so taken with one another.

PHOCION. [*Very formally.*] Indeed. Our conversations have been most infrequent.

AGIS. [*Hurt.*] I hope I haven't interrupted your conversation. Perhaps that is why you treat me so coldly.

PHOCION. Agis!

AGIS. Pardon me.

PHOCION. Wait!

[AGIS *exits.*]

HERMOCRATE. Now why is Agis so forward? In all these years I've never seen him so interested in anything as much as you. [*Pause.*] How well do you know him? Have you revealed yourself to him? Do you abuse my feelings?

PHOCION. I'm so happy I could burst with joy! You've just told me you're jealous.

HERMOCRATE. No.

PHOCION. In so many words, yes. You've made me so happy—my heart thanks you for such injustice. Hermocrate is jealous. He cherishes me, he adores me. So what if he insults me! He may be unjust, but he loves me! [*Pause.*] Agis is not far off; I still see him—have him come back, call him, sir. I'll go look for him myself—I'll speak to him, and you'll see whether I merit your lovely suspicions.

HERMOCRATE. No, Aspasie. I see my mistake. Your frankness is reassuring. Don't call him. Forgive me. No one must know that I love you yet. Give me time to think.

PHOCION. I consent and I forgive. Here comes your sister. I'll leave you two alone. [*Aside.*] Dear gods, pardon my scheme. How I pity his weakness.

[PHOCION *exits and* LÉONTINE *enters.*]

LÉONTINE. There you are. I've been asking after you everywhere. No one can sit still today.

HERMOCRATE. What do you want, Léontine?

LÉONTINE. Where do you stand with Phocion? Do you still plan to send him away? He holds you in such high esteem, speaks so well of you, that I promised him that he could stay. I gave him my word, brother. And don't try to change my mind. I never retract a statement.

HERMOCRATE. I could never change your mind, Léontine. Since you made a promise, he will stay as long as you like, sister.

LÉONTINE. [*A pause.*] How obliging you've become. It shocks me, brother. In truth, Phocion deserves the favor.

HERMOCRATE. I have measured his full worth.

LÉONTINE. And besides, it will be so nice for Agis to have a playmate, don't you think? No one should be alone at that age.

HERMOCRATE. [*With a little sigh.*] That or any other age.

LÉONTINE. You're right. One has moments of sadness. Even I get bored now and then. Or very often. Or all the time.

HERMOCRATE. Who doesn't get bored? Is not man born for society?

LÉONTINE. Did we know what we were doing when we forsook mankind and came to this retreat? It was such a rapid decision. Such a painful decision to make so . . . rapidly.

HERMOCRATE. Go on, sister. I haven't your courage.

LÉONTINE. After all, mistakes can be remedied. Man can, fortunately, change his mind.

HERMOCRATE. And change for the better.

LÉONTINE. [*Tentatively.*] A man at your age would be welcome everywhere if he wanted to change his station.

HERMOCRATE. And you, who are younger and more attractive than I . . . permit me to say I am not anxious for *you.*

LÉONTINE. Oh, brother, few young men are your equal . . . permit me to say the gift of your heart would not go unopened.

HERMOCRATE. As for yours . . . men would fall in line to gain your heart and give you theirs.

LÉONTINE. [*Shyly.*] Would you be surprised if I said I have some prospects?

HERMOCRATE. I'd be more surprised if you had not.

LÉONTINE. And you?

HERMOCRATE. [*With a smile.*] Who knows? My lips are sealed.

LÉONTINE. How wonderful for you, brother. [*Pause.*] Hermocrate. The gods invented marriage. The gods are married. We have no more wisdom than the gods . . .

HERMOCRATE. [*Softly.*] Ergo . . .

LÉONTINE. Ergo . . . I believe a husband is as worthy as a hermit. Think. Adieu.

[LÉONTINE *exits.*]

HERMOCRATE. I see the both of us are in a rare and tender state. I wonder who she has set her sights upon. Maybe someone as young for her as . . . Aspasie is . . . for me. Oh, how weak man is. [*Long pause.*] If this be man's destiny, I suppose we must submit.

Act III

[HERMIDAS *and* PHOCION *are alone in the garden.*]

PHOCION. Come talk to me, Corine. Infallible success is mine. Would you have believed I'd conquer both philosophers? Hermocrate and Léontine fell one after the other. Now they both want to marry me secretly. I can't begin to tell you how many measures they've already taken for their imaginary nuptials. Why, it's impossible to chart where love has led their wise heads. They're off the map. [*Sighs.*] Agis. We need to talk. I think I've blown it with him. He loves me as Aspasie. Could he hate me as Princess Léonide?

HERMIDAS. No my lady. Finish him off. After all that Léonide has done and will do for him, he'll find her more lovable than plain Aspasie.

PHOCION. I daresay I agree with you. But his family perished because of mine.

HERMIDAS. Your father inherited the throne—he didn't usurp it.

PHOCION. I love him. I fear him. But I must act certain of success. Have you had my letters sent to the estate?

HERMIDAS. I sent them with the messenger Dimas gave me. You'll soon have news. You addressed them to Ariston. What are his orders?

PHOCION. I bade him to follow the messenger with guards and a coach. Agis will leave this garden a prince. Post yourself at the gate, Corine, and come get me the moment Ariston arrives. Go put the crowning touch on all that you have done for me.

HERMIDAS. You're not through with Léontine yet—here she comes-a-courting.

[HERMIDAS *exits and* LÉONTINE *enters.*]

LÉONTINE. Dearest Phocion, one thought: the die is cast.

PHOCION. Yes, may the heavens be praised.

LÉONTINE. [*Dramatically.*] I shall depend on no one but myself and my love. We shall be united for all eternity. You sent for the coach, didn't you? I told you I didn't want to create a spectacle near the house, but I fear the measures we've taken don't appear entirely decent. Instead of leaving together, wouldn't it be better if I went ahead first and waited for you in the city?

PHOCION. Leave by yourself? How cunning of you, my pet.

LÉONTINE. Love emboldens me. Two hours hence—I shall be hence. But Phocion, you will fly to my side?

PHOCION. The sooner you leave, the sooner I'll fly.

LÉONTINE. You can't give me anything but love.

PHOCION. Yours is priceless.

LÉONTINE. No other man in the world could make me take this step.

PHOCION. An innocent little step, really, and you run no risk if you run now!

LÉONTINE. I love your enthusiasm—may it last forever!

PHOCION. And may you always be eager in return—because right now your turtle steps try my patience.

LÉONTINE. I must confess to you that a sadness—ineffable—fleeting—takes hold of me at times.

PHOCION. I only feel joy.

LÉONTINE. There's my brother. He cannot find me in emotional undress.

[LÉONTINE *exits.*]

PHOCION. Again with the brother! There's really no end to these two!

[HERMOCRATE *enters.*]

PHOCION. I thought you'd be busy arranging our departure.

HERMOCRATE. Oh, my charming Aspasie, if you only knew how divided I feel!

PHOCION. Oh, if you only knew how weary I feel dividing you! Again and again. One can never be too sure with you.

HERMOCRATE. Forgive my agitation. My heart promises to be more decisive in the future.

PHOCION. Ah! Your heart takes so many attitudes, Hermocrate, you can be as agitated as you like, just hurry, unless you want the wedding to take place here.

HERMOCRATE. [*Sighs.*] Ahhhh . . .

PHOCION. Sighs expedite nothing.

HERMOCRATE. I have one last thing to tell you, something that pains me very much.

PHOCION. One more last thing more? You never conclude, do you?

HERMOCRATE. I shall entrust everything to you. I sacrificed my heart, and soon I shall be yours. Then there will be no more secrets between us.

PHOCION. Except?

HERMOCRATE. I've raised Agis ever since he was a boy. I cannot abandon him so quickly. Do you think he might live with us for awhile? We can send for him after the honeymoon. He can be our common interest.

PHOCION. Who is he?

HERMOCRATE. You've heard tell of Cléomenes. Agis is his son. He escaped from prison in his infancy.

PHOCION. Your confidence is in safe hands.

HERMOCRATE. I've sheltered him so carefully over the years. What would he become in the hands of a princess who breathes his death?

PHOCION. Come now. She is reputed to be fair and generous.

HERMOCRATE. Her blood is neither one nor the other.

PHOCION. They say she would marry Agis—if only she knew him. They are the same age, after all.

HERMOCRATE. Whatever she wants is beside the point. The righteous hate Agis bears against her would prevent such a union.

PHOCION. I would have believed that the glory of pardoning one's enemy might equal the honor of hating her forever. Especially when the enemy is innocent.

HERMOCRATE. No, the throne is too high a price for this pardon. Friends are fomenting a war against her. Agis will enlist.

PHOCION. Will no one defer to the Princess? Submit to her rule? Or will they just kill her?

HERMOCRATE. Since hers is only an inherited guilt, they need not kill her, just imprison her.

PHOCION. I think that's all you better confess for now, dear. Finish packing.

HERMOCRATE. Adieu, dear Aspasie. I've only another hour or two to spend here.

[HERMOCRATE *exits, and* DIMAS *and* HARLEQUIN *enter.*]

PHOCION. Agis must be waiting for an opportunity to speak to me. This hate he bears for me makes me tremble. More counselors? Will I never be rid of them? And what do you want?

HARLEQUIN. Your servant, my lady.

DIMAS. I salute you, my lady.

PHOCION. Not so loudly, please.

DIMAS. Never fear, we're alone.

PHOCION. What do you want?

HARLEQUIN. A trifle.

DIMAS. I'm here to square your debts.

HARLEQUIN. To see how much we're worth together.

PHOCION. Out with it. I'm pressed for time.

DIMAS. Have I done good work?

PHOCION. You've both served me well.

DIMAS. And your plan is working?

PHOCION. I have one last thing to reveal to Agis, who, as you speak, is waiting for me.

HARLEQUIN. Very good. If he's waiting, we won't press.

DIMAS. It's a black, marvelous affair we've sold.

HARLEQUIN. There are no comparable rascals in the kingdom.

DIMAS. I threw your heart all over the neighborhood.

HARLEQUIN. Portraits to trap faces—

PHOCION. Get to the point.

DIMAS. Your scheme is soon to bloom. How much will you yield for the harvest?

PHOCION. What do you mean?

HARLEQUIN. Buy the rest of the adventure. Our price is reasonable.

DIMAS. Give us your business, or I'll squeal.

PHOCION. Didn't I promise to make your fortune?

DIMAS. Give us your word in gold.

HARLEQUIN. After all—

HARLEQUIN and DIMAS. Henchmen are forgotten once the dirty work is done.

PHOCION. What insolence!

DIMAS. Could be, could be.

PHOCION. You anger me with this impertinence. Here is my answer. Should you foil my plan, should you commit an indiscretion, you'll atone for it in a prison cell. You don't know who I am. But I warn you I have the power to lock you both away. If, on the other hand, you remain silent, I shall keep every promise I made you. Choose. As for the present, I order you to leave. Right your wrong with swift obeisance.

DIMAS. [*To* HARLEQUIN.] Well, do we keep up the sass?

HARLEQUIN. No, that's the garden path to jail. I prefer anything to four stone walls.

[*They exit.*]

PHOCION. I did well to upbraid them.

[AGIS *enters.*]

PHOCION. Agis. At last.

AGIS. We meet again, Aspasie. At last I can speak to you in perfect liberty. I almost hate Hermocrate and Léontine for all the hospitality they've shown you; you're never alone. But you are so lovable, who would not love you? How sweet it is to love you, Aspasie.

PHOCION. What pleasure to hear you say that, Agis. Tell me, this tenderness, this charming candor, is it proof of everything? Nothing could rob me of it?

AGIS. No—the only way would be to cease breathing.

PHOCION. I've something to tell you. You don't know me.

AGIS. I know your charms; I know the sweetness of your soul; nothing could tear me from them. They're enough for me to adore my whole life long.

PHOCION. O gods! The more I cherish love, the more I fear losing it. I've kept my birth from you, Agis.

AGIS. You don't know who I am, either—nor can you know the terror I feel to unite my life with yours. O cruel Princess, I have so many reasons to despise you!

PHOCION. Who are you talking to—about, Agis? Which princess do you hate so much?

AGIS. I shrink from pronouncing her name. She who reigns, Aspasie. My enemy and yours. Princess Léonide who—someone's coming.

PHOCION. Hermocrate, the eternal interrupter. I'll come back as soon as he leaves. Our destiny hangs on a word. You hate me—without knowing it.

AGIS. Me, Aspasie?

PHOCION. No more for now. Break with Hermocrate.

[PHOCION *exits.*]

AGIS. [*Alone.*] I don't understand what she means. I can't leave Hermocrate without telling him my plans.

[HERMOCRATE *enters.*]

HERMOCRATE. [*Troubled.*] What I have to say to you, my prince, I don't know where to begin.

AGIS. What is wrong?

HERMOCRATE. Something that you could never have imagined, something I'm ashamed to confess to you, but something, after much reflection, I feel I must tell you.

AGIS. That's quite a preamble. [*Pause.* HERMOCRATE *is silent.*] What has happened to you?

HERMOCRATE. I find I am as weak as any other man.

AGIS. My lord, to what type of weakness do you refer?

HERMOCRATE. The most common weakness of all, the most excusable for everyone else—but the most unexpected for me. [*Pause.*] You know what I've thought of the passion called love.

AGIS. Yes, and to speak frankly, you've exaggerated a bit on that topic.

HERMOCRATE. If you like, but what could you expect? A solitary man who meditates, who studies, who kept commerce with his mind, never his heart. A man shrouded in an austerity of his own design can hardly be expected to bear judgment on certain things. He would go too far.

AGIS. You fell into excess.

HERMOCRATE. What didn't I say against love? To me this passion was crazy, extravagant, unworthy of a reasoning soul; I called it delirium when I didn't know what I was talking about. I consulted neither nature nor reason. I was criticizing the very heavens.

AGIS. Yes, because in the end, man is born to love.

HERMOCRATE. Exactly. Everything revolves around that feeling.

AGIS. A feeling that might one day avenge itself upon you and your scorn for it.

HERMOCRATE. Too late.

AGIS. What?

HERMOCRATE. I have been duly punished.

AGIS. Seriously?

HERMOCRATE. Prepare yourself for a change in character. If you love me, come with me. I'm getting married.

AGIS. This is the source of your confusion.

HERMOCRATE. Oh, Agis, it is very painful to switch philosophies!

AGIS. I congratulate you for it. The only gap in your knowledge was the purpose of man's heart.

HERMOCRATE. I have received quite a lesson of late, I assure you. Passion's industry has truly come to call. And just in time I feel to . . . I was seen several times in the forest—someone developed an attraction for me— the person tried to cease and desist, but could not. Lest her true sex risk unwelcome, she disguised herself, became the most handsome of men. She came here, and I instantly recognized the deception. I wanted her to go; I even thought *you* were the object of her attention—she swore this was false. She said: "I love you. My hand, my fortune belong to you, along with my heart. Give me yours in return or cure mine—yield to my affections or teach me to conquer them; teach me indifference or share my love." This was said to me with such eyes, in such dulcet tones, they would have conquered the most ferocious and obstinate of philosophers.

AGIS. Sir, this tender lover disguised, have I seen him here? She came here?

HERMOCRATE. She is still here.

AGIS. I only see Phocion.

HERMOCRATE. He is she. And not a word to Léontine.

[LÉONTINE *enters.*]

AGIS. [*Aside.*] Treacherous woman! What has she gained by deceiving me?

LÉONTINE. [*As nonchalant as she can muster.*] I've come to tell you of a short stay I intend to make in town.

HERMOCRATE. With whom shall you be staying, Léontine?

LÉONTINE. Tatiana—I have news from her—she entreats me to visit.

HERMOCRATE. Then, as I am leaving within the hour, we shall both be gone.

LÉONTINE. You're leaving, my brother? Where shall you be?

HERMOCRATE. With Criton.

LÉONTINE. Really? In town like me! How peculiar that we both have things to do in town. I am recalling our previous conversation. Does your trip carry any mystery on board?

HERMOCRATE. That is a question that makes me . . . question the motive of *your* trip. Surely you remember your words, my dear?

LÉONTINE. Hermocrate, let's speak with open hearts. We've found each other out. I'm not going to Tatiana's.

HERMOCRATE. Since you adopt a frank tone, I too shall come clean, I'm not going to Criton's.

LÉONTINE. My heart is taking me on a trip.

HERMOCRATE. Mine has packed my bags.

LÉONTINE and HERMOCRATE. I'm getting married!

LÉONTINE. How astonishing. [*Pause.*] Now that it's out in the open, I believe my beloved and I can get married right here and save travel expenses.

HERMOCRATE. You're right. My heart's delight is here too. We needn't leave either.

LÉONTINE. We can have a double wedding! [*Pause.*] I, for one, don't know who your heart's delight is. [*Pause.*] I'm marrying Phocion.

HERMOCRATE. Phocion!

LÉONTINE. Yes, Phocion!

HERMOCRATE. You mean—the man who sought us out, the man whose cause you championed?

LÉONTINE. The very one.

HERMOCRATE. Hold on—I'm marrying him too. I—he—we—me! We can't both marry him.

LÉONTINE. Him? You marry a him?

HERMOCRATE. Nothing could be truer.

LÉONTINE. You and Phocion? Is this a new philosophy? Phocion loves me with an infinite tenderness; he had my portrait copied unbeknownst to me.

HERMOCRATE. Your portrait! It's mine, not yours, that he had copied without my knowledge.

LÉONTINE. You are mistaken. Here is his portrait—don't you recognize him?

HERMOCRATE. Here, sister, here is its double; yours is a man; mine is a woman. That makes all the difference.

LÉONTINE. O misery!

AGIS. Enough! *I'm* marrying her, and I didn't get a portrait!

HERMOCRATE. You too?

AGIS. Me three!

LÉONTINE. I am beside myself with indignation!

HERMOCRATE. This is no time for indignation, Léontine. This imposter has to explain himself—herself!

[LÉONTINE *and* HERMOCRATE *exit.*]

AGIS. This is despair.

[PHOCION *enters.*]

PHOCION. Agis, look at me. What's wrong?

AGIS. What have you really come to do here? Which member of our unhappy trio gets to marry you? Hermocrate, Léontine, or Agis?

PHOCION. I am discovered.

AGIS. Don't I at least get a portrait? Everybody else did.

PHOCION. The others would never have received my portrait if I hadn't wanted to give you the person.

AGIS. I yield you to Hermocrate. Goodbye perfidious one. Goodbye cruel . . . cruel . . . person! I don't know what to call you. What does one call someone like you? I never met anyone like you. This shall kill me.

PHOCION. Stop, dear Agis—listen to me.

AGIS. Let me go, I say.

PHOCION. No, I'll never let you go. And if you don't pay attention, you'll be the most ungrateful of men.

AGIS. *I* will? I—whom you deceive?

PHOCION. I tricked everyone else for you! There was no other way—my snares are proof of my tenderness. You insult the tenderest heart imaginable. You cannot know all the love that you owe me; all the love I bear for you, you cannot know. You will love me, you will hold me in esteem, and you will crave pardon.

AGIS. I don't understand.

PHOCION. To gain your heart I did everything I could to abuse those who stood in my way. You were the sole object of my machinations.

AGIS. How can I believe you, Aspasie?

PHOCION. Dimas and Harlequin, who know my secret, will second this pledge. Interrogate them. My love is not ashamed to seek the confirmation of servants.

AGIS. How can what you're saying be possible, Aspasie? Then no one has ever loved as much as you.

PHOCION. That is not all. This Princess, whom you call your enemy and mine—

AGIS. She will never spare the son of Cléomenes. If you truly love me, she will make you cry over my death one day.

PHOCION. I am in a position to make you judge of *her* fate.

AGIS. I would only ask her to let us arrange our fate together.

PHOCION. Arrange her life yourself then. You have already delivered her heart.

AGIS. Her heart? Princess Léonide—is you?

PHOCION. The full extent of my love is yours entirely.

[AGIS *falls to his knees*.]

AGIS. My heart cannot answer you with words.

[HERMOCRATE *and* LÉONTINE *enter*.]

HERMOCRATE. What do I see? Agis on bended knee? [*He shows a portrait to* PHOCION.] This is a portrait of—

PHOCION. Me.

LÉONTINE. [*Showing portrait*.] And this one, varlet, is—

PHOCION. Me. Shall I withdraw them and return yours?

HERMOCRATE. This is no time for pleasantries. Who are you?

[HERMIDAS, HARLEQUIN, *and* DIMAS *enter*.]

PHOCION. I shall tell you. But first let me speak to Corine.

DIMAS. Master, I warn you, there's a garden full of pikestaffers and ruffian soldiers and fancy carriages.

HERMIDAS. Ariston has arrived.

PHOCION. [*To* AGIS.] My lord and master, come receive the homage of your subjects. Your royal guard awaits you. It is time to leave. [*To* LÉONTINE *and* HERMOCRATE.] You, Hermocrate, and you, Léontine, who first refused to let me stay, learn now the motive of my artifice. I wished to surrender the throne to Agis, and I wanted to be his. Had I used my true identity, I would have rebuffed his heart. I disguised myself to catch it. For this plan to bear fruit, I had to abuse your hearts by turns. There is no cause for complaint. Hermocrate, I leave your heart to the care of your eminent reason. As for yours, Léontine, the revelation of my sex must have already doused the embers of the feelings inspired by my hoax.

3

EATING CROW

✳ ✳ ✳

EATING CROW

EUGÈNE LABICHE

First presented at the Théâtre du Palais-Royal on 25 June 1853

Cast
in order of appearance

ANTOINE

DE CRIQUEVILLE

A PORTER

CATICHE

GENERAL RENAUDIER

PAGEVIN

EMERANCE

MONTDOUILLARD

AN ENGLISHMAN

A WAITER

A CAKESELLER

ARTHUR

BARTAVELLE

DE FLAVIGNY

A BUSINESSMAN

KERKADEC

DE SAINT-PUTOIS

MADAME DARBEL

PARTY GUESTS

Act I

A quai on the Seine by the Pont Neuf. Just before dawn. A parapet in the rear. Buildings can be seen in the distance. There are houses at stage left and stage right with doors opening onto the street. The house at stage right bears a wine merchant's sign. ANTOINE *is installed in front of the wineseller's shop with his shoeshine kit, equipped with mudscrapers; he is sitting on a chair at the back of which is nailed a placard bearing the words: "Antoine Waxes Boots — Clips Dogs — Buys Broken Bottles — Pay in Advance!"*

ANTOINE. [*Blowing on his fingers.*] Shit shit shit . . . this cold pinches me in more ways than one . . . ten below zero here by the clever knight! Even King Henry's horse has a red nose! This bitching cold will be my ruin, my ruin! No dogs or cats to clip — they'd get the flu! There's no mud to speak of on this stinking pavement — what lousy weather! [*Blows again on his fingers.*] Shit shit shit . . . Christ, what a pinching cold!

[*Draped in an overcoat,* CRIQUEVILLE *enters left and dramatically advances to the footlights.*]

CRIQUEVILLE. Yes, it's me! That's right, I've come to hurl myself into the brine! It's not funny, it's just the way things go! This spot looks ideal . . . I come to angle for my life. Let us prepare to —

ANTOINE. Shine your shoes, mister?

CRIQUEVILLE. He can go to hell. . . . He thinks he'll fish me out and collect a reward. It'll all be over soon! [*He removes his coat and appears in white pants with a fine nankeen jacket. To* ANTOINE.] My friend, would you be so kind as to hold my coat until I should return?

ANTOINE. [*Looking at* CRIQUEVILLE'*s ensemble with astonishment.*] What . . . too hot, mister?

CRIQUEVILLE. [*Aside.*] It's all I have left of my wardrobe.

ANTOINE. You must be Russian.

CRIQUEVILLE. Now is the hour! [*He advances several steps toward the parapet and stops.*] Funny . . . you'd think I had the jitters. Let us then prepare — then — to go then. [*He runs toward the parapet and stops.*] Mother of God, the Seine is frozen. How's that for luck? I could wait for it to melt. No, there are ways. Yoo-hoo, bootblack!

ANTOINE. Black your boots, mister?

CRIQUEVILLE. No, tell me, do you know how to break ice?

ANTOINE. Beg pardon?

[CATICHE *enters, preceded by a* PORTER *carrying her trunk. Day is slowly breaking.*]

CATICHE. [*To the* PORTER.] Hold it right there!

CRIQUEVILLE. Great, now we have a crowd!

CATICHE. [*To* CRIQUEVILLE.] Mister, could you read me out this address, please?

CRIQUEVILLE. Do I look like I have time on my hands? [*Aside.*] A man can't drown himself in peace. [*Reads.*] Let's see . . . "Monsieur Albert de Criqueville." That's me.

CATICHE. Now there's a piece of luck. It's me! Catiche!

CRIQUEVILLE. Catiche! Darling! Who are you?

CATICHE. The daughter of Old Man Greluche.

CRIQUEVILLE. Greluche? In Vauchelles? In Picardy?

CATICHE. Your old hometown—I grew up there. We went to the same grade school! You don't mind if I . . .

[*She kisses him.*]

CRIQUEVILLE. Gladly. [*Aside.*] Another delay.

ANTOINE. [*Aside.*] What a dish! Now why couldn't I have grown up in Picardy?

CRIQUEVILLE. Why have you come to Paris?

CATICHE. To cook—the deputy mayor gave me a letter telling me to come cook for you.

CRIQUEVILLE. A capital idea. Can you cook?

CATICHE. I make omelettes. Sort of.

CRIQUEVILLE. Sort of. And?

CATICHE. That's it.

CRIQUEVILLE. It's a good thing chickens are plentiful.

CATICHE. Then I'm hired?

CRIQUEVILLE. No, I'm leaving Paris momentarily; I'm going on a pleasure cruise.

CATICHE. Well, that's a kick in the shins. I just know I would have had a great time cooking for you. You seem so refined.

CRIQUEVILLE. Toujours gai! Good day. Good day.

ANTOINE. I'd take her in, if I had the eggs.

CATICHE. I'll keep going then—I've got lots of names; I just would have preferred you, you know, us being from the same hometown and all. Picardy and everything.

CRIQUEVILLE. Yes . . . bon voyage!

CATICHE. Hey, you don't mind if I . . .

[*She kisses him.*]

CRIQUEVILLE. [*Aside.*] One last kiss before the tolling of the bell.

ANTOINE. We didn't have girls like that back in Savoie.

CATICHE. [*To the* PORTER.] Let's go. . . . Step on it, honey!

[*She exits right.*]

ANTOINE. Now that was a nice slice of woman!

CRIQUEVILLE. Can you break ice?

ANTOINE. What ice?

CRIQUEVILLE. That ice.

ANTOINE. Hell, just stomp on it.

CRIQUEVILLE. Well, then, might you do me the honor of descending onto the riverbank below us and making an opening in the Seine four to five feet in diameter? Do you know what diameter means?

ANTOINE. It's . . . just like you said—diameter.

CRIQUEVILLE. Precisely. I'll give you twenty cents for your pains.

ANTOINE. [*Aside.*] Paid to break ice? That's a dumb stunt! [*Aloud.*] Does your dog need a bath?

CRIQUEVILLE. Yes, now hurry up!

ANTOINE. Right away. Keep an eye on my box, please. [*Exiting.*] I don't see any dog.

CRIQUEVILLE. [*Alone.*] In just fifteen minutes . . . [*To the sky.*] it's going to be beautiful out today! My God, I'm dressed as if I were going to take a stroll at Longchamps! [*Looking at his jacket.*] Truth to tell, I can't claim to have paid for this tux. Drowning on a Friday . . . isn't that bad luck! Are we in Lent yet? If I were able to get by just one more day. . . . I don't have the means to hang on that long. [*Looking at his change.*] Twenty-four cents! And twenty of it goes to that savoyard. . . . To think that a year ago I had forty thousand francs to my name—I could have opened a hardware store like everybody else, but since I had a bachelor's degree in literature, I thought I was a poet. Since I was a poet, I just had to commit some poetry . . . and generally, when one commits some poetry, one just has to read it aloud to somebody. Few poets have the courage of solitary verse. I said to my bosom friends, "Come with me, I will read you something first-rate!" The bums wouldn't budge! So I took to giving dinners—to stuff my elegies with truffles—an open bar—everybody came, and I mean everybody—I was fêted, I was flattered, I was crowned the prince of poets, the sultan of the sonnet—there was even a certain gentleman who had the good taste to remark that I looked like Pindar right before he borrowed three hundred francs. And that's why I find myself on the bank of the Seine with twenty-four cents in my pocket and a violent love in my heart. [*To the audience.*] Oh, didn't I tell you? Well, I'll tell you. Her name is Clotilde Renaudier. Imagine for yourselves a divine assemblage of all the graces . . . [*Searching in his pocket.*] Hold on, I have here five hundred lines that paint her from head to heel. [*Taking out paper.*] It's very short! [*Reading.*] "Three resolings—fifty-nine francs." That's my bootmaker's bill—paid up, I'll have you know. [*Looking in pocket.*] Now where could I have put those verses?

[RENAUDIER *enters from upstage right.*]

RENAUDIER. Where in the devil can a man get a hack around here? [*He sees* CRIQUEVILLE.] There's a doorman—you, sir!

CRIQUEVILLE. Sir?

RENAUDIER. Monsieur de Criqueville!

CRIQUEVILLE. General Renaudier! [*To audience.*] Clotilde's father.

RENAUDIER. What are you doing here?

CRIQUEVILLE. As you can see . . . I'm taking a stroll.

RENAUDIER. In a planter's costume?

CRIQUEVILLE. I'm off to Longchamps today.

RENAUDIER. [*Aside.*] Looks pretty damn funny. [*Aloud.*] Well, I'm glad to see you. You wrote me three days ago to ask for my daughter's hand.

CRIQUEVILLE. Yes, sir, general, sir.

RENAUDIER. My first thought was to have your ears cut off.

CRIQUEVILLE. What?

RENAUDIER. Then I thought it was an April Fool's joke.

CRIQUEVILLE. In March?

RENAUDIER. Exactly! [*Sternly.*] You are without position.

CRIQUEVILLE. I have a bachelor's degree.

RENAUDIER. That doesn't count. It isn't that you disgust me personally. On the contrary, you suit me fine.

CRIQUEVILLE. Oh, your generalissimo-ship.

RENAUDIER. Any man whose father served with the 7th Hussards—

CRIQUEVILLE. You're too kind.

RENAUDIER. I sabered in the 8th—

CRIQUEVILLE. My uncle was blown to bits in the 9th!

RENAUDIER. Now those are credentials! Clotilde comes with a hundred thousand francs as a dowry—what are you worth?

CRIQUEVILLE. I admit that, to match that gift in kind, I would still need—

RENAUDIER. How much?

CRIQUEVILLE. A small balance.

RENAUDIER. Balance away then, my lad, balance away.

CRIQUEVILLE. Right away . . . I'm going to take care of it. I'm out in the cold today for that very reason.

RENAUDIER. I'm in a real hurry to marry her off—especially after last night's adventure.

CRIQUEVILLE. What adventure?

RENAUDIER. General Doblin gave a costume ball. I went Spanish.

CRIQUEVILLE. That must have suited you.

RENAUDIER. No, it was too tight. Wasn't room enough to eat in. On our way out, I left Clotilde in the vestibule for just one second while I brought the carriage around. I'm hardly down the stairs when I hear a cry — I turn around and what do I see, a monk is trying to kiss Clotilde.

CRIQUEVILLE. Good God! A monk!

RENAUDIER. He was in costume! I jump in and start cuffing him. Unfortunately my bolero got in the way, and the holy father slipped away.

CRIQUEVILLE. You didn't recognize him?

RENAUDIER. No, but he was heavily perfumed. I got his hankie, and it gave off a strong odor that I would recognize a hundred years from now. Catch a whiff of this.

CRIQUEVILLE. Smells like . . . no, it's definitely essence of bergamot.

RENAUDIER. Bergamot? Hmmm, rhymes with clot. And sot.

CRIQUEVILLE. And blot.

RENAUDIER. Rot.

CRIQUEVILLE. Yacht.

RENAUDIER. That's all I have to say. If I ever get my hands on him —

[ANTOINE enters.]

ANTOINE. Your hole is ready, sir.

RENAUDIER. What does that mean?

CRIQUEVILLE. Just a little errand.

RENAUDIER. I'm off. So, we have an agreement then: just find a hundred thousand francs, get a job, and my daughter is yours.

CRIQUEVILLE. Get a job?

RENAUDIER. A good one.

CRIQUEVILLE. A good job can't cost more than a bad one.

RENAUDIER. That's the spirit. Only hurry, because I have promised to marry her before she comes of age.

CRIQUEVILLE. And that day?

RENAUDIER. Dawns in two months.

CRIQUEVILLE. Two months! Goodbye, your generalship.

RENAUDIER. Goodbye, my boy. Don't stay out too long. You'll catch your death.

CRIQUEVILLE. You are very kind.

RENAUDIER. Bergamot . . . not . . . bot . . . rot . . . pepperpot . . . hottentot . . . polka dot . . .

[He exits grumbling.]

CRIQUEVILLE. Two months — could there be a better push to a man leaning over the edge?

ANTOINE. Where's his dog?

CRIQUEVILLE. I guess I won't be going to Longchamps today. How odd.

I walked out the door this morning perfectly resolved . . . and now . . . it's no use . . . I'm just not going to be happy about this drowning thing.

ANTOINE. Your hole is ready, sir.

CRIQUEVILLE. Alright already. My poetic soul does not recoil, ye gods! It asks only to spring forward. I await this, the liquid envelope—the corporeal casement, I compare myself to a gatekeeper who doesn't want to pull the doorknob! [*To audience.*] You know, I love me in this. [*He finds a cigar in his pocket.*] Look—a very dry havana, lost in the recesses of my sports jacket. It would be a tragedy to get it wet. I'll just smoke it. Give me a light!

ANTOINE. Here, sir. If you don't get a move on, the ice'll freeze over again.

CRIQUEVILLE. One moment, you devil. [*Aside.*] He's a pain. I should at least be allowed the reprieve of a final cigar.

[*He begins to stroll.*]

ANTOINE. He's waiting for his dog.

CRIQUEVILLE. How droll. When is a cigar not a cigar? This is no mere havana—it is my life that I am smoking—draining it down to the final lees, I mean, puff. [*He finishes.*] Crac! All settled. Scout's honor.

ANTOINE. Sir.

CRIQUEVILLE. Yes.

ANTOINE. Can I have the butt?

CRIQUEVILLE. Will you please leave me in peace? [*Aside.*] He is really ferocious, that one. [*Aloud.*] Here are your twenty cents.

ANTOINE. Thank you, sir.

CRIQUEVILLE. Down to four. Here goes. Do you carry beeswax by any chance?

ANTOINE. Pardon me?

CRIQUEVILLE. [*Gaily.*] How about a shine? One must enter eternity properly. [*Placing his foot on the box.*] Shine 'er up.

ANTOINE. Your boots are spotless!

CRIQUEVILLE. It's my nickel—here's four cents.

ANTOINE. That's the spirit—keep the workers working; if everyone were like you, the economy would recover in no time.

CRIQUEVILLE. You're not happy?

ANTOINE. Sure I am—H—A—P—P—Y, happy.

CRIQUEVILLE. [*Aside.*] Another man who scorns destiny! I've got an idea! Suppose he were to join me? He can even go first. [*Aloud.*] Antoine.

ANTOINE. Sir?

CRIQUEVILLE. Now truthfully, man to man . . . do you much enjoy yourself in this sorry world of woe?

ANTOINE. It depends on the day. As long as there's mud in the streets, who's complaining.

CRIQUEVILLE. Yes, but, after scraping shit off your fellow man for ten years, where does that get you?

ANTOINE. Married.

CRIQUEVILLE. Your wife will cheat on you.

ANTOINE. Children.

CRIQUEVILLE. They won't be yours.

ANTOINE. Come on.

CRIQUEVILLE. And after that, you will be covered with infirmities — very ugly ones. [*Limping.*] You'll walk like this.

ANTOINE. But sir —

CRIQUEVILLE. Believe me, you'd be better off taking my arm and going! [*Takes his arm.*]

ANTOINE. Where are we going?

CRIQUEVILLE. To find out what lies at the bottom of the hole you dug.

ANTOINE. In the river? No, let go of me!

CRIQUEVILLE. You're afraid!

ANTOINE. You better fucking believe it! You mean just walk calmly into the river like we were going out for sandwiches.

CRIQUEVILLE. Come here.

ANTOINE. No.

CRIQUEVILLE. Have no fear. I want to make you my heir.

ANTOINE. [*Approaching slowly.*] No kidding.

CRIQUEVILLE. [*Searching through his pockets.*] First, my wardrobe. A false collar. You'll have to have it bleached.

ANTOINE. [*Examining it.*] Looks clean to me.

CRIQUEVILLE. Two pair of white gloves.

ANTOINE. Oh. I prefer black.

CRIQUEVILLE. You'll dye them. My library. Can you read?

ANTOINE. Sure I can. Books even — just watch me. [*He opens the book and begins to recite.*] "Perch'd on a lofty oak, Sir Crow . . ."

CRIQUEVILLE. Stop — I know that one.

ANTOINE. Well, I don't; let me finish. "Held in his beak a cheese. . . . Sir Fox, who smelt it in the breeze, thus to the holder spoke — "

CRIQUEVILLE. You're boring me.

ANTOINE. "Ha, how do you do, Master Crow? How beautiful you are! How fair!" [CRIQUEVILLE *whistles a song between his teeth.*]

CRIQUEVILLE. I'm sorry I lent him my library.

ANTOINE. "Sir Crow, overcome by praise, must show how musical his croak. Down fell his luncheon from the oak — "

CRIQUEVILLE. [*Interested.*] Hmmm.

ANTOINE. "Which snatching up, Sir Fox thus spoke. . . ."

CRIQUEVILLE. Keep going.

ANTOINE. "The flatterer, my good sir does liveth on his listener—This lesson, if you please—"

CRIQUEVILLE. [*Walks about in his excitement.*] Enough—that fable is a revelation! Every flatterer lives at the expense of those who listen to him. A fresh start! Yes, that's it! Take men by flattery. Caress their vanity. Swoon over their ugliness—and live—succeed—thrive at everything! That's the trick. [*Pause.*] But it's so insipid, so base, so low. After all, I'd just be giving back what I took from the world. Haven't flatterers devoured me, knawed me down to my last penny? So why am I hesitating? Look at me—ready to throw myself in the water like a thirteen-year-old girl?

ANTOINE. Sir, the ice is freezing over.

CRIQUEVILLE. Let it ice! Let it freeze! Let it snow!

ANTOINE. You've put out your cigar.

[ANTOINE *holds out his hand to take it.*]

CRIQUEVILLE. I'll hang onto this!

ANTOINE. [*Aside, scornfully.*] He must be some cheap six-hundred-franc clerk.

CRIQUEVILLE. What risk do I run? The river's not going anywhere. And if I succeed, I'll marry Clotilde. To boot, the experience is artistic— it's great grist. A man, lost on a quai, in a nankeen jacket, in the dead of winter, no money, no credit, no asylum, a man who crashes society with one single word—flatter, flatter, flatter! It's an investment like no other. I want to see what it nets me. Sir Crow had better hang onto his cheese—here comes Sir Fox. Antoine!

ANTOINE. Yessir?

CRIQUEVILLE. I need a groom. I'll take you in my service.

ANTOINE. Me, a groom?

CRIQUEVILLE. And a page and a valet and a houseboy. Your fortune is made.

ANTOINE. My fortune? I accept. [*Aside.*] He must be a banker.

[*The sound of someone playing a piano is heard from the house stage left.*]

CRIQUEVILLE. Jesus, what a horrible racket! [*Pause.*] My brilliant debut. [*He walks under the window of the house and applauds.*] Bravo! Bravo! Bravo! [*Aside.*] God, it's even flatter now. All the better. I could use the exercise. [*To* ANTOINE.] Do as I do. [*Applauding louder.*] Bravissimo! Bravissimo!

ANTOINE. Bravissimo! Bravissimo!

[PAGEVIN *appears at the window.*]

PAGEVIN. [*Aside.*] What does that idiot want out of me? [*Graciously to* CRIQUEVILLE, *who bows to him.*] Come upstairs, my good man, come upstairs.

CRIQUEVILLE. It works! [*To* PAGEVIN.] Gladly, sir. [*To* ANTOINE.] Wait three minutes, then come upstairs. [*Piano starts up again.* CRIQUE-VILLE *exits, applauding.*] Bravo! Charming, absolutely charming.

ANTOINE. He's going to get the tar beat out of him. I think I'll move my establishment over to the winesellers.

[ANTOINE *moves his shoeshine box.*]

Act II

The drawing room of PAGEVIN *the tailor. Doors in the rear wall and on the sides. A casement window upstage left. A stove downstage right. Piano down left. A woman's portrait on the rear wall.*

PAGEVIN. The devil take me, I think he's coming up. What nerve. Where did my cane go?

EMERANCE. [*Behind the piano.*] Daddy, you're going to get in a fight.

PAGEVIN. I don't like to be made fun of. Keep playing that piano.

EMERANCE. But Daddy—

PAGEVIN. I order you to keep playing.

[*She begins again.* CRIQUEVILLE *appears in the rear doorway.*]

CRIQUEVILLE. Bravo. Brava! Bravissima!

PAGEVIN. Sir, do you take us for imbeciles?

CRIQUEVILLE. [*Aside.*] Oh, no, he's angry.

PAGEVIN. [*Brandishing his cane.*] I'm in no mood for—

CRIQUEVILLE. [*Interrupting.*] What a gorgeous cane you have there! It must be a malacca, no? [*Taking it from him.*] May I?

PAGEVIN. But—

CRIQUEVILLE. It's a female rush. She's worth 250 francs—and that's not counting her knob.

[*He moves to put it against the wall.*]

PAGEVIN. That much? All right, sir . . . what are you doing here?

CRIQUEVILLE. You asked me to come up, so here I am. But I shall never regret the twenty-three steps of your stairway if Mademoiselle would do me the honor of playing another one of these delicious musical morsels.

EMERANCE. Gladly, sir.

PAGEVIN. My daughter isn't learning piano to entertain sidewalk casanovas.

EMERANCE. Mademoiselle is your daughter? A beautiful talent, sir, a splendid talent.

PAGEVIN. Sir, she has no talent at all.

EMERANCE. But Daddy! [*She starts to cry.*]

CRIQUEVILLE. She does!

PAGEVIN. She doesn't!

[EMERANCE'*s wailing increases in volume.*]

CRIQUEVILLE. I must take issue with your opinion!

PAGEVIN. The landlord is ready to kick us out, she's scorched his ears so often.

CRIQUEVILLE. [*Aside.*] Out of luck.

PAGEVIN. Emerance, close the piano.

CRIQUEVILLE. Emerance! What a pretty name.

PAGEVIN. [*Aside.*] I'll give him a pretty name, just wait. [*To* EMERANCE.] Go to your room, Emerance.

EMERANCE. Right away, Daddy.

[*She exits.*]

CRIQUEVILLE. [*Aside.*] A bad start. Look—a stove. Score one for the knight in nankeen.

[CRIQUEVILLE *warms himself at the stove.* PAGEVIN *goes for his cane.*]

PAGEVIN. [*Aside.*] He's hogging my heat!

CRIQUEVILLE. [*Aside.*] Vienna sausages. I at least have to get lunch out of this.

PAGEVIN. Sometimes jokes don't—

CRIQUEVILLE. [*Aside.*] Again with the cane! [*Aloud.*] Saint's alive, what a beautiful rush you have there! She must be a malacca! [PAGEVIN *growls.* CRIQUEVILLE *pretends to search his pockets.*] Might you consent to part with her?

PAGEVIN. [*Softened.*] Well, if I could get a good price. [*Aside.*] Maybe he'll give me 250 francs.

CRIQUEVILLE. A friend of mine fancies canes. I'd be glad to take you to him. But you musn't hit anything with her. She's very delicate.

[CRIQUEVILLE *manages to get the cane against the wall and then sees the portrait.*]

CRIQUEVILLE. By Jove, what an exquisite canvas! Is it a Murillo?

PAGEVIN. [*Impatient.*] No, it's a Galuchet.

CRIQUEVILLE. A Galuchet, you say. A beautiful talent, sir, a splendid talent.

PAGEVIN. He's some scribbler who owed me twenty-five francs and slapped that together as payment. It's my wife.

CRIQUEVILLE. Your wife? What a sweet disposition—the very picture of domestic virtue!

PAGEVIN. Alas sir, I lost her.

CRIQUEVILLE. [*Taking out a handkerchief and starts to cry.*] So young and so beautiful—

PAGEVIN. No. I lost her on the Champs-Elysées. In the crowd. I suspect a notary clerk.

CRIQUEVILLE. [*Quickly returning his handkerchief to his pocket.*] I was just about to say—now there is the face of a woman who could get lost on a broad thoroughfare—in a crowd with a notary clerk.

PAGEVIN. Imagine it, sir, in front of a macaroon stand. [*Pause.*] Why am I telling you my business?

[CATICHE *appears upstage, talking to someone in the wings.*]

CATICHE. Yoo-hoo, you—can you wait a minute? That's right, I'm talking to you—

PAGEVIN. Now what?

CRIQUEVILLE. [*Aside.*] Looks like I'm in for a kiss.

CATICHE. Monsieur Pagevin, please.

PAGEVIN. That's me. Yes?

CATICHE. This is a letter from our sheriff telling me to cook for you.

PAGEVIN. As a matter of fact, I *am* looking for a cook. I've had to do for myself for too long. [*Opening her letter.*] Let's see.

CATICHE. Oh, goodness! My hometown honey. [*Moves to kiss him.*] May I?

CRIQUEVILLE. Let's wait until the class reunion.

CATICHE. You know what? I've been to two more houses since I saw you, but they both wanted cooks who know how to cook.

CRIQUEVILLE. That's absurd. Just tell them you can and you'll learn by doing.

CATICHE. You think?

PAGEVIN. [*Finishing the letter.*] Your references are excellent. What are your specialties?

CATICHE. Damn. [CRIQUEVILLE *signals her.*] Everything! Pastry too!

PAGEVIN. You're hired.

CATICHE. That was easy.

CRIQUEVILLE. [*Aside.*] I hope he likes omelettes.

CATICHE. Yoo-hoo, you down there—haul it up.

PAGEVIN. Is she bringing up a mule?

[ANTOINE *enters with* CATICHE's *bag on his back.*]

ANTOINE. Here you go, miss. I climbed up behind her. Her instep is a feast for the gods.

PAGEVIN. I'll show you the kitchen. Can you make Eggs Sardou?

CATICHE. Everything! Pastry too!

PAGEVIN. Sir. It's time for my lunch.

CRIQUEVILLE. Sir. You are too kind.

PAGEVIN. So I won't keep you.

CRIQUEVILLE. [*Disappointed.*] You are too kind.

PAGEVIN. Follow me.

[CATICHE, ANTOINE, *and* PAGEVIN *exit right.*]

CRIQUEVILLE. [*Alone.*] Is the system faulty? It can't be. I just fell on a stringy old crow to start with. I'll have to seek more tender birds. [*Starts to leave.*]

[ANTOINE *re-enters.*]

ANTOINE. He didn't even pay my fee. A master tailor.

CRIQUEVILLE. He's a tailor?

ANTOINE. In a big way.

CRIQUEVILLE. I could use a suit. We'll stay.

ANTOINE. We better. I sold my business.

CRIQUEVILLE. How much did you get for it?

ANTOINE. Three sixty-five.

CRIQUEVILLE. That's only worth a pair of gloves.

ANTOINE. You and gloves.

CRIQUEVILLE. Where's the money?

ANTOINE. Gone, sir. I met this guy from Bordelais . . . a very nice guy. When he found out I was from Limoges, he made such a flattering speech about the people of Limousin. . . . Well, I just had to lend it to him.

CRIQUEVILLE. Then the system does work.

ANTOINE. And then I bought him a drink with your twenty-four cents.

CRIQUEVILLE. Clod.

ANTOINE. But now that I have this good job. . . . Speaking of which, we've forgotten one small thing.

CRIQUEVILLE. What?

ANTOINE. My salary.

CRIQUEVILLE. You were expecting money for such a tremendous opportunity?

ANTOINE. Well, yes.

CRIQUEVILLE. You, a child of Limoges . . . the most generous, the most beautiful, the most . . . large region in all of central France! The region that produces the handsomest of men, the handsomest of horses—

ANTOINE. You've been there!

CRIQUEVILLE. [*Aside.*] I'm wafting my incense. [*Aloud.*] I mean finally, when one sees a big, strong horse . . . what does one say? One says—

CRIQUEVILLE and ANTOINE. "It's a Limousine!"

ANTOINE. Master, you will pay me what you can.

CRIQUEVILLE. [*Aside.*] It's a simple little system.

ANTOINE. What a delicious smell. What time do you break for lunch, sir?

CRIQUEVILLE. When do you?

ANTOINE. Any time.

CRIQUEVILLE. Then it's not too late.

[ANTOINE *opens the stove.*]

ANTOINE. Look look, somebody's home. Sausages! They need a turn.

[*He turns them over.*]

PAGEVIN. [*From the wings.*] Stop it. That's enough.

[PAGEVIN *enters.*]

ANTOINE. What's the matter?

PAGEVIN. That cook wants to kiss me just because I'm from Soissons. Have you ever heard of such a thing?

CRIQUEVILLE. From Soissons, did you say? My compliments, sir.

PAGEVIN. [*Aside.*] You're still here?

CRIQUEVILLE. The Soissonais . . . the most generous, the most beautiful, the most . . . large region in all of central France.

PAGEVIN. [*Turning his back.*] Good day, sir.

CRIQUEVILLE. Does it only work on servants?

PAGEVIN. [*To* ANTOINE.] Young man, take this man, carry him into the street, and I will give you ten sous.

ANTOINE. Impossible. I am his groom.

PAGEVIN. His groom. [*Aside, looking at* CRIQUEVILLE *with suspicion.*] He's very lightly dressed. [*Aloud.*] Monsieur doesn't feel chilly?

CRIQUEVILLE. I just got back from Brazil.

PAGEVIN. Really. I do business over there. Do you know the General—

CRIQUEVILLE. Very. We—

PAGEVIN. Santa Guarda?

CRIQUEVILLE. A dear friend. Since my intention is to winter in Paris, I'd like to order a complete wardrobe—and livery for my groom.

ANTOINE. [*Aside.*] Is it possible? His groom in livery?

CRIQUEVILLE. Might you be so kind as to give me . . . well . . .

PAGEVIN. What?

CRIQUEVILLE. The address of Monsieur Dusautoy?

PAGEVIN. What did you say?

CRIQUEVILLE. The address of the best tailor in Paris.

PAGEVIN. Best? Best? There are lots better than Dusautoy!

CRIQUEVILLE. Come now. Who, for instance?

PAGEVIN. Me, for instance.

CRIQUEVILLE. You mean to say you are a—

PAGEVIN. Tailor, yes.

ANTOINE. [*Aside.*] What a stupe. I just told him that.

PAGEVIN. And, without boasting, the House of Pagevin is known—

CRIQUEVILLE. Known? I should say it's known, it's known as being a little tacky—off the rack—

PAGEVIN. Off the rack? Me?

ANTOINE. Oh my God.

PAGEVIN. Sir, my workshop is on the premises. Please take the trouble of examining my art.

CRIQUEVILLE. Really sir, I only buy the best.

PAGEVIN. Sir, the fact that you have offended me gives me the right to demand this of you.

CRIQUEVILLE. Well, I don't want to be impolite. I warn you though, my taste is extremely finicky.

PAGEVIN. So much the better. Follow me, sir, and you shall choose.

ANTOINE. Yeah. Let's go choose.

CRIQUEVILLE. [*Passing in front of* PAGEVIN.] Just to be polite.

ANTOINE. [*Aping his master.*] Just to be polite.

[ANTOINE *and* CRIQUEVILLE *exit left.* EMERANCE *enters and tries to stop her father, who is about to exit.*]

EMERANCE. Daddy!

PAGEVIN. What?

EMERANCE. The new cook—she's putting *fines herbes* in the eggs Sardou.

PAGEVIN. Can't you see I'm doing business?

[PAGEVIN *exits and* MONTDOUILLARD *enters.*]

MONTDOUILLARD. Hello? Anybody in?

EMERANCE. [*To herself.*] Well, I've never heard of *fines herbes* in eggs Sardou.

MONTDOUILLARD. [*Sees* EMERANCE.] Ah!

[*He tiptoes to her and takes her by the waist.*]

EMERANCE. Oh!

MONTDOUILLARD. Shhh, it's me.

EMERANCE. Monsieur Montdouillard!

MONTDOUILLARD. Call me Sulpice. I dream of hearing your rosy lips stammer out my Christian name!

EMERANCE. Stop. Or I'll tell Daddy.

MONTDOUILLARD. Vixen. I've brought you a bag of *marrons glacés*.

EMERANCE. I'll get fat.

MONTDOUILLARD. Careful, there's a note at the bottom.

EMERANCE. Again? That makes number nine.

MONTDOUILLARD. I'm that kind of guy. When I give a girl a bag of *marrons glacés*, there's bound to be a note at the bottom. It's a little piece of lava in the ice. Oh, my little imp, my sprite.

EMERANCE. But Monsieur Montdouillard—

MONTDOUILLARD. Call me Sulpice. Or I'll expire at your feet.

EMERANCE. Don't make fun of me—let me go!

MONTDOUILLARD. Don't wiggle, my tasty cuckoo. Don't you know why I come here every other day for another badly made fifty-franc waistcoat?

EMERANCE. No.

MONTDOUILLARD. It's time you learned: it's to see you! Smell you! Breathe you!

EMERANCE. Then you love me.

MONTDOUILLARD. Love and waistcoats, that's my motto.

EMERANCE. Why don't you speak to my father?

MONTDOUILLARD. Why would I want to do that?

EMERANCE. So we can get married.

MONTDOUILLARD. Mademoiselle, your insistence is inexplicable. It lacks modesty.

EMERANCE. But . . . but . . .

MONTDOUILLARD. Not another word. It seems to me that I've told you that certain necessary papers have to come through.

EMERANCE. But it's been six months already!

MONTDOUILLARD. I told you that city hall burned down. They're digging as fast as they can.

[CATICHE *enters*.]

CATICHE. Miss.

EMERANCE. What? What do you want?

CATICHE. Where is the stove?

MONTDOUILLARD. A new cook.

EMERANCE. Which stove?

CATICHE. [*Gesturing*.] You know, the kind for flipping the eggs Sardou.

EMERANCE. Flip them? Follow me. [*Aside*.] What a funny cook.

[EMERANCE *exits left*.]

MONTDOUILLARD. [*Pinching* CATICHE's *waist*.] Hello, Miss Alsace-Lorraine.

CATICHE. Don't touch me.

MONTDOUILLARD. Do you like *marrons glacés?*

CATICHE. Yeah, but I don't like wiseguys.

[CATICHE *punches him and exits left.*]

MONTDOUILLARD. [*In pain.*] Jesus! [*Alone.*] Emerance is bewitching . . . and the cook to boot. Womankind—the finest product in all creation. I adore them wholesale! They do me good. Woman is my sole occupation—until two in the afternoon. The instant the Stock Exchange opens, my heart shuts tight. I bolt the door and hide the key. I'm an inside trader on the high market. From two to four, I speculate, and after, oh, after, I make wicked. One must make the most of every day. And now it is time for me to marry. What happiness for husbands the day Montdouillard is unpistoled. [*Notices* PAGEVIN, *who enters.*] Good day, Pagevin.

PAGEVIN. [*Bowing.*] Sir.

MONTDOUILLARD. Is my nineteenth waistcoat finished yet?

PAGEVIN. They're sewing the buttons on as we speak.

MONTDOUILLARD. Hurry it up, shall we?

[CRIQUEVILLE *enters, newly dressed. He speaks to the wings.*]

CRIQUEVILLE. And for the hat, do you hear, a fine gold braid, eight centimeters wide. [*He greets* MONTDOUILLARD.] Sir.

MONTDOUILLARD. Sir.

PAGEVIN. [*To* CRIQUEVILLE.] If you'll wait a moment, I'm yours. [*Aside.*] I'll just add up his bill.

MONTDOUILLARD. My waistcoat cannot wait.

PAGEVIN. Coming right up. [*He exits shouting.*] The nineteenth waistcoat of Monsieur Montdouillard!

CRIQUEVILLE. [*Aside.*] Nineteen waistcoats! He's a collector.

MONTDOUILLARD. [*Moving upstage.*] Now where the devil did that little Emerance go?

CRIQUEVILLE. [*Moving downstage, displaying his suit.*] I have a new formula! [*Pulling out a notebook.*] And I will write it down on the very first page of my notebook. "Let us flatter, but let's not swindle."

MONTDOUILLARD. [*Eyeing him with a lorgnette.*] That man is wearing the pattern of my seventh waistcoat—the one I blinded the Marquise de Clafoutis and La Duchesse de la Dinde with.

CRIQUEVILLE. It's astonishing how sausages can perfume the breeze. I should turn them over. [*He opens the stove.*] God, I'm famished.

MONTDOUILLARD. Pagevin better be done soon. Lunch is at noon at the Café de Paris.

CRIQUEVILLE. [*Aside.*] The Café de Paris! [*Closes stove.*] That's a lot pricier than these stinking sausages. I must aim my sights higher. [*Greets* MONTDOUILLARD.] Sir.

MONTDOUILLARD. Sir.

CRIQUEVILLE. [*Aside.*] I just have to crank the right tune out of my canary. [*Aloud to* MONTDOUILLARD, *who has opened his jacket and revealed his vest.*] My God, what a pretty waistcoat . . . what a handsome waistcoat!

MONTDOUILLARD. Frankly, how do you find it?

CRIQUEVILLE. Superb, delicious, staggering, stupendous, yummy!

MONTDOUILLARD. And in good taste?

CRIQUEVILLE. Glistening with good taste — from front to back!

MONTDOUILLARD. I have the finest waistcoats on the the Stock Exchange.

CRIQUEVILLE. [*Aside.*] Just pull that chain.

MONTDOUILLARD. I've got nineteen new ones.

CRIQUEVILLE. You know, I've always thought that this particular part of the wardrobe is the veritable touchstone of elegance and distinction.

MONTDOUILLARD. I too. [*Aside.*] He is very spiritual.

CRIQUEVILLE. I would go even further; I dare to put forth with Buffon . . .

MONTDOUILLARD. Buffon?

CRIQUEVILLE. A writer who wrote of animals; yes, sir, I dare to put forth with Buffon that the waistcoat *is* the man.

MONTDOUILLARD. No! You think?

CRIQUEVILLE. [*Aside.*] Lunchtime. [*Aloud.*] I have yet to have the honor of meeting you, have I not? Would you like to wager that, based upon a simple inspection of your scrumptious waistcoat, I could list both your qualities and your faults?

MONTDOUILLARD. What shall we wager?

CRIQUEVILLE. Whatever you like. Lunch perhaps — at the Café de Paris?

MONTDOUILLARD. You're on.

CRIQUEVILLE. Let us begin with your qualities. Oh, now don't be shy; don't hide your waistcoat. It's my gospel.

MONTDOUILLARD. Gladly shall I spread for you.

CRIQUEVILLE. [*With a lorgnette.*] First of all, I read — that you are a charming man.

MONTDOUILLARD. That's easy.

CRIQUEVILLE. With a distinguished mind, an agreeable commerce.

MONTDOUILLARD. [*Flattered and astonished.*] But — that's so . . .

CRIQUEVILLE. Endowed to the highest degree with a head for business — a genius for speculation.

MONTDOUILLARD. Very curious.

CRIQUEVILLE. Stop if I make a mistake.

MONTDOUILLARD. None so far. Keep going.

CRIQUEVILLE. Tall, generous, brave, loyal.

MONTDOUILLARD. It's unheard of! He's leaving nothing out.

CRIQUEVILLE. But . . . but . . . horribly dangerous around women.

MONTDOUILLARD. [*Modestly.*] Well, I am a bit of a scamp.

CRIQUEVILLE. In short, sir, this admirable waistcoat reveals to me one extremely rare gift . . . the gift endowed upon the superior man, the truly accomplished man . . .

MONTDOUILLARD. Which gift is that?

CRIQUEVILLE. You don't like compliments. You detest flattery.

MONTDOUILLARD. Upon my very soul, it's simply staggering!

CRIQUEVILLE. So you see, sir—

MONTDOUILLARD. Yes, I see, very good with the qualities—but now for the faults! My faults?

CRIQUEVILLE. [*Aside.*] I could eat a horse. [*Aloud.*] Permit me. [*With lorgnette . . . a pause.*] Not a single one.

MONTDOUILLARD. You win! [*Aside.*] It's amazing. He is very spiritual. [*Aloud.*] I like you. I want us to be friends. What a dear. What is your name?

CRIQUEVILLE. De Criqueville.

MONTDOUILLARD. I'm Montdouillard. Let's eat.

CRIQUEVILLE. Oh, some other time. There's no rush.

MONTDOUILLARD. No, today. I insist. [*Aside.*] I'll make a friend pay.

CRIQUEVILLE. Well, if you insist. You go ahead, I'll follow—I'm waiting for my servant.

MONTDOUILLARD. All right. I'll put the oysters on the shell and have you presented to all my intimates. Now, you have to promise me that you'll re-read my waistcoat.

CRIQUEVILLE. I'd only bore you.

MONTDOUILLARD. No no, in front of everybody—they'll love it. Adieu. [*As he exits.*] He's charming, simply charming!

CRIQUEVILLE. You know, that was no fun at all. He was too easy—I could have handed him over to Antoine. [ANTOINE *enters magisterially, in grand livery, carrying the overcoat of his master on his arm.*] Well, I've quite a handsome houseboy. What do you have there?

ANTOINE. [*Solemnly.*] I have the honor of carrying the topcoat of Monsieur.

CRIQUEVILLE. Are you happy with your livery?

ANTOINE. Oh, yes, but greatness won't turn my head. Although I am a domestic, I will always remember that I come from the people.

CRIQUEVILLE. [*To the audience.*] You see how a little bit of braid can make a man drunk! [*To* ANTOINE.] We're leaving.

ANTOINE. I follow my master's orders.

[*They are about to leave.* PAGEVIN *enters.*]

PAGEVIN. Where do you think you're going? You've forgotten something. [*Handing a paper to* CRIQUEVILLE.]

CRIQUEVILLE. And what is that?

PAGEVIN. The bill for 663 francs.

CRIQUEVILLE. Of course. I'll just look this over at home.

[*He tries to leave.*]

PAGEVIN. Excuse me—cash on delivery.

CRIQUEVILLE. You wouldn't happen to have change for a thousand-franc note?

PAGEVIN. Yes, I would.

CRIQUEVILLE. You would? Very good. I'll just go get it.

[*He tries to leave.*]

PAGEVIN. But I just told you I had it.

ANTOINE. He has it!

PAGEVIN. Just give me your thousand and—

CRIQUEVILLE. Of course, of course. [*Aside.*] What song can I sing?

PAGEVIN. Well?

CRIQUEVILLE. [*Quickly.*] My God, what a gorgeous waistcoat! What a simply staggering waistcoat!

PAGEVIN. You were saying?

CRIQUEVILLE. [*Aside.*] Wrong tune. [*Aloud.*] I'm admiring my groom! What a livery!

PAGEVIN. [*Holding out the bill.*] If you please.

CRIQUEVILLE. [*To* ANTOINE.] Turn around. What a cut. What elegance. Dusautoy can't hold a candle to you. Ensembles this superb ought to be signed, like a painting. Pagevin *fecit*.

PAGEVIN. The 663 francs will be ample reward.

CRIQUEVILLE. [*Aside.*] Wrong tune.

PAGEVIN. All added up.

CRIQUEVILLE. Just a minute. I can't believe it. I've noticed there's nothing in your buttonhole—no medal of honor—no royal charter—

PAGEVIN. Me, oh sir, in my humble profession . . .

CRIQUEVILLE. Perhaps you never asked for one.

PAGEVIN. No sir, never . . . how could I . . . never . . . only . . . five times.

CRIQUEVILLE. [*Aside.*] Do re mi fa so la ti do! [*Aloud.*] And did anyone respond?

PAGEVIN. Oh hell, what's the use . . . nobody answered me.

CRIQUEVILLE. That's not even polite.

PAGEVIN. It's far from Paris to Brazil, I guess.

CRIQUEVILLE. What do you mean, Brazil?

PAGEVIN. By the intervention of General—

CRIQUEVILLE. Santa Guarda.

PAGEVIN. Your friend.

CRIQUEVILLE. Intimate! We're like this.

PAGEVIN. Since I had made three full dress uniforms for him—I had let myself hope—

CRIQUEVILLE. [*Mysteriously.*] Shhh.

PAGEVIN. What?

CRIQUEVILLE. [*To* ANTOINE.] Stand back, Antonio.

ANTOINE. Antonio?

[CRIQUEVILLE *leads* PAGEVIN *to the other end of the stage.*]

CRIQUEVILLE. [*Mysteriously.*] Your affair is going by giant steps.

PAGEVIN. No! Do you know something?

[*He puts the bill back in his pocket.*]

CRIQUEVILLE. [*Aside.*] A farewell to arms.

PAGEVIN. Tell me!

CRIQUEVILLE. Shhh. Stand back, Antonio.

ANTOINE. Antonio?

CRIQUEVILLE. I pleaded your case with all my might to General Santa . . . uh, General Santa . . . Whoozy . . . General Santa Barbara.

PAGEVIN. Oh, sir . . . I can't thank you enough.

CRIQUEVILLE. Mind you . . . it didn't go like greased lightning. "A tailor," he said, "isn't that rank a little . . . silly?"

PAGEVIN. What?

CRIQUEVILLE. [*With fire.*] "What do you mean, silly?" I cried out. "Is there a greater, nobler, more useful profession in society? Answer me, General Santa Anna. Suppress the tailors and what would become of morality?"

ANTOINE. [*Opening the stove.*] Presto! They're done.

[*He removes a sausage and eats it.*]

CRIQUEVILLE. "Without tailors, whence civilization? If mankind is left to dress itself, it will fall into the savage state of nakedness—or at least to the level of hideous baker boy outfits. Suppress the tailors and all of Brazil will look like bakers' assistants!"

PAGEVIN. Well said! Bravo! Bravo!

CRIQUEVILLE. [*Aside, looking at* ANTOINE.] Look at him eating over there. "The flatterer liveth on his listener"—there's the fable in action.

PAGEVIN. So do you think I'll obtain the . . .

CRIQUEVILLE. Shhh. It's been done.

PAGEVIN. I've been named?

CRIQUEVILLE. Knighted! It'll come in the mail today or tomorrow. Or the day after tomorrow. One of these days.

PAGEVIN. Is it big?

CRIQUEVILLE. Enormous.

PAGEVIN. What color?

CRIQUEVILLE. [*Aside.*] I'm dying of hunger. [*Aloud.*] Yellow, green, blue, and currant on lilac.

PAGEVIN. Five colors. My five colors have been hoisted! I still have something to ask you.

CRIQUEVILLE. Excuse me, but lunch awaits me at the Café de Paris. My hat.

PAGEVIN. Here it is.

ANTOINE. [*Aside.*] The Café de Paris? If I'd known that . . .

[*He throws the sausage on the stove.*]

PAGEVIN. Depend, sir, on my eternal gratitude.

CRIQUEVILLE. [*Exiting, lightly striking* PAGEVIN's *cheek.*] Yes, yes, good Pagevin . . . adieu.

ANTOINE. [*Exiting, same business.*] Yes, yes, good Pagevin . . . adieu.

PAGEVIN. [*Accompanying them.*] Watch your step. The stairs were just waxed. Hold the rail. [*Re-entering.*] What a charming young man! Finally I've been named. I am a knight of the order of . . . of . . . hold on! What order? [*Remembers.*] Hey, you forgot the bill. [*Rushing to the door.*] Sir—that's six hundred and sixty-three—

Act III

The boulevard in front of the Café de Paris. Table and chairs. In the background, café windows. Upstage center is the flight of stairs that leads into the café. As the curtain goes up, an ENGLISHMAN *is seated at a table at the right.* ANTOINE *is standing at the foot of the staircase with his master's overcoat on his arm. There are sounds and music of great mirth inside.*

ANTOINE. He's eating, he's having lunch inside there with a bunch of beautifully gloved petty bourgeois boobs while I've been invited to wait by the door and starve to death.

CRIQUEVILLE. [*From inside.*] Such a heart-stopping waistcoat! My God, what an artistic waistcoat!

MONTDOUILLARD. [*From inside.*] He's a genius!

ENGLISHMAN. Waiter.

WAITER. Sir?

ENGLISHMAN. I asked you for a glass of Swiss absinthe.

WAITER. Here you are, sir.

ANTOINE. An Englishman looking to stimulate his appetite. Mine is hyper-overstimulated. [*Loud burst of music from inside.*] Are they having a wedding in there? I shouldn't have been so particular about the tailor's sausages.

[CRIQUEVILLE *appears at the stage left window, a glass of champagne in his hand.*]

CRIQUEVILLE. The Café de Paris serves a most refined luncheon.

ANTOINE. Master . . . could you swipe me a sandwich?

CRIQUEVILLE. I'm not putting mayonnaise in my new suit pockets. Here, have a drink.

ANTOINE. [*After draining the glass.*] Delicious . . . but a little low on nutrition and not very thick.

[*He returns the glass.*]

CRIQUEVILLE. You know Antoine, Paris is full of crows—I've been asked to dine for the entire week.

ANTOINE. What about me?

CRIQUEVILLE. You can come along—like today.

ANTOINE. That's it?

[*Voices from inside call out "Criqueville! Criqueville!"*]

CRIQUEVILLE. They cannot do without me. Coming, coming.

[CRIQUEVILLE *closes the window and disappears.*]

ANTOINE. Well, if the job weren't so prestigious.

[CATICHE *enters with a basket under her arm.*]

ANTOINE. Look, it's Lady Picarde!

CATICHE. Hello, Monsieur Antoine. I'm coming back from the market.

ANTOINE. [*Sniffing the basket.*] Oooh, minx. That smells good. What have you got in there?

CATICHE. A duck.

ANTOINE. Smoked?

CATICHE. No, silly, raw.

ANTOINE. Mustn't touch. It looks like your tailor eats well.

CATICHE. Oh, I'm not working for him anymore.

ANTOINE. Already?

CATICHE. We just couldn't get along. He doesn't like omelettes.

ANTOINE. To think, in the nineteenth century, there are tailors who don't like omelettes. That's progress.

CATICHE. I only worked two hours for him, but he paid me for a whole week.

ANTOINE. That's the least he can do.

CATICHE. Fortunately, the people right below him hired me. But their ideas about what to eat are just as crazy. Do you know what they asked me to get for dinner?

ANTOINE. No, but I'm sure I'd eat it.

CATICHE. A duck with olives and a crème au chocolat!

ANTOINE. Foreigners!

CATICHE. I don't know what I'm going to do about this. I've always bought eggs.

ANTOINE. That duck might start with olives, but he's gonna end up in an omelette.

CATICHE. Gotta run!

ANTOINE. Good luck. [CATICHE *exits*.] What a tasty Picardess.

[*The* ENGLISHMAN *enters and sits at a table to the left.*]

ENGLISHMAN. Waiter!

WAITER. Sir?

ENGLISHMAN. Another glass of Swiss absinthe.

ANTOINE. [*Looking at the* ENGLISHMAN.] The sight of that makes me hungrier and hungrier. I can't stand it anymore. Waiter!

WAITER. Absinthe, sir? Right away.

ANTOINE. No, would you tell Monsieur Criqueville that an extremely important gentleman wishes to speak to him.

WAITER. I'll fly.

[*He exits.*]

ANTOINE. I'll ask him for five francs and get myself a steak.

CRIQUEVILLE. [*Appears at the flight of stairs.*] Who is asking for me?

ANTOINE. Shhh. Come closer.

CRIQUEVILLE. [*Descending.*] Well?

ANTOINE. It's me.

CRIQUEVILLE. What the hell do you want?

ANTOINE. Can I have some lunch money?

CRIQUEVILLE. Do I look like I have anything on me?

ANTOINE. Then give me the key—I'll go look for them.

CRIQUEVILLE. What key?

ANTOINE. To your house. By the way, where do we live?

CRIQUEVILLE. We don't live anywhere.

ANTOINE. [*Aside.*] No money and no house—well, if the job wasn't such a good opportunity. [*Aloud.*] But I can't live like this! Am I supposed to eat this coat on my arm? My stomach dreams of other meals.

CRIQUEVILLE. Then listen, my friend, remember the fable. Be like the fox and go hunt some crow. Just act like Sir Fox and make the crows sing!

ANTOINE. [*Speaking.*] On the Boulevard des Italiens?

CRIQUEVILLE. They're everywhere you look! Look! There's a cakeseller!

[A CAKESELLER *is walking upstage, offering her wares to the* ENGLISHMAN.]

ANTOINE. You think?

CRIQUEVILLE. I know. Go on.

ANTOINE. I'll try. [*He goes and grabs her by the waist.*] Hey there, little mother.

CAKESELLER. [*Pushing him away.*] Hands off!

ANTOINE. How fresh and pretty you are this morning.

CAKESELLER. Buy something from me.

ANTOINE. Buy? I couldn't possibly. I've just had an enormous lunch. [*Following her.*] Oh, but how fresh and pretty you are this morning.

[*She exits,* ANTOINE *following.*]

CRIQUEVILLE. He'll do just fine.

[GENERAL RENAUDIER *descends the stairs and speaks to the* WAITER.]

RENAUDIER. Adrian, I'd like—

CRIQUEVILLE. Renaudier!

RENAUDIER. Criqueville! I was about to send word to you.

CRIQUEVILLE. To me?

RENAUDIER. Are you making good time? Have you completed your balance?

CRIQUEVILLE. Not yet.

RENAUDIER. And your position?

CRIQUEVILLE. I'm positioning myself.

RENAUDIER. Well, for God's sake, hurry up.

ENGLISHMAN. Waiter! Waiter! Garçon!

[*The* WAITER *approaches. They converse in low tones.*]

RENAUDIER. I want to caution you that someone is presenting a future for my daughter this very evening.

CRIQUEVILLE. Tonight? This morning you said two months.

RENAUDIER. Two months—if nothing turned up before. But, if I find someone else first—I can't wait around for you 'til doomsday.

CRIQUEVILLE. But General—

[*The* WAITER *has left the* ENGLISHMAN *and come up to* RENAUDIER.]

WAITER. Sir.

RENAUDIER. What? What do you want?

WAITER. Ummm . . . I don't know how to put this sir, it's just that that Englishman over there. [*The* ENGLISHMAN *gets up and salutes* RENAUDIER, *who returns the gesture.*] He asked me to ask you whether you'd care to eat against him.

RENAUDIER. Eat against him?

WAITER. As a challenge. He came all the way from London just for this. The loser pays for dinner.

CRIQUEVILLE. A duel to indigestion.

RENAUDIER. [*Angry.*] I've never heard of anything so grotesque. Off with the both of you. The man's an orangutan. Goodbye, Criqueville.

CRIQUEVILLE. But General—

RENAUDIER. Tempus fugit, my boy, tempus fugit.

[RENAUDIER *exits left,* CRIQUEVILLE *follows him.*]

ENGLISHMAN. [*Getting up.*] Oh! Shocking! The gentleman didn't want to eat against me. What a poltroon.

[*He exits right and* CRIQUEVILLE *returns.*]

CRIQUEVILLE. This is a fine mess. Tonight a future is presented to my beloved and it's my fault. I lunch, I swill champagne and don't get around to business. It's just that a hundred thousand francs and a good job aren't held out to you on every corner like a pinch of snuff.

[MONTDOUILLARD *in another new waistcoat, descends the staircase, followed by* BARTAVELLE, ARTHUR, *and the other guests. They surround* CRIQUEVILLE *with handshakes.*]

ARTHUR. Good Criqueville—

BARTAVELLE. My new best friend—

MONTDOUILLARD. Albert, would you like a cigar?

CRIQUEVILLE. My pleasure, Montdouillard.

MONTDOUILLARD. Call me Sulpice.

ARTHUR. [*Low to* CRIQUEVILLE.] Throw that away. Montdouillard is a blowhard who smokes ten-cent cigars. Here, have one of these—pure havana.

[*He presents his cigar case.*]

CRIQUEVILLE. Thank you. Tomorrow, I'll have you taste mine.

BARTAVELLE. [*Low.*] Don't smoke that—his havana was made in Brussels. [*Offering his cigar case.*] Here's a true havana.

CRIQUEVILLE. You're too kind. [*Offering one.*] Let me offer you, in kind, one of mine—it's so sweet. [*Aside.*] Montdouillard's two-center.

[BARTAVELLE *accepts it, examines it, starts to light it.*]

CRIQUEVILLE. Oh no, smoke it later, right before dinner. [*Aside.*] They don't mind waving their cigars around, but it's not like they add up to a dowry.

MONTDOUILLARD. Waiter! Serve the coffee quickly. I have to get to the Stock Exchange.

ARTHUR. Bah, the exchange! You'll go tomorrow.

MONTDOUILLARD. Impossible. I'm working on my biggest deal ever.

ARTHUR. What deal is that?

MONTDOUILLARD. My Bulgarian loan. In four days, it'll be completely underwritten, and then I'll float it. We have no competitors, and that's a stroke of fortune.

CRIQUEVILLE. A stroke of fortune. I'd like to cram myself inside that action.

WAITER. The coffee is ready.

[*Everyone moves upstage to sit.*]

CRIQUEVILLE. [*Stopping* MONTDOUILLARD.] You were saying that the Bulgarian loan—

MONTDOUILLARD. A magnificent transaction. The returns are already at hundred-franc options. And I've set aside a sweet five thousand for Papa.

CRIQUEVILLE. Ah, you've set some aside. [*Cajoling him.*] Good little Saint Sulpice. [*Caressing his waistcoat.*] My God, what pretty material, what spellbinding material.

MONTDOUILLARD. [*Strutting and preening.*] You know, I find him very spiritual, but the coffee is getting cold.

CRIQUEVILLE. Tell me, Sulpice, might there be a way to obtain just a small portion of your returns?

MONTDOUILLARD. For you, dear child, there's always a way.

CRIQUEVILLE. Oh, dear friend.

MONTDOUILLARD. I think—*entre nous*—we can go to bed on this.

[*They move upstage to get their coffee.*]

CRIQUEVILLE. [*Aside.*] I'll ask for a thousand—that should square my account. [*He sees* BARTAVELLE *alone at right.*] Bartavelle, what's wrong? Are you ill?

BARTAVELLE. I'm worried sick.

CRIQUEVILLE. How can that be? A man with your beautiful horses. [*To audience.*] With this one, it's horses.

BARTAVELLE. [*Sadly.*] Oh, Criqueville. I have a mare who won't eat. You know Mauviette.

CRIQUEVILLE. [*Affecting the most vivid distress.*] Oh my God, my God, Mauviette, the mare who's off her feed.

BARTAVELLE. And then I worry that Pichenette—

CRIQUEVILLE. Not another?

BARTAVELLE. No. A dancer. I think she's cheating on me.

CRIQUEVILLE. Oh, well, who can ever say—

BARTAVELLE. It's not that it hurts. . . . It's that it *humiliates*. This morning at her place I found a mash note at the bottom of a bag of *marrons glacés*.

MONTDOUILLARD. [*Aside.*] Oooops!

CRIQUEVILLE. And so you suspect that the candymaker—

[*They rise and leave the scene,* CRIQUEVILLE *taking his glass.*]

BARTAVELLE. No, not the candymaker. I suspect five of my closest friends.

CRIQUEVILLE. Come now, let's not think of that. Think of your horses. You have so many.

MONTDOUILLARD. Especially that magnificent team waiting for you in front of Tortoni's.

BARTAVELLE. [*Scornfully.*] That pair? A law clerk's nags! I'm going away for a few days. I need a friend to exercise my team.

CRIQUEVILLE. I'm here for you, Bart.

BARTAVELLE. Criqueville, I couldn't possibly impose on you.

CRIQUEVILLE. Why not?

BARTAVELLE. You have your own to manage.

CRIQUEVILLE. Well, what I mean to say is—[*Aside.*] Wheels—I don't have a house—I can sleep inside the coach.

BARTAVELLE. [*Puts down his glass.*] I'm leaving within the hour. How about going to visit your stables?

CRIQUEVILLE. No! I mean, I can't today. I have the Masons. And then, you're going to laugh at this, I know you, but just at present, I'm on foot. [*Everyone laughs boisterously.*] I've sold everything!

BARTAVELLE. Perfect. Use my carriage.

CRIQUEVILLE. It's just that I don't know whether . . .

BARTAVELLE. Don't be proud. I won't take no for an answer.

CRIQUEVILLE. Well . . . if you insist.

BARTAVELLE. I'll go tell my driver to be at your service.

CRIQUEVILLE. [*Aside.*] Free housing.

MONTDOUILLARD. Two o'clock. Son of an Arabian foothill!

ARTHUR. What did you just say?

MONTDOUILLARD. Son of an Arabian foothill. It's an industrial oath. It came to me one day when I lost five thousand francs on the mines. Adieu, my pets. By the way, I have a meeting at four with Flavigny. If you see him, tell him to wait for me.

ARTHUR. That's perfect. I have to ask him to give a job to a friend.

CRIQUEVILLE. What? Who is this Flavigny that can hand out jobs?

BARTAVELLE. A bigwig with the railroad commission.

MONTDOUILLARD. And a complete pushover. I just read his last report to the stockholders. He's an unbearable blowhard.

CRIQUEVILLE. And he has jobs to spare?

MONTDOUILLARD. His pockets are full of them.

CRIQUEVILLE. [*Aside.*] That's the pocket to pick.

MONTDOUILLARD. Until later.

[*Everyone leaves except* CRIQUEVILLE.]

CRIQUEVILLE. I have a coach and a dowry. Well, at any rate I have them tomorrow. Man's a funny piece of machinery. All he takes for lubrication is a little piece of sugar.

[ANTOINE *enters.*]

ANTOINE. I can't take this anymore.

CRIQUEVILLE. Antoine! So, how did it go with your cakeseller?

ANTOINE. She's a harpy. I flattered her all the way to the city gates! All I could get off her was one lousy cream horn.

CRIQUEVILLE. Success then.

ANTOINE. A very light success. Hey, you're smoking. Give me your butt, sir.

CRIQUEVILLE. Stop bothering me. While you were gone, I got ourselves a carriage.

ANTOINE. Sure you did.

CRIQUEVILLE. Look over there—in front of Tortoni's.

ANTOINE. It's no surprise to me. Master is so clever.

CRIQUEVILLE. You think?

ANTOINE. Oh, master, I never know how you're going to get all that you aim for . . .

CRIQUEVILLE. Go on . . .

ANTOINE. But as soon as you speak, I just sit there . . . like an idiot . . . mouth wide open.

CRIQUEVILLE. [*Aside.*] I like his rustic style.

ANTOINE. And so fine . . . as fine as ink . . . as fresh as stink . . . as right as rain . . . and a great build. Geez, what a beautiful physique.

CRIQUEVILLE. [*Aside, astonished.*] He's a really nice guy. [*Aloud.*] Here, have a cigar.

ANTOINE. O, thank you sir. [*To the audience.*] As dumb as dirt. [*To* CRIQUEVILLE.] I'll go take a look at our rig.

[ANTOINE *exits and* FLAVIGNY *enters.*]

CRIQUEVILLE. So unspoiled.

FLAVIGNY. [*To the* WAITER.] Adrian! Do you know if Montdouillard is here?

WAITER. He just went out, Monsieur de Flavigny.

CRIQUEVILLE. Flavigny, huh?

FLAVIGNY. I'm early. I'll just wait for him here. [*He sits.*] Bring me a glass of port.

WAITER. Right away.

CRIQUEVILLE. [*Aside.*] Flavigny! My government job. Let's try some civil service. [*He approaches* FLAVIGNY *and salutes him.* FLAVIGNY *snubs him.*] Maybe he's nearsighted.

FLAVIGNY. Adrian! A match.

CRIQUEVILLE. Do you need a light, sir?

FLAVIGNY. [*Coldly.*] Thank you.

CRIQUEVILLE. [*Aside.*] Snowball. [*After a silence.*] A lovely day. [FLAVIGNY, *put out, takes out a newspaper and turns his back.*] I think his is a losing personality.

FLAVIGNY. Adrian! What time is Montdouillard getting back?

CRIQUEVILLE. [*Butting in impressively.*] At four o'clock, sir, at four o'clock.

FLAVIGNY. [*Coldly.*] Thank you, sir.

CRIQUEVILLE. [*After a silence.*] What a charming man Montdouillard is. Mind — manners — form — all distinctive.

FLAVIGNY. You're easily impressed.

[*He takes up his newspaper.*]

CRIQUEVILLE. [*Aside.*] Hmm . . . looks like for this one, I'll have to tear down the other guy. Some people are like that. [*Aloud.*] To me he's always seemed like a wigmaker who's just won first prize in the lottery.

FLAVIGNY. To whom are you referring?

CRIQUEVILLE. Montdouillard.

FLAVIGNY. [*Smiling.*] Ahh. [*He puts down his paper.*] But you were just saying —

CRIQUEVILLE. Well, in front of the waiter. I didn't want to deprive him of his only admirer.

FLAVIGNY. [*Laughs.*] Well, I suppose he does have some success with servants.

CRIQUEVILLE. What can I say? A man who changes his waistcoat five times a day — that dazzles the help.

FLAVIGNY. Right, right.

[*He moves his chair a little closer.*]

CRIQUEVILLE. It's the same way with little Bartavelle. Oh excuse me, is he a friend of yours?

FLAVIGNY. Yes, but go ahead.

CRIQUEVILLE. A man whose mind is only on his horses, yet who always looks like he's on foot.

FLAVIGNY. [*Moving his chair closer.*] Can I offer you a glass of port?

CRIQUEVILLE. Thank you.

FLAVIGNY. I notice that you are friends to these gentlemen.

CRIQUEVILLE. I meet them in society, but just between us, I have little esteem for these boulevard loafers.

FLAVIGNY. That speaks highly of you.

CRIQUEVILLE. I like to count among my friends only those men who are serious, those with lucid, practical, penetrating minds, men who honor science and industry.

FLAVIGNY. Well spoken.

CRIQUEVILLE. I just read an article by one of these truly useful men and I'm just thunderstruck with admiration before the immense sweep of his superior intelligence.

FLAVIGNY. [*Cold again, taking up his journal.*] How fortunate for you.

CRIQUEVILLE. [*Aside.*] He thinks I mean one of his friends.

FLAVIGNY. [*Ironically.*] Might one know the name of this marvel?

CRIQUEVILLE. The byline on the piece was Flavigny.

FLAVIGNY. What? You read that?

CRIQUEVILLE. Did I read it? I read it and re-read it!

FLAVIGNY. [*Flattered.*] Well, how about that?

CRIQUEVILLE. [*Aside.*] Here kitty kitty kitty.

FLAVIGNY. And is Flavigny one of your intimates?

CRIQUEVILLE. If intimacy means admiration, then yes, sir. As for his person, I have a picture in my mind—a noble old gentleman.

FLAVIGNY. What?

CRIQUEVILLE. But still spry . . . hair whitened by study.

FLAVIGNY. Permit me—

CRIQUEVILLE. [*Enthusiastically.*] It was only a simple report, sir—a stockholder's report—ordinarily the shallowest of things.

FLAVIGNY. [*Laughing.*] The report or the stockholders?

CRIQUEVILLE. Both! But under his magic plume, my horizons were forever broadened—what sap, what vigor, what precision!

FLAVIGNY. You mean in the conclusion.

CRIQUEVILLE. All of it, sir! Beginning, middle, and end, every single syllable—it was all so beautiful, right down to the numbers! Numbers are usually mere thistles of discourse, but he knew how to transform them into so many sweet, harmonious flowers! I stained the pillow with my tears!

FLAVIGNY. [*Aside.*] He has a way with words.

CRIQUEVILLE. So you see, sir, I could die happy having shaken the hand of this venerable savant.

FLAVIGNY. Oh I'm sorry, venerable is just too much.

CRIQUEVILLE. [*Rising with menace.*] Do you dare to insult him?

FLAVIGNY. [*Also rising.*] No, but—

CRIQUEVILLE. [*vehemently.*] I won't stand for it, do you hear me? I will not stand for it!

FLAVIGNY. Calm down. I can arrange for you to shake Monsieur Flavigny's hand, if it would give you so much pleasure.

CRIQUEVILLE. Where? When? Let's go!

FLAVIGNY. No need. [*Extending his hand.*] Put 'er there!

CRIQUEVILLE. What? Sir . . . you're . . . and still so young . . . so . . .

FLAVIGNY. Enough. I'm afraid you're going to try and flatter me.

CRIQUEVILLE. Me, flatter? You don't know me.

FLAVIGNY. Might I learn the name of my new friend?

CRIQUEVILLE. Albert de Criqueville.

FLAVIGNY. I shall never forget it. Come visit me—we can finish this conversation—I've had so much, I mean so much from listening to you.

CRIQUEVILLE. [*Aside.*] Glutton.

FLAVIGNY. But you must excuse me now. I have to go inside, write a letter, blah blah blah. [*To the* WAITER.] Let me know as soon as Montdouillard gets here.

WAITER. Yes, sir.

FLAVIGNY. [*Laughing.*] Poor Montdouillard. You'll never guess why I'm waiting for him.

CRIQUEVILLE. To talk waistcoats.

FLAVIGNY. No, he wants to get married.

CRIQUEVILLE. Poor wretch.

FLAVIGNY. After five, I can wash my hands of him. I'm presenting him to the father-in-law. His intended is the daughter of General Renaudier.

CRIQUEVILLE. [*Leaping up.*] Clotilde!

FLAVIGNY. Good day.

[FLAVIGNY *exits into the café.*]

CRIQUEVILLE. Montdouillard wants to marry my Clotilde and the meeting is at five. I have to stop this at any cost.

[*He starts up the stairs and bumps into* PAGEVIN, *who has entered with a package under his arm.*]

PAGEVIN. Ouch!

CRIQUEVILLE. Lout!

PAGEVIN. It's you.

CRIQUEVILLE. Pagevin! Dear friend.

PAGEVIN. Listen, it hasn't arrived yet.

CRIQUEVILLE. What?

PAGEVIN. You know . . . the thing . . . from Brazil . . .

CRIQUEVILLE. Shhh! The winds are bad.

PAGEVIN. And then I wanted to ask you . . . which order is it?

CRIQUEVILLE. [*Aside.*] Jesus Christ! [*Aloud.*] The Order of the White Blackbird.

PAGEVIN. I'm so excited! [*Pause.*] Wait, there's no such thing as a white blackbird.

CRIQUEVILLE. Brazil is a very strange country. But I see you're in a rush. I won't keep you.

PAGEVIN. By the way, we forgot the bill this morning.

[*He pulls it out of his pocket.*]

CRIQUEVILLE. What is this? You're doing your shopping on foot?

PAGEVIN. I'm waiting for a bus. It's 663 francs.

CRIQUEVILLE. My tailor on a bus! I won't stand for it—where are you headed?

PAGEVIN. The Bastille. Six hundred and—

CRIQUEVILLE. Antonio! [*To* PAGEVIN.] You shall have my carriage.

PAGEVIN. You've got a carriage?

ANTOINE. Sir.

CRIQUEVILLE. Take the excellent Monsieur Pagevin in my coupé to the Bastille. Then return.

PAGEVIN. But really, why don't we just settle the bill—

CRIQUEVILLE. Go go, thanks aren't necessary. Good Monsieur Pagevin.

ANTOINE. Give me your package, good Monsieur Pagevin.

[ANTOINE *drags* PAGEVIN *offstage right.*]

CRIQUEVILLE. One up, one down.

[MONTDOUILLARD *enters.*]

MONTDOUILLARD. I'm late. Did Flavigny get here?

CRIQUEVILLE. He just left.

MONTDOUILLARD. Son of an Arabian foothill!

CRIQUEVILLE. You see that carriage over there headed for the Bastille.

MONTDOUILLARD. No, it can't be. [*Calling out.*] Flavigny! Flavigny! He can't hear me. I'll take a hack. [*He exits, shouting,* CRIQUEVILLE *with him.*] Driver! Driver!

CRIQUEVILLE. Two down, one to go.

FLAVIGNY. [*Entering.*] Where the hell is Montdouillard?

CRIQUEVILLE. He just left.

FLAVIGNY. How?

CRIQUEVILLE. [*Pointing in the other direction.*] That hansom cab that's on its way to the Madeleine . . .

FLAVIGNY. That imbecile! There's been some misunderstanding. I've got to catch up with him. Quick! A cab! [*Exiting.*] Driver! Driver! [*The* ENGLISHMAN *returns to his table at the left. The* WAITER *goes over to talk to him.*]

CRIQUEVILLE. Three up, three down.

[ANTOINE *enters.*]

ANTOINE. Monsieur, the tailor is full of gratitude. [*Aside.*] And I ordered a second pair of pants. But I'm still starved.

WAITER. [*Approaching* CRIQUEVILLE.] Sir, it's that Englishman again.

CRIQUEVILLE. What does he want?

WAITER. He's wondering whether you'd care to eat against him.

CRIQUEVILLE. Tell him to take a hike. [*He notices* ANTOINE *and gets an idea.*] No, don't say anything. [*To* ANTOINE.] Antoine, how healthy is your appetite?

[*The* ENGLISHMAN *walks slowly up the stairs.*]

ANTOINE. I could eat our team of horses.

CRIQUEVILLE. More than sufficient. Put on my topcoat. Like that—now hide your hat.

ANTOINE. What are you up to now?

CRIQUEVILLE. [*To the* ENGLISHMAN.] My lord, permit me to introduce you to a young banker. [*Low.*] Hide your hat.

ENGLISHMAN. So you want to eat against me, do you?

ANTOINE. I'd eat my father now if I could.

CRIQUEVILLE. First one full pays the bill—don't lose, you hear me?

ENGLISHMAN. I've already blown up two of my friends. [*Showing him the door.*] After you.

ANTOINE. No, after you.

ENGLISHMAN. Waiter! Roast beef for eight!

[*They exit into the café.*]

CRIQUEVILLE. [*Alone.*] Let no one say I don't feed my servants. What a busy day. Today I sow, tomorrow I reap. How shall I kill time waiting for my groom? I feel like a little ice cream. [*Searching his pockets.*] I don't know why I bother. [*Sees a businessman at a nearby table.*] Don't be shy—this man wasn't put on this earth for nothing. Waiter, a dish of vanilla—

ANTOINE. [*Opening the window, his mouth full.*] Waiter—beef with cabbage for eight!

CRIQUEVILLE. Looks like he's keeping up the French side. [*Goes to sit at the businessman's table.*] Sir, could I read your *Constitutionnel* after you?

BUSINESSMAN. Certainly.

[*He moves to remove his hat from the table.*]

CRIQUEVILLE. Leave it, leave it, I don't mind.

BUSINESSMAN. But sir—

CRIQUEVILLE. And such a lovely hat it is—is it a beaver?

[*The* WAITER *brings the ice cream.*]

Act IV

The next day. An office antechamber. A writing table to the right. Near the table, a chair with a removable cushion. The main entrance is upstage. Doors at either side, one with the sign "Office of the Director," the other, "Administration."

KERKADEC. [*Holding a stack of papers, speaking offstage.*] Good Monsieur de Saint-Putois . . . rest assured . . . it will come out right. [*Returning to his table.*] And that's one railroad director who annoys me at all speeds.

[FLAVIGNY *enters from the Administration door.*]

FLAVIGNY. My friend, see whether Saint-Putois can see me.

KERKADEC. Right away, sir. [*He gives a letter to* FLAVIGNY *and exits left.*]

FLAVIGNY. Another request for that first-class inspector post. It fell open yesterday and already we have fourteen applicants. But my hands are tied without the agreement of my colleague Saint-Putois, and vice versa. That's our arrangement.

[MONTDOUILLARD *enters from upstage in a new waistcoat, speaking to the wings.*]

MONTDOUILLARD. Have the carriage wait for me.

FLAVIGNY. Montdouillard.

MONTDOUILLARD. Finally.

FLAVIGNY. That's nice of you—after yesterday.

MONTDOUILLARD. Don't even speak to me about that! I followed a beastly cab all the way to the Bastille—

FLAVIGNY. I went in the opposite direction all the way to the Etoile.

MONTDOUILLARD. And who do I find inside—my tailor!

FLAVIGNY. And me, a ballistics expert and a woman from Alsace!

MONTDOUILLARD. Son of an Arabian foothill! I completely missed my interview with General Renaudier.

FLAVIGNY. I saw him this morning. He'll be at Madame Darbel's at three this afternoon. Nab him there.

MONTDOUILLARD. [*Displaying his waistcoat.*] Well, I am dressed for it.

FLAVIGNY. You're not going to present yourself wearing that vest, are you?

MONTDOUILLARD. You don't find that my waistcoat suits me?

FLAVIGNY. You look like you're wearing a bed of tulips.

MONTDOUILLARD. [*Vexed.*] A bed of tulips! You are alone in your opinion. [*Aside.*] What a shame Criqueville isn't here.

FLAVIGNY. You've come to see Saint-Putois.

MONTDOUILLARD. Yes, I've come to talk to him about my Bulgarian loan.

KERKADEC. [*Entering.*] You may enter, gentlemen.

FLAVIGNY. Let's go, but believe me, change that vest.

MONTDOUILLARD. You're just jealous.

[*They exit.* CRIQUEVILLE *enters, speaking to* ANTOINE, *who is in the wings.*]

CRIQUEVILLE. Get a move on!

[ANTOINE *appears, still carrying his master's overcoat; he is very pale.*]

ANTOINE. I'm right here, master.

CRIQUEVILLE. Is Monsieur de Flavigny in his office?

KERKADEC. He just went into the Director's office with Monsieur Montdouillard.

CRIQUEVILLE. [*Aside.*] Both here? My dowry and my job!

KERKADEC. If you care to wait.

CRIQUEVILLE. Certainly.

[KERKADEC *exits.*]

ANTOINE. I don't feel very well—that Piccadilly porkbelly!

[*He sits.*]

CRIQUEVILLE. What's wrong with you?

ANTOINE. Master, I feel very melancholy. My stomach is inconsolable.

CRIQUEVILLE. You're not still hungry, are you?

ANTOINE. As God is my witness, I will never be hungry again.

CRIQUEVILLE. It appears to me that your digestion was in fine fettle yesterday.

ANTOINE. I had to win, master—for the glory of France!

CRIQUEVILLE. Or die?

ANTOINE. Or pay! Oh, sir—if only you could have seen that Brit maneuvering through the steaks, the legs of lamb, the roast beefs—haoup! haoup!

CRIQUEVILLE. And yourself?

ANTOINE. Me, I held my own at first. But after about an hour, I began to feel myself blowing up in your coat, and it was a little tight on me to start with. The Englishman looked at me, I didn't budge; finally, they brought the coffee, and I said to myself it's over, but the damned teabag ordered a huge plate of beans—with pork—I leaped up, popped a button, and my livery peeked through.

CRIQUEVILLE. Clumsy.

ANTOINE. On the contrary, that's what saved me. Finding himself eating at the same table with a servant, milord lost his appetite all of a sudden, got up, flung me a "most shocking," paid the check, and disappeared. [*Sadly.*] I could really rub myself down with a cup of tea.

CRIQUEVILLE. Courage! We've almost made our goal! [*Exaltedly.*] Antoine, today is our Austerlitz!

ANTOINE. Or our Waterloo! For all our effort, we've yet to see the color of a twenty-franc note.

CRIQUEVILLE. Patience — the fable was right — every flatterer lives at the expense of —

ANTOINE. Lives, I'll grant you, but he doesn't get rich. He doesn't get rich — there's the snag. We don't even have a roof over our heads.

CRIQUEVILLE. We're doing just fine in Bartavelle's carriage.

ANTOINE. Maybe you are — inside — but not on the seat up top. Besides, an apartment on wheels!

CRIQUEVILLE. Stop whining. We've been staying in the nicest neighborhood — the Boulevard des Italiens.

ANTOINE. It's too noisy.

CRIQUEVILLE. If you prefer the Marais, just tell me. It's only a crack of the whip away.

ANTOINE. Laugh now, but you'll see that one fine morning we'll wake up in the animal pound.

CRIQUEVILLE. Relax. In one hour our vagabond days will be over. I'll have a job, a dowry, and a home.

ANTOINE. How about a teapot?

[CATICHE *enters with a cup and saucer.*]

CATICHE. Where is the office of the presiding Monsieur?

CRIQUEVILLE. You're here, too!

CATICHE. Yes sir, the others showed me the door — they kept ordering olive creams and chocolate ducks; they just didn't want what I had to offer.

CRIQUEVILLE. Poor girl.

CATICHE. But they paid me for a week just the same. I've been paid twice since yesterday.

CRIQUEVILLE. Fourteen days in forty-eight hours — not bad.

ANTOINE. She knows the ropes.

CATICHE. I'm looking for my boss's office so I can bring him his tea.

ANTOINE. Did you say tea?

[*He drinks it down.*]

CATICHE. What are you doing?

ANTOINE. Much better.

CATICHE. Now I'll have to get some more.

ANTOINE. More?

CATICHE. In the kitchen.

ANTOINE. Never leave me. Come, let me tell you my troubles — did I mention that I love you . . .

[*They exit to the kitchen.* MONTDOUILLARD *enters.*]

MONTDOUILLARD. [*Speaking offstage.*] Old boy, we're all set — signed and delivered . . .

CRIQUEVILLE. [*Aside.*] Montdouillard. Now it's time to make the cash register ring.

MONTDOUILLARD. Criqueville! What a pleasant surprise. [*Aside.*] It couldn't hurt to find out what he thinks of my waistcoat. [*He opens his suit.*]

CRIQUEVILLE. What a radiant figure.

MONTDOUILLARD. I've just met with Saint-Putois. He's nearly consented to be named President of the Administrative Council for my Bulgarian loan. We should pull in all the small fry and raise the futures another fifteen francs on his name alone.

CRIQUEVILLE. And a hundred . . . that makes 115.

MONTDOUILLARD. Exactly. [*Aside.*] That's funny, he hasn't said a word about my waistcoat. [*He opens his suitcoat wider.*]

CRIQUEVILLE. My dear friend, I have a little favor to ask of you. You were so kind yesterday as to offer me some of your returns.

MONTDOUILLARD. I never go back on my word.

CRIQUEVILLE. If it's not too vulgar, put me down for a thousand.

MONTDOUILLARD. Excellent. [*Taking out notebook.*] Let me just draw up your portfolio. That's one thousand at 115 francs.

CRIQUEVILLE. What did you say?

MONTDOUILLARD. Let's put them at a hundred francs — that means you'll owe me a hundred thousand even.

CRIQUEVILLE. How do you mean, a hundred thousand?

MONTDOUILLARD. For the premium — the premium!

CRIQUEVILLE. Excuse me; I thought you'd offer them to me at cost.

MONTDOUILLARD. At cost? Me? That's a good one! I only sell at cost when stocks fall below cost.

CRIQUEVILLE. [*Aside.*] How dumb can I be? I completely forgot. [*Going into ecstasies over the waistcoat.*] Oooh! Is that new? It's even prettier than yesterday's!

MONTDOUILLARD. The fact is — really?

CRIQUEVILLE. Mouth-watering.

MONTDOUILLARD. It doesn't remind you, even slightly of —

CRIQUEVILLE. Of what? Remind me of what?

MONTDOUILLARD. A bed of tulips?

CRIQUEVILLE. Who said that? I'll kill him. What calumny! [*Aside.*] For tulips everywhere.

MONTDOUILLARD. [*Aside.*] What a great guy. [*Finding a ticket in his pocket.*] Look, if you want to go to the Hippodrome, someone gave me a pair on the aisle.

CRIQUEVILLE. Thank you. [*Taking his arm.*] So, Sulpice, you won't refuse me a thousand shares at cost.

MONTDOUILLARD. [*Disengaging his arm.*] Not on your life.

CRIQUEVILLE. Not even for a friend?

MONTDOUILLARD. Friends that cost a hundred thousand francs, thanks but no thanks. [*Offering the tickets.*] If you want to go to the Hippodrome.

CRIQUEVILLE. Fuck the Hippodrome.

MONTDOUILLARD. Good day. I have an appointment at three.

CRIQUEVILLE. [*Running after him.*] Montdouillard.

MONTDOUILLARD. I'm in a rush. [*Exiting.*] A thousand shares at cost — that's a hot one.

[*He exits through the rear.*]

CRIQUEVILLE. [*Alone.*] Turned down flat. Damn. [*Pacing.*] Let's see, let's see. Would La Fontaine have driveled such nonsense in the face of this great century of progress? No! I just played him wrong. I only played a little ditty when I should have sung a whopping aria — for a hundred thousand francs, I need a whopping aria! Flavigny! We shall see!

FLAVIGNY. [*Entering.*] If I'm not mistaken, Monsieur de Criqueville.

CRIQUEVILLE. You deigned to invite me to come trouble you at your office, and, as you see — I've already abused your invitation.

FLAVIGNY. Abuse? You could never do that.

CRIQUEVILLE. Perhaps I will, since I have come to ask you for a favor.

FLAVIGNY. Granted.

CRIQUEVILLE. [*Shaking his hand.*] Oh, Monsieur de Flavigny!

FLAVIGNY. Call me Horace.

CRIQUEVILLE. I am scared stiff that you might find my request a little — indiscreet. [*Aside.*] He's going to say no.

FLAVIGNY. Indiscreet? Impossible — coming from you.

CRIQUEVILLE. Oh, Horace [*Aside.*] What was I saying?

FLAVIGNY. I haven't forgotten our conversation from yesterday. You were developing such truthful assessments, such reasoned opinions.

CRIQUEVILLE. [*Aside.*] I should think so; I trashed everyone but him.

FLAVIGNY. Out with it. For me it will be a rare happiness to be able to oblige such an honest man.

CRIQUEVILLE. I'll get to the point. My dear Monsieur de Flavigny — Horace — I have resolved to consecrate my leisure time to serious, productive work.

FLAVIGNY. You?

CRIQUEVILLE. Further, I shall not blush to add that my fortune — given its limited nature — forces my hand in the matter.

FLAVIGNY. [*Aside.*] And here I thought he was loaded. [*He puts his hat on his head.*] I hope you don't mind; I feel a draft.

CRIQUEVILLE. Without further preamble, I have come then to ask you for a place in your administration. I feel I could never accept a position anywhere else — it is under a master such as yourself that I wish to serve.

FLAVIGNY. And have you thought about what kind of a job you'd like?

CRIQUEVILLE. I have learned that a position for a first-class inspector has opened up.

FLAVIGNY. [*Suppressing his surprise.*] And you do realize that the position offers a salary of ten thousand francs.

CRIQUEVILLE. Ten thousand francs! [*Controlling his pleasure.*] I wasn't aware of that. [*Gaily.*] The figure however does nothing to alleviate my intense desire to get the job.

FLAVIGNY. Really. [*Aside.*] This one has chutzpah. [*Aloud.*] I would be very happy, certainly, to say to you right now — welcome aboard, but you see, our hiring decisions do not depend on my consent alone. You need two signatures of approval, mine and Monsieur de Saint-Putois's.

CRIQUEVILLE. [*Lively.*] Do but give me yours; I feel certain that yours is really the deciding vote.

FLAVIGNY. I assure you it is not.

CRIQUEVILLE. Modesty! As if anyone could dare to countermand the author of the famous stockholder's report of the second of January —

FLAVIGNY. Now stop.

CRIQUEVILLE. That work of such lucidity! so remarkable, so eloquent, so juicy, so — here, here's a pen and some ink.

FLAVIGNY. So you really want to work here. My pleasure.

[*He goes to* KERKADEC's *desk, writes something, and seals it up.*]

CRIQUEVILLE. [*Aside.*] I stunned him into submission. His head's up his ass.

FLAVIGNY. [*Handing him the paper.*] Here you are.

CRIQUEVILLE. Horace. If I can ever do you a favor, you can count on me.

FLAVIGNY. That means a lot.

[FLAVIGNY *exits right.*]

CRIQUEVILLE. Well, I have the desk, now it's just a question of conquering the chair. [*To* KERKADEC, *who is entering.*] My good man, tell the Director that I am here.

KERKADEC. I'm afraid that is impossible. He receives no one.

CRIQUEVILLE. What?

KERKADEC. His orders.

CRIQUEVILLE. I have an appointment — he's expecting me.

KERKADEC. You and what army. He's a crab; he sees nobody—once a humpback, always a humpback, that's what I say. But I'll tell him you're here.

[KERKADEC *goes into the Director's office.*]

CRIQUEVILLE. A humpback! Why didn't anybody tell me? [*He spies the cushion on* KERKADEC's *chair.*] It's a stroke of genius. [*He takes the cushion and stuffs it into his back.*] *Similia similibus!* Homeopathic flattery!

[SAINT-PUTOIS *enters, growling.*]

SAINT-PUTOIS. I won't put up with this! I told you no appointments; I can't get a moment's peace in my own office!

CRIQUEVILLE. Pardon me, sir.

SAINT-PUTOIS. What does this joker want? [*He sees* CRIQUEVILLE's *hump.*] Oh. Wait. Wait. [*Very gently.*] Go ahead, my friend, speak . . . you have nothing to fear.

CRIQUEVILLE. I see that I've come at a bad time. I'll just walk back home. All that way.

SAINT-PUTOIS. No, please stop. [*Aside.*] His is much bigger than mine.

CRIQUEVILLE. You are going to find me very bold, me, a stranger, an unknown, a poor—

[SAINT-PUTOIS *cannot refrain from staring at* CRIQUEVILLE's *back.*]

SAINT-PUTOIS. Pardon me—is it congenital or was it caused by an accident?

CRIQUEVILLE. Are you referring to my . . . ?

SAINT-PUTOIS. Yes.

CRIQUEVILLE. Congenital.

SAINT-PUTOIS. Mine too.

CRIQUEVILLE. Your what?

SAINT-PUTOIS. You didn't notice? I have one shoulder which is a little— bigger—than the other one.

CRIQUEVILLE. No! You? [*He looks.*] Which one?

SAINT-PUTOIS. What? [*Aside.*] I guess next to his, mine hardly shows. He seems like a very brave young man. [*Aloud.*] Come now, tell me your story. Won't you sit down?

[*They sit down face to face, in profile to the audience.*]

CRIQUEVILLE. [*To audience.*] We ought to be in pictures.

SAINT-PUTOIS. Go on, I'm listening.

CRIQUEVILLE. Monsieur de Saint-Putois, I'm twenty-six years old, with some education, full of good will.

SAINT-PUTOIS. Yes. [*Aside.*] Yes, sir, it does me good to look at him. His puts mine in the shade.

CRIQUEVILLE. My first idea was to throw myself into a military career.

SAINT-PUTOIS. Ah!

CRIQUEVILLE. But the review board—

SAINT-PUTOIS. Say no more; you could never manage the backpack.

CRIQUEVILLE. So then I had to start thinking about creating another career for myself . . . and. . . . May I tell you my dreams, sir? My dream is to enter into the administration that you yourself direct with such a firm hand—

SAINT-PUTOIS. I can flatter myself that I am one of the principal columns around here.

CRIQUEVILLE. [*Aside.*] A twisted column.

SAINT-PUTOIS. I could use a new assistant. This is perfect.

CRIQUEVILLE. Excuse me, but some people led me to believe that I might be able to set my sights higher.

SAINT-PUTOIS. So you're ambitious! That's great! And should some job happen to open up . . .

CRIQUEVILLE. One has.

SAINT-PUTOIS. Oh. Which one?

CRIQUEVILLE. The first-class inspector's position.

SAINT-PUTOIS. Hell, you're on the ball, kid.

CRIQUEVILLE. Under your direction sir, I would hope—

SAINT-PUTOIS. Well, as far as I'm concerned, I see no obstacles. I prefer you to all the other candidates.

[KERKADEC *has entered and begun to look for his cushion.*]

KERKADEC. I thought it was right here.

CRIQUEVILLE. Oh, Jesus.

KERKADEC. [*Looking around.*] Where has it gone to?

SAINT-PUTOIS. [*Aside.*] At least this one won't try hitting on my wife. [*Aloud.*] But surely you realize that I cannot hire you all by myself. My colleague, Monsieur de Flavigny must second my recommendation—

CRIQUEVILLE. Will this do? [*Shows him* FLAVIGNY's *letter.*] Horace and I have talked.

SAINT-PUTOIS. Already? So much the better. Let's see. [*Aside, opening the letter.*] Humpbacks are so grasping.

KERKADEC. [*Looking everywhere.*] Dammit, somebody just walked off with it.

CRIQUEVILLE. [*Moving away from* KERKADEC.] Get the hell away from me.

SAINT-PUTOIS. [*After reading the letter, aside.*] Oh, the poor cripple— what a shame.

[*He crumples the paper and throws it onto the ground.*]

CRIQUEVILLE. Well, sir?

SAINT-PUTOIS. Well, sir, it's impossible.

CRIQUEVILLE. What?

SAINT-PUTOIS. There are obstacles. Humps—mountains! [*Moving toward his office.*] I'm terribly, terribly sorry, my good man.

CRIQUEVILLE. But sir . . . what happened?

[SAINT-PUTOIS *exits.*]

KERKADEC. [*Catching sight of* CRIQUEVILLE'*s hump.*] Aha! You didn't have that hump when you came in.

CRIQUEVILLE. You shut up!

KERKADEC. Give me back my hump!

CRIQUEVILLE. Here, take your lousy good-for-nothing cushion. [*He hands it to him.*] Rejected—after Flavigny's recommendation. [*Picks up the letter.*] There it is—he'll be furious that Saint-Putois turned me down. [*Reads it.*] "Don't hire him." What? "Don't hire him." Some friends! I practically broke the incense burner right under his nose.

FLAVIGNY. [*Off right.*] Joseph, lock up my office.

CRIQUEVILLE. [*Going to him.*] I was looking for you, sir.

FLAVIGNY. Why?

CRIQUEVILLE. So I could not thank you. [*He shows him the letter*].

FLAVIGNY. [*Calmly.*] You read it then? What do you want, my boy? The position has already been promised to someone whom I am interested in placing.

CRIQUEVILLE. I thought I was your friend.

FLAVIGNY. I like you, certainly. I find you charming, obliging, even complimentary. But in this world it doesn't suffice to simply say "Oh, what a tasty waistcoat," or "Oh, what a beautiful horse," or "Oh, what a magnificent report," and then expect to land a job worth ten thousand francs. It just doesn't work that way.

CRIQUEVILLE. Please, sir.

FLAVIGNY. In this century, our century, there's only one thing that can't be easily seduced and that is money! Look at a one-franc piece. It has no ears, it has no vanity, it cannot be flattered. It can't be flattered, but it can be placed. As for all these charming adulations that please us so much, I'm all for them—to pay for those we always keep a little small change handy.

CRIQUEVILLE. Small change?

FLAVIGNY. Pocket money. Cigars, dinners, tickets to the theater.

CRIQUEVILLE. The Hippodrome.

FLAVIGNY. Exactly. But when we're talking big money, the serious money —that's another affair entirely. That we keep.

CRIQUEVILLE. For whom?

FLAVIGNY. Either for those who can serve our interests or for those who can destroy our interests—the ones we fear.

CRIQUEVILLE. Thanks for the tip, sir, I'll be sure to turn a profit from it. Someday. [*To himself, discouraged.*] All that's left for me is my cigar butt. A re-lit cigar is . . . very sad. A re-lit cigar is . . . never good.

MONTDOUILLARD. [*Entering.*] Kiss me, my friend!

CRIQUEVILLE. What happened?

MONTDOUILLARD. I've just come back from my interview with General Renaudier.

CRIQUEVILLE. What?

MONTDOUILLARD. His daughter is absolutely enchanting. Tomorrow at Madame Darbel's ball, I shall go a-courting.

CRIQUEVILLE. [*Aside.*] Tomorrow! Clotilde become the wife of that pack of waistcoats! Oh, no—I'll fight this! I'll go to war! But how?

[ANTOINE *enters.*]

ANTOINE. Master, the carriage is waiting below.

MONTDOUILLARD. Are you dining with us?

CRIQUEVILLE. [*Dryly.*] Thank you, no.

MONTDOUILLARD. Suit yourself. [*Taking* FLAVIGNY's *arm and leading him away.*] What cheek to ask me for a thousand shares at cost.

FLAVIGNY. He flat-out asked me for a job worth ten thousand francs.

MONTDOUILLARD. What a kidder.

[*They exit, laughing.*]

CRIQUEVILLE. [*Thoughtfully, to himself.*] One keeps the serious money, in case the ones to fear . . .

ANTOINE. Who are we going to flatter now, master?

CRIQUEVILLE. Nobody! No more flattery—we're not going to sing for our supper—we're going to swallow it whole!

ANTOINE. But I've lost my appetite.

CRIQUEVILLE. I've got enough for twelve—follow me!

[*They exit.*]

Act V

A drawing room at Madame Darbel's, decorated for a party. A pedestal table at left equipped with writing utensils. Three doors in the back wall, as well as doors at the sides. At the rise of the curtain, as FLAVIGNY, BARTAVELLE, *and* ARTHUR *arrive,* MADAME DARBEL *goes up to greet them.*

MADAME DARBEL. Gentlemen! Arriving so late to my party—I won't forgive you.

FLAVIGNY. Permit us, Madame, to plead extenuating circumstances.

BARTAVELLE. Mine is the fifty leagues I had to travel in order to attend your charming soirée.

FLAVIGNY. Mine is this bouquet I offer you now which wasn't ready at the florist's.

ARTHUR. Mine, Madame—

MADAME DARBEL. [*Taking the flowers.*] I accept the flowers, but not the excuses. And I'm imposing a fine on the guilty by announcing on their behalf, at midnight, a collection for the poor.

FLAVIGNY. Watch what you're doing—you'll only encourage laziness.

BARTAVELLE. Charity is what keeps people poor.

ARTHUR. That was a good one—that's just what I was going to say.

FLAVIGNY. Excuse me?

ARTHUR. I was just going to say that.

[GENERAL RENAUDIER *enters.*]

MADAME DARBEL. Ah, the General.

RENAUDIER. [*Greeting her.*] My lady.

MADAME DARBEL. And our dear Clotilde. Didn't you bring her?

RENAUDIER. She's in the small salon with her aunt.

MADAME DARBEL. We have yet to see her young fiancé.

RENAUDIER. Lord Montdouillard.

FLAVIGNY. No doubt he's still trying on vests.

ARTHUR. That was a good one—that's just what I was going to say.

FLAVIGNY. Excuse me?

ARTHUR. I was just going to say that.

FLAVIGNY. You're completely unbearable.

[*Music is heard.*]

MADAME DARBEL. The orchestra has begun. Messieurs, I commend you to the ladies.

BARTAVELLE. I absolutely have to find Criqueville. I need my carriage.

[RENAUDIER, ARTHUR, BARTAVELLE *and the* GUESTS *move into the other rooms.*]

MADAME DARBEL. Well, what are you waiting for, Monsieur de Flavigny?

FLAVIGNY. The return on my bouquet.

MADAME DARBEL. [*Offering her hand, which he kisses.*] Speculating on flowers, sir? That's not nice.

MONTDOUILLARD. [*From offstage.*] Son of an Arabian foothill!

MADAME DARBEL. [*Pulling her hand away.*] Silence—someone is coming.

[MONTDOUILLARD *appears, magnificently attired, with a breathtaking waist-coat.*]

MONTDOUILLARD. What a darling party.

FLAVIGNY. Well, if it isn't the Count of Monte Cristo himself!

MADAME DARBEL. As handsome as the sun.

MONTDOUILLARD. [*Greeting her.*] Madame. Frankly, what do you think of me?

FLAVIGNY. Horribly handsome.

MONTDOUILLARD. I just love simple things.

MADAME DARBEL. It shows, it shows. And gracious sakes, but you're throwing off some scent!

MONTDOUILLARD. [*Contentedly.*] Oh, a dab here, a dab there.

FLAVIGNY. [*Aside.*] Somebody break a window. And push him and his stink out.

MONTDOUILLARD. It's a toilet water composed especially for me — Eau de Montdouillard. Try as you might, my parfumer won't sell you any.

FLAVIGNY. [*Aside.*] I hope not.

MONTDOUILLARD. I water myself with it whenever I go out in society. It wears so well and completely intoxicates the ladies.

MADAME DARBEL. Ladies?

FLAVIGNY. That plural is bound to appear very singular to Clotilde.

MONTDOUILLARD. [*Gaily.*] Has she arrived?

MADAME DARBEL. [*Reproachfully.*] Well before you, sir.

MONTDOUILLARD. It's all my hairdresser's fault. I'll run and beg my pardon with her.

[MONTDOUILLARD *rushes out left.*]

MADAME DARBEL. Poor Monsieur Montdouillard. Happiness has made him almost witty.

FLAVIGNY. May it only happen to me the same way.

[CRIQUEVILLE *enters from the back and eavesdrops.*]

MADAME DARBEL. Patience! No one must know of our marriage plans — just yet.

CRIQUEVILLE. [*Aside.*] Their marriage plans?

MADAME DARBEL. For now I must abandon you to pain and solitude.

FLAVIGNY. Oh — right —

MADAME DARBEL. [*Picking up a newspaper.*] See whether this lifts up your downcast spirits.

FLAVIGNY. A newspaper?

MADAME DARBEL. It contains a slanderous article about you — someone is attacking your administrative capabilities.

FLAVIGNY. What?

MADAME DARBEL. Complain all you like, my little ingrate—people are still envious of you.

FLAVIGNY. Let's see. This article is signed Z. I don't know him. One of my friends must be skulking behind it. [*Aloud.*] "We have just completed the soporific shareholders report that Minister Flavigny has presented"—It starts well enough—"a poor, obscure style, narrow, banal views, a self-assured mediocrity, a memorable testament to the extreme incapacity of certain administrations, those whose sole useful talent is an imposition of their droning nonentical style on the dupes and gulls of the day." [*Folding the paper.*] Most gracious. Just the opposite of the crushing compliments my friend de Criqueville paid me yesterday. I'd be mighty pleased to know the name of Monsieur Z.

CRIQUEVILLE. [*Who has approached quietly.*] Z, that's me.

FLAVIGNY. What?

CRIQUEVILLE. I'm a freelance journalist.

FLAVIGNY. A journalist! [*Sweetly.*] Hooligan!

CRIQUEVILLE. Monsieur de Flavigny!

FLAVIGNY. [*Calmly and soberly.*] Monsieur de Criqueville, there are two ways to bite. The way of the lion and the way of the serpent. I think that Monsieur Z chose the wrong method for the occasion. I often read, even gratefully, the disinterested critiques of loyal citizens. But when they've been dictated in a spirit of hate or self-interest, then it's my habit to pay absolutely no attention to them.

[*He throws the newspaper in* CRIQUEVILLE*'s hat, bows coldly, and leaves stage left.*]

CRIQUEVILLE. [*Crumpling the paper.*] He's right, my approach was common and vulgar and unsuccessful.

MONTDOUILLARD. [*Quickly crossing upstage, left to right, giving his hand to a lady.*] No, my dear, try as you might, my parfumer won't sell you any.

[*He tosses the paper in the fire. After* MONTDOUILLARD *has passed through,* RENAUDIER *comes by the same way, sniffing and stopping at the middle door.*]

CRIQUEVILLE. I'm so angry I could duel to death the next person I see.

MONTDOUILLARD. [*From offstage.*] The very first schottische, I promise you.

CRIQUEVILLE. Montdouillard—I shall relieve myself on him.

MONTDOUILLARD. [*Entering stage right.*] Oh, how charming my future is, how delicious, how intoxicating! [*Seeing* CRIQUEVILLE.] Hello, Albert. [*Standing in front of him and spreading his suit to reveal his waistcoat.*] Now, what do you have to say about number twenty-three?

CRIQUEVILLE. [*Savoring the words.*] Horrible! Hideous! Ridiculous! Fruity!

MONTDOUILLARD. Fruity!

CRIQUEVILLE. You look like an old Louis Quinze footstool—a faded footstool!

MONTDOUILLARD. *Faded!*

CRIQUEVILLE. It feels so good to speak one's mind.

MONTDOUILLARD. Oh, I get it.

CRIQUEVILLE. I find that hard to believe.

MONTDOUILLARD. I tell you I get it. It's because I refused you those shares of my Bulgarian loan.

CRIQUEVILLE. Oh, you and your loan. You haven't even issued it yet.

MONTDOUILLARD. Give me three days—and there isn't any competition.

CRIQUEVILLE. Who knows?

MONTDOUILLARD. [*Worried.*] What? What did you say?

CRIQUEVILLE. Another corporation could start up overnight.

MONTDOUILLARD. You know something.

CRIQUEVILLE. My lips are sealed.

MONTDOUILLARD. [*Aside.*] Holy shit, a takeover. [*Aloud.*] See here, Criqueville—speak! Albert, baby—Big Al—what's happening?

CRIQUEVILLE. No, Sulpice.

MONTDOUILLARD. We'll have lunch tomorrow.

CRIQUEVILLE. [*Coldly.*] I'm fasting.

[*The orchestra starts up again.*]

MONTDOUILLARD. There's the orchestra. I promised Clotilde we'd lead the quadrille. I'll get back to you, I'll get back to you.

CRIQUEVILLE. I would rather you didn't.

MONTDOUILLARD. Al, baby, don't cut me off.

[*He exits upstage right.* RENAUDIER *enters stage right, sniffing the air.*]

RENAUDIER. There's that bergamot again—he's in this room—no. He must have gone that way.

[*He exits through the same door as* MONTDOUILLARD.]

CRIQUEVILLE. I've failed—no dowry, no job—I'm biting, but my gums are flapping in the empty air.

[ANTOINE *enters from upstage with a plate of refreshments.*]

CRIQUEVILLE. What are you doing here, Antoine?

ANTOINE. Keep it down, master, keep it down. Where is Madame Darbel?

CRIQUEVILLE. How should I know? What do you want with her?

ANTOINE. Shhh . . . I'm on a secret mission.

CRIQUEVILLE. You?

ANTOINE. You remember your pretty Picardess? The humpback paid her for a week.

CRIQUEVILLE. What do I care?

ANTOINE. Now she's cooking—well, at least for the time being—for that lady dancer friend of your friend Bartavelle.

CRIQUEVILLE. Mauviette.

ANTOINE. No, Pichenette. And I tell you, there's a girl who isn't terribly particular about the color of money. You know, she has promised me twenty francs just for taking this little package of letters to Madame Darbel. Can you believe it? It's not even heavy. I guess when a woman wants to avenge herself—

CRIQUEVILLE. Re-venge herself. On whom? Give them to me.

[*He tears the package from* ANTOINE.]

ANTOINE. Oh. Read me something spicy.

CRIQUEVILLE. I recognize that signature—No mistake about it.

ANTOINE. Why are you keeping them?

CRIQUEVILLE. I'll take care of this. Now go.

ANTOINE. What about my twenty francs?

CRIQUEVILLE. I'll double your wages.

ANTOINE. Zero times two is zero.

CRIQUEVILLE. Get out of here.

ANTOINE. At what time will my master be returning this evening?

CRIQUEVILLE. Very funny. I don't know.

ANTOINE. The apartment will be parked at the corner of rue Joubert. My master will find his bed candle in the streetlamp.

CRIQUEVILLE. Alright already.

[ANTOINE *exits stage right.*]

FLAVIGNY. [*From the second salon, to the guests.*] Gentlemen, supper awaits us.

CRIQUEVILLE. Speak of the devil. A word with you, Monsieur de Flavigny.

FLAVIGNY. With me, sir?

CRIQUEVILLE. Sir, when a gentleman makes a mistake, the best way for him to erase it is to confess it. I recognize my mistake, and I beg you to forget that nasty article. It's in the fire.

FLAVIGNY. You are going to ask me for something now.

CRIQUEVILLE. True.

FLAVIGNY. A job.

CRIQUEVILLE. First, I wish some advice.

FLAVIGNY. Despite my extreme incapacity.

CRIQUEVILLE. Ashes to dust.

FLAVIGNY. Out with it.

CRIQUEVILLE. A somewhat compromising correspondence addressed to a dancer has just fallen into my hands.

FLAVIGNY. Yes—

CRIQUEVILLE. A dancer named Mauviette—no, Pichenette. She is of your acquaintance, I believe?

FLAVIGNY. Yes—

CRIQUEVILLE. The letters are signed—

FLAVIGNY. Yes—

CRIQUEVILLE. Let us not incriminate the gentleman in question—let us call him X. I was Z a short while ago. Let us call him X. The alphabet is handy that way. [*Slowly pulling out the letters.*] Here is the entire Pichenette—X collection. Do you have a minute?—"Dear little angel"—

FLAVIGNY. Am I not free to write whatever—isn't X—isn't he free to write to whomsoever he wishes? He's just a boy.

CRIQUEVILLE. Yes, but he is supposed to get married.

FLAVIGNY. What? How do you know?

CRIQUEVILLE. I know so many things.

FLAVIGNY. What do you plan to do?

CRIQUEVILLE. Advice first. Suppose I were to love—no, let us stick to the alphabet. Suppose that Z loves, better, idolizes, the woman that X wants to marry.

FLAVIGNY. You? That's grotesque.

CRIQUEVILLE. Please . . . let us remain gallant to the image of Madame Darbel. X is therefore my rival. I have a weapon against him; must I use it?

FLAVIGNY. [*Agitated.*] Sir, such conduct—

CRIQUEVILLE. Is quite unbecoming, except in war—and in the theater. Between rivals in love, these little stabs in the back are permitted. Besides, I plan to warn X. This time I don't want to bite like a serpent, but like a lion—face to face.

FLAVIGNY. [*Aside.*] I shall not yield, by God, I shall not yield.

CRIQUEVILLE. Your advice?

FLAVIGNY. I'll give it to you in all sincerity, with brutal frankness if you like!

CRIQUEVILLE. You do me great honor.

FLAVIGNY. You said to yourself: "Monsieur de Flavigny refused to hire me for a position," a position that you didn't deserve. "I have in my hands letters which can destroy all of his hopes for happiness. With these letters I shall grab him by the balls, as it were, and force him to say—your money or your life."

CRIQUEVILLE. [*Coldly and with much dignity.*] You are in the wrong, sir. I ask nothing of Monsieur de Flavigny. I had the misfortune of offending him. I possess a correspondence injurious to his well-being. I can make use of it: I will burn it.

[*He lights the packet of letters with a candle.*]

FLAVIGNY. [*Moved.*] Sir—what you have done—is a great thing—a noble gesture.

CRIQUEVILLE. [*Moved.*] Isn't it?

FLAVIGNY. A very great thing.

[*He runs to the table and writes.* MONTDOUILLARD *enters and sees* FLAVIGNY *writing.*]

MONTDOUILLARD. What the hell is Flavigny signing? It must be a rival Bulgarian loan.

FLAVIGNY. [*Handing a paper to* CRIQUEVILLE.] Monsieur de Criqueville, here is my support.

MONTDOUILLARD. [*Aside.*] His support?

FLAVIGNY. I can also answer for Saint-Putois.

MONTDOUILLARD. [*Aside.*] Saint-Putois, too? He's poaching all of my subscribers!

FLAVIGNY. We are even.

CRIQUEVILLE. Not yet.

FLAVIGNY. How do you mean?

CRIQUEVILLE. Your hand?

FLAVIGNY. [*Shaking.*] With a full heart, sir, with a full heart.

CRIQUEVILLE. [*Aside.*] Now that I don't want anything more out of him, I can make him my friend.

MONTDOUILLARD. Criqueville, I'm no chump; let's put our cards on the table. You're putting together another corporation in competition against me.

CRIQUEVILLE. Me? You're joking.

MONTDOUILLARD. Will you deny it?

CRIQUEVILLE. No.

MONTDOUILLARD. Shhh. [*He makes sure no one can hear him.*]

CRIQUEVILLE. You guessed.

MONTDOUILLARD. Criqueville, I've come to propose a merger of our two companies.

CRIQUEVILLE. Just what I've been thinking. Let's merge immediately.

MONTDOUILLARD. State your terms.

CRIQUEVILLE. Montdouillard, at this moment a total imbecile is on the brink of marrying the woman I love.

MONTDOUILLARD. Yes, well, you can tell me all about it tomorrow.

CRIQUEVILLE. To supplant this joker, I would need quite a cushy dowry.

MONTDOUILLARD. Oh, I get it. Criqueville, in business, I'm a very plain dealer. I set aside five thousand shares for myself. I'll offer you two hundred of them.

CRIQUEVILLE. Twenty thousand francs is a shoemaker's dowry.

MONTDOUILLARD. Four hundred.

CRIQUEVILLE. A bootmaker.

MONTDOUILLARD. Dammit!

CRIQUEVILLE. Let's understand each other—I want a thousand shares at cost.

MONTDOUILLARD. Never.

CRIQUEVILLE. Then the merger is off. Good day.

[*He feigns leaving.*]

MONTDOUILLARD. Criqueville!

CRIQUEVILLE. Agreed?

MONTDOUILLARD. [*Holding out his hand.*] You'll have them in the morning. But we have merged?

CRIQUEVILLE. Until death.

[RENAUDIER *enters, sniffing.*]

RENAUDIER. I lost the trail again.

CRIQUEVILLE. There's my dowry.

MONTDOUILLARD. [*Aside.*] What a numbskull—I was prepared to go to two thousand.

[CRIQUEVILLE *goes up to* RENAUDIER.]

CRIQUEVILLE. General Renaudier, I have accomplished my Herculean labors. I've kept strict time—just barely—so I ask you for the hand of your daughter.

MONTDOUILLARD. She's *my* wife!

RENAUDIER. [*Coming between the two, to* CRIQUEVILLE.] I'm sorry, my boy, but it's too late.

CRIQUEVILLE. Too late?

RENAUDIER. She's already spoken for. [*Stopping suddenly, he turns to* MONTDOUILLARD.] Ah, I smell, I smell. . . . [*He rips* MONTDOUILLARD*'s handkerchief out of his hand and smells it.*] That's it! What is that smell?

MONTDOUILLARD. It's essence of bergamot.

RENAUDIER. And that rhymes with shitpot! [RENAUDIER *rears back and gives* MONTDOUILLARD *a boot in the rear, who screams. The other guests rush in.*]

GUESTS. [*Severally.*] What's the matter?

RENAUDIER. What the matter is that I am giving my daughter in marriage to Monsieur Albert de Criqueville.

CRIQUEVILLE. Finally!

GUESTS. [*Severally.*] What?

MONTDOUILLARD. But sir!

RENAUDIER. Sir, I am at your service—I laid a hand on you.

MONTDOUILLARD. [*With great dignity.*] A foot, Monsieur. I assure you that your hand would have felt differently.

ANTOINE. [*Rushing up to* CRIQUEVILLE, *whom everyone is complimenting.*] Master, somebody stole our house.

CRIQUEVILLE. [*Low.*] Rent a carriage by the hour.

ANTOINE. On what money?

CRIQUEVILLE. We're only keeping it until tomorrow. As soon as the stock exchange opens, I am cashing in my assets.

MONTDOUILLARD. [*Aside, looking at* CRIQUEVILLE.] That man is definitely going places; I'd better make a friend out of him. [*Aloud.*] God, what a pretty waistcoat. Oh, what a handsome waistcoat.

CRIQUEVILLE. [*Laughing.*] I can name that tune. [*To* MONTDOUILLARD.] Thank you. Tomorrow I'll give you a ticket to the Hippodrome. [*To* FLAVIGNY.] Small change.

MONTDOUILLARD. A ticket to the Hippodrome!

CRIQUEVILLE. [*To* FLAVIGNY.] Well, dear sir, you were right. In this world, the one way to succeed is to make yourself feared.

FLAVIGNY. I know a better way.

CRIQUEVILLE. Which way is that?

FLAVIGNY. A little heart and a lot of work.

CRIQUEVILLE. [*Aside.*] I'd do well to make a friend of him.

GUESTS. Yes, if in this world, you want to succeed, you have to, by turns, flatter to please.

CRIQUEVILLE. [*To the audience.*]

> Master Public, perched in its stalls
> Held in its hands a vote.
> Master Actor, hunting for glory,
> Holds quite tight to this saying:
> Goodnight, gracious public!
> With your precious vote
> Make three parts:
> Hold out your hands and
> Give one part to the actors,
> A small piece to the author,
> But the lion's share to La Fontaine.
> Oh, give the best piece to La Fontaine.

THREE FRENCH COMEDIES
Turcaret, The Triumph of Love, and Eating Crow
Translated and with an Introduction by James Magruder

In this entertaining book, a playwright and theater critic presents up-to-date and witty translations of three classic comedies of French theater: Alain-René Lesage's satire *Turcaret*, Pierre Marivaux's love comedy *The Triumph of Love*, and Eugène Labiche's farce *Eating Crow*. James Magruder's translations capture the humor and imagination of the original texts and significantly extend the English-language repertory of French comedies.

Magruder's enlightening introduction sets each play within the context of its author's oeuvre and the theatrical culture of its time. *Turcaret*, written in the eighteenth century, is the tale of a high-stakes entrepreneur who, along with every other character, is irredeemably craven and genially amoral. This play of sexual intrigue, greed, and bad manners, says Magruder, was revolutionary in the history of drama for its lack of a moral cynosure. A second eighteenth-century play, *The Triumph of Love*, makes self-reflection and self-consciousness both the substance of and obstacles to the action, as it focuses on the tireless efforts of Princess Léonide to woo Agis and his guardians. *Eating Crow*, written in the nineteenth century and never before translated into English, is a hilarious story of excesses that takes aim at stockbrokers, skinflints, dowagers, dandies, and paralegals, among others.

"This volume is indispensable; it raises the standards of what we should expect in translation and offers an enticing possibility that American theater may be able to begin a real conversation and active relationship with classical dramatic literature."
— TONY KUSHNER

JAMES MAGRUDER is resident dramaturg at CenterStage in Baltimore. His translation of *The Triumph of Love*—which has been produced off-Broadway and in Baltimore, Cleveland, and La Jolla, California—was praised by Vincent Canby in the *New York Times* as an "unhackneyed translation . . . that retains the flavor of Marivaux's flowery locutions . . . but also . . . gives the charade a contemporary edge."